Chinese Entrepreneurship in a Global Era

As we enter the twenty-first century it is clear that the economic growth China has enjoyed has been extraordinary. Although Western countries continue to dominate the world economy and financial markets, the capital markets of Hong Kong, Singapore, Shanghai, and Shenzen have matured considerably and are eager to become major global players.

As business owners in the rest of East Asia are predominantly of Chinese descent, or under Chinese cultural influence, the economic vitality of the rest of the region has been credited to the adaptability, flexibility and ingenuity of Chinese entrepreneurship nurtured by a particular (Confician) heritage. In *Chinese Entrepreneurship in a Global Era*, Raymond Wong and contributors analyze the tremendous changes in the global, regional and local environments in which Chinese entrepreneurs operate, and ask whether a new breed of Chinese entrepreneurs has developed in response to these changes.

Including theoretical discussion and empirical case studies on Chinese entrepreneurship in Hong Kong, China, Singapore, Thailand and Vietnam, the book will be an invaluable resource to students and scholars of Chinese and East Asian business and entrepreneurship.

Raymond Sin-Kwok Wong is Professor of Sociology at the University of California–Santa Barbara, USA.

Chinese Worlds

Chinese Worlds publishes high-quality scholarship, research monographs, and source collections on Chinese history and society. "Worlds" signals the diversity of China, the cycles of unity and division through which China's modern history has passed, and recent research trends toward regional studies and local issues. It also signals that Chineseness is not contained within borders—ethnic migrant communities overseas are also "Chinese worlds."

The series editors are Gregor Benton, Flemming Christiansen, Delia Davin, Terence Gomez and Frank Pieke.

Chinese Entrepreneurship in a Global Era

Edited by
Raymond Sin-Kwok Wong

Routledge
Taylor & Francis Group

LONDON AND NEW YORK

First published 2008
by Routledge
2 Park Square, Milton Park, Abingdon, Oxon OX14 4RN

Simultaneously published in the USA and Canada
by Routledge
270 Madison Ave, New York, NY 10016

Routledge is an imprint of the Taylor & Francis Group, an informa business

© 2008 Editorial selection and matter, Raymond Sin-Kwok Wong;
Individual chapters, the contributors

Typeset in Times New Roman by
Taylor & Francis Books

British Library Cataloguing in Publication Data
A catalogue record for this book is available from the British Library

Library of Congress Cataloging in Publication Data
Chinese entrepreneurship in a global era / edited by Raymond Sin-Kwok
  Wong.
    p. cm.
  1. Entrepreneurship – China. 2. China – Commerce. 3. China –
  Economic conditions. I. Wong, Raymond Sin-Kwok.
  HB615.C627 2008
  338′.040951 – dc22   2007051695

ISBN 978-0-415-46218-1 (hbk)
ISBN 978-0-203-89488-0 (ebk)

To
Ming-Yan and Hanwey
and
in memory of Amy

Contents

Illustrations

Figures

Tables

xii *Illustrations*

Contributors

Yanjie Bian is Professor of Sociology at the University of Minnesota and Chair Professor of Social Science and Director of the Survey Research Center at Hong Kong University of Science and Technology. He has led the Chinese General Social Survey project since 2003, and is currently conducting research on the roles of social networks in employment processes and economic organizations in China.

Dung-Sheng Chen is currently the Director-General of Humanities and Social Sciences, National Science Council of the Republic of China, Taiwan, and Professor of Sociology at the National Taiwan University. His research interests include urban sociology, sociology of organizations, and deliberative democracy and public participation.

Denggao Long is a Professor in the School of Humanities and Social Sciences at the Tsinghua University in Beijing, China. He received his Ph.D. in economic history at Yunnan University in 1993. He was a visiting scholar at Yale University (2003) and Harvard University (2005–6).

Edmund Terence Gomez is Research Coordinator at the United Nations Research Institute for Social Development (UNRISD). He also holds the post of Associate Professor at the Faculty of Economics and Administration, University of Malaya. Among the books he has published include *Chinese Enterprise, Transnationalism and Identity* (RoutledgeCurzon, 2004), *The State of Malaysia: Ethnicity, Equity and Reform* (RoutledgeCurzon, 2004), *The Chinese in Britain, 1800–Present: Transnationalism, Economy and Identity* (Palgrave, 2008), and *The State, Development and Identity in Multi-ethnic Societies: Ethnicity, Equity and the Nation* (Routledge, 2008).

Hsin-Huang Michael Hsiao is Executive Director of the Center for Asia-Pacific Area Studies, and a Research Fellow of the Institute of Sociology, both at Academia Sinica; and Professor of Sociology at the National Taiwan University. His current research interests include civil society and democracy, local sustainable development, and the middle class in the Asia-Pacific.

Qiming Han is the Head of Library Technology at Housatonic College in Bridgeport, Connecticut, U.S.A. His research interests include American economic history, business history, and Chinese-American relations.

Hong Liu is Chair of Chinese Studies and Professor of East Asian Studies at the University of Manchester, where he is also the founding director of the Centre for Chinese Studies. He is the author of *Singapore Chinese Society in Transition: Business, Politics and Socio-economic Change, 1945–1965* (New York, 2004), *Images, Metaphors and Postcolonial Transformation: A Study of Sino-Indonesian Interactions, 1949–1965* (Singapore, 2008), and editor of *The Chinese Overseas* (four volumes, London, 2006).

Sue-Ching Jou is Professor of Geography at National Taiwan University. She obtained her doctoral degree in geography at the University of Minnesota, U.S.A. Her research interests focus on urban policy and politics, and cross-border investment of Taiwanese capital.

Raymond Sin-Kwok Wong is Professor at the Department of Sociology, University of California–Santa Barbara. His research interests include social inequality and stratification, sociology of education, quantitative methodology, and economic development in East Asia.

Henry Wai-Chung Yeung is Professor in the Department of Geography, National University of Singapore. He is the author of *Entrepreneurship and the Internationalisation of Asian Firms: An Institutional Perspective* (Edward Elgar, 2002), and *Chinese Capitalism in a Global Era* (Routledge, 2004), and editor of the *Handbook of Research on Asian Business* (Edward Elgar, 2007), and *Remaking the Global Economy: Economic-Geographical Perspectives* (Sage, 2003).

Preface and acknowledgments

Though my particular research interests in Chinese entrepreneurship date only to the late 1990s, I have long been interested in economic development in East Asia, for both personal and academic reasons. Like many other researchers who grew up and received education in the region during the second half of the twentieth century, I was drawn by the phenomenal achievement of many Asian economies in the past few decades. The entry of communist China into the global economic arena in the late 1970s and its meteoric rise in economic power has been particularly captivating, not least for its impact on the economic and political future of not only the region, but also our closely interconnected world under global capitalism. An informed understanding of economic development in the region, I believe, will help us assess the region's past and future success and, for better or worse, the continual transformation of global capitalism.

The importance of Chinese entrepreneurs in the economic development of East Asia is a well rehearsed argument. In trying to extend our knowledge on the subject of Chinese entrepreneurship, I was struck by a rather unfortunate tendency among academic researchers to echo, rather than critically examine, the stereotypical notions perpetrated in the mass media that the region's success is largely due to entrepreneurship cultivated by *unique* Chinese cultural heritage, traits, and/or practices. Much of the region's economic success is undoubtedly attributable to the hard working and diligent peoples in its lands. Yet, diligence and tenacity are hardly the unique cultural traits of Asians or any particular ethnic group. Equally problematic is the reactive stance that emphasizes the negative or dark side of Chinese culture or Confucianism, and blames this for inherent failures in Asian economies, particularly during the Asian economic crisis in 1997. To me, such contradictory claims represent an *essentialized* and distorted understanding of Chinese culture and cultural influences on economic practices. They shortcircuit scholarly examination of the economic vitalities and vulnerabilities of the region, and obfuscate our understanding of entrepreneurial activities and their functioning in larger social and economic contexts. I was particularly concerned that the neglect of changes in the global economic system (in terms of the pace and the spread of technological development, movement of capital and labor, and dissemination of Western organizational practices) would forestall the recognition of changes and transformations in Chinese enterpreneurship over time.

Harboring such misgivings about prevalent views on the subject, I was fortunate to participate in a Taipei conference organized by Michael Hsiao and Terence Edmund Gomez in 2001, where I voiced my reservations. I was initially apprehensive of the reception of my arguments and empirical findings, which contradicted and challenged conventional wisdom on Chinese enterprises and entrepreneurship. To my delight, I found a group of like-minded scholars who share a similar skepticism and dissatisfaction. It is perhaps not coincidental that we are all scholars born and educated in the region during the postwar period. The encounter encouraged me to further my investigation of the subject. With support from the Pacific Rim Research Program of the University of California, I later organized a conference in Hong Kong to explore the possibility of a new breed of Chinese entrepreneurs in the making and to examine the conditions under which Chinese entrepreneurs operate today. Many of the papers presented at that conference are collected in the present volume.

To the participants of the two conferences, I am grateful for insightful and stimulating exchanges. To the Pacific Rim Research Program of the University of California, the Institute of Social, Behavioral, and Economic Research (ISBER) at the University of California–Santa Barbara, the Academic Senate of the University of California–Santa Barbara, the National Science Foundation, the Fulbright Scholar Program, and the Hong Kong University of Science and Technology, I am thankful for their research support. Without their generous support, many of my ideas on Chinese entrepreneurship would never have been developed and tested. Finally, my heartfelt thanks to my wife, Ming-Yan Lai, whose unconditional support and encouragement has helped renew my passion and energies to work on this project. Last but not least, I would like to thank my son, Hanwey, for his patience and understanding during the preparation of this book, and the fun and joy that he brings into my life.

Raymond Wong
Santa Barbara, California
November 2007

Part I

Introduction

1 A new breed of Chinese entrepreneurs?

Critical reflections

Raymond Sin-Kwok Wong

As we enter a new millennium, it is apparent that the center of world economic activities, at least in terms of manufacturing, has shifted eastward from the United States and Europe to China and its neighboring countries throughout East and Southeast Asia (Dicken 2003; Sklair 1999). Although Western countries continue to dominate the world economy and financial markets, the capital markets of Hong Kong, Singapore, and, to a lesser extent, Shanghai and Shenzen have matured considerably and are eager to become major global players in the foreseeable future. For instance, the dual listing of the Industrial and Commercial Bank of China (ICBC) in Hong Kong and Shanghai in October 2006, valued at about US$21.9 billion, represents the world's largest IPO ever and easily surpasses the US$18.4 billion raised by Japan's NTT Docomo in 1998. In fact, buoyed by several major offerings from companies in China, including the Bank of China, Hong Kong has surpassed New York and rivals London as the world's biggest market for initial public stock offerings in 2006, clearly indicating China's growing significance in international finance.[1] While much of the Asian economic ascendance became notable only after China entered the global economic scene in the 1980s, the trend can be traced back at least a decade earlier when the Four Little Dragons (Hong Kong, Singapore, South Korea, and Taiwan) became world manufacturers and exporters.

Because business owners in East Asia are predominantly of Chinese descent or under Chinese cultural influence (as in the case of the Republic of Korea), the economic vitality of the region has been conveniently credited to the adaptability, flexibility, and ingenuity of Chinese entrepreneurship nurtured by a particular (Confucian) cultural heritage. Indeed, the prominence of Chinese entrepreneurs in the global economic market received so much media coverage that the contribution of Chinese culture or the Chinese way of conducting business to economic development and success has become almost common sense. Ironically, such faith in Chinese culture belies the fact that for almost three quarters of the last century, virtually the same cultural arguments have been used to account for the economic backwardness of China and its neighbors (Dirlik 1995). Even more telling is the dramatic about-face during the recent Asian economic crises. Just as the hype of Chinese influence reached a zenith, the burst of economic crises in the summer of 1997 – first in Thailand, then spreading like wildfire to nearby countries Malaysia, Indonesia, Hong Kong, Taiwan, and the Republic of Korea – triggered a chorus of blame on "Chinese culture" for fostering and breeding cronyism as well as the over-zealousness, excessive exuberance, and irrationality in speculative investments that brought about the crises. Indeed, we have come full circle in assessing the role of Chinese (Confucian) culture in economic development or the lack thereof. The fact that the same national/ethnic culture has been used in different times to account for both economic failures and successes calls attention to the inherent inadequacy of the cultural argument and the need for sociological inquiries into the "social constructiveness" of the subject matter.

New bottle, old wine?

Sociologically speaking, without an adequate explanation of *how* and *why* Chinese culture under different social, economic, and political environments can inhibit or foster entrepreneurship, the cultural and/or any other actor-centered arguments will always have limited explanatory power. Culture does not and cannot exist in a social vacuum. Rather, it reflects embedded social and structural relationships that bind or circumscribe the behaviors of social and economic actors (Berger and Luckmann 1966; Granovetter 1985). Therefore, culture *per se* does not determine economic behaviors. Cultural effects are mediated through the social and economic environment where business entrepreneurs find themselves situated. Without taking the larger socioeconomic contexts into account, the claims of cultural determination will simply be a non-reflective rehash of old cliché that lacks scientific clarity and validity. Thus, instead of debating whether cultural explanations are unscientific, essentialist, and perhaps even calculative manipulations by the media and politicians, it is more productive to probe into and scrutinize the social construction of "Chinese entrepreneurs."

Indeed, given the tremendous changes in the global, regional, and local environments in which Chinese entrepreneurs operate their businesses in recent years, there is an urgent need to update our understanding of this social construct and explore whether a "new breed of Chinese entrepreneurs" has developed in response to these changes. In other words, our understanding of contemporary Chinese entrepreneurship should no longer be based solely on the traditional *actor-centered* approach that emphasizes the importance of Chinese family business networks (which no doubt would continue to be functional in modern settings), but rather focus on the complex and intricate interrelations between individual entrepreneurs and their rapidly changing environment and the transformation thereof. Of course, to identity something as new, we must demonstrate how the present development is *different* from the past.

There is, however, no consensus yet on what constitutes the "changed" environments in which Chinese entrepreneurs operate. Disregarding those who take a relatively static stance and refuse to recognize any new development, there are currently two competing views on this particular matter. One emphasizes some fundamental alterations in the way businesses are organized and conducted today. The other takes an incremental view that stresses a high degree of continuity and the sustained importance of traditional (cultural) factors under the new environment. As cogently argued in the following chapter by Yeung, the incremental view highlights the blending of the old and the new in the formation of *hybrid capitalism*, which underscores an incomplete, partial, and contingent *ongoing* transformation in an evolving set of capitalist norms, institutions, and structures.

In view of these competing understandings, the present edited volume seeks to offer a wide-ranging exploration and evaluation of Chinese entrepreneurship in contemporary Asian contexts. Through a collection and juxtaposition of various case studies, we also try to illuminate whether and how a new breed of Chinese entrepreneurs has indeed been formed and is in operation, or is still in the making, or yet simply an exaggeration. Together, the eight following chapters offer both theoretical discussion and empirical examination of the formation of "new Chinese entrepreneurs." While the book does not offer any definitive conclusion, the empirical evidence assembled provides rich materials to enhance our understanding and stimulate further exploration of the subject matter.

The book is divided into three parts, Part I being this introduction. Part II consists of three chapters that give theoretical and empirical overviews of the environment and operation of Chinese entrepreneurship and observable changes over time. As mentioned earlier, Yeung's chapter (Chapter 2) attempts to map out the changing dynamics of Chinese capitalism in relation to globalization and how these changes and transformations led to the emergence of "hybrid capitalism" and a new breed of Chinese entrepreneurs. While still maintaining the continuing significance of Chinese culture, Yeung nonetheless asserts that there are indeed fundamental changes in the ways Chinese owners organize their entrepreneurial activities under globalization. Because of the new development, Chinese entrepreneurs are no longer bound by an enclosed community like their predecessors. On the other hand, Long and Han adopt the neo-institutional economic framework to explore in Chapter 3 how Chinese entrepreneurs in the past failed to behave similarly as their Western counterparts because of a lack of institutional support that enhances socialized transactions rather than inherent cultural predispositions. This suggests the possibility of change over time that Wong documents in Chapter 4 with an empirical investigation of the historical changes of Chinese entrepreneurship in Hong Kong. Using data from several micro-censuses in Hong Kong, the results from Wong demonstrate that not only has the range of economic activities expanded, but there are also fundamental changes in the composition of business entrepreneurs that mirror fundamental demographic changes in the general population.

To further our understanding of the current state of Chinese entrepreneurship, Part III of the volume includes five case studies that range from
Hong Kong and China to Malaysia, Singapore, Thailand, and Vietnam.
Together, they provide a rich contextual exploration of the changing conditions and business operations of contemporary Chinese entrepreneurs.
Gomez (in Chapter 5) documents for the first time a new and genuine
development of inter-ethnic business relationship between Bumiputeras and
non-Bumiputeras in Malaysia that results from a generational shift in the
formation of a *unified* national identity cutting across racial and ethnic lines.
Another noteworthy recent development in Chinese entrepreneurship is the
rise of transnational entrepreneurs who "live dual lives: speaking two languages, having homes in two countries, and making a living through continuous regular contact across national borders" (Portes et al. 1999:217;
2002;see also Yeung in Chapter 2). In Chapter 6 Liu illuminates this phenomenon by examining how new immigrants from China become transnational entrepreneurs in Singapore and how they differ from conventional
immigrant entrepreneurs. Liu's analysis usefully explores the systematic
relationship of such transnational entrepreneurship to globalization, state,
and transnational networks.

The studies by Chen, Jou, and Hsiao (Chapter 7) and Bian (Chapter 8)
both examine the role of *guanxi* or social networks in business transactions.
While Bian stresses the importance of social networks in the start-up of
businesses, Chen, Jou, and Hsiao explore the specific conditions under
which pre-existing network relations would be maintained, transformed to
adopt Western efficiency principles, or even dissolved over time. Through
their case studies of Taiwanese ventures in Thailand and Vietnam, Chen et
al. pinpoint specifically that the degree of embeddedness within the global
production network has profound implications for the transformation in
management and organizational structures. The typology of business start-
ups developed by Bian offers a refreshing understanding of the importance
of social networks in contemporary China. Bian demonstrates that not only
do entrepreneurial opportunities exist in a person's network, but many of
them appear before a firm is founded (see also Burt 1992; Aldrich 1999).
Consistent with Long and Han's argument in Chapter 3, Bian's analysis
shows that it is precisely the lack of a proper functioning "market" that
gives embedded social networks their maximum utility in information,
opportunity, and mobilization of resources. Finally, Wong in Chapter 9
examines the changing patterns of management practices and philosophies
among Hong Kong entrepreneurs in the 1990s, demonstrating that the predominant management style of Chinese entrepreneurs in Hong Kong follows the Western mode, with emphasis on rationality and efficiency, rather
than the traditional, paternalistic style. Together, these case studies suggest
some important changes in Chinese entrepreneurship that cut across countries and/or locations. In the next section, I will map out the new and
changing environment for Chinese entrepreneurship implied in these case

studies and explore its significance for enhancing our understanding of Chinese entrepreneurs today.

New and changing environment

Though amenable to different interpretations, if we examine closely the range of economic activities that contemporary Chinese entrepreneurs engage in and how their business operations and transactions are structured today, there is clear evidence of significant departures from the conventional image of Chinese entrepreneurs established in past studies. For instance, they are no longer confined to the low-rung jobs of petty traders, street hawkers, and small-scale industrial manufacturers with limited skills, knowledge, and capital (note especially the arguments and evidence in chapters by Long and Han, Wong, and Liu). Although many businesses continue to be small, franchises, chain stores and multi-division conglomerates dominate the local markets of many East Asian economies in terms of sales volume and market penetration. At the same time, visible if small segments of business entrepreneurs engage in activities that require significant capital outlay and sophisticated technical skills, not much different from their counterparts in developed economies. Furthermore, many have become transnational entrepreneurs in relocating or operating part or all of their economic activities in neighboring countries. Predictably, such development has significant implications not only for the organizational structures but also for the management practices of the businesses. In order to compete against local and international companies, the management practices of Chinese firms tend to depart significantly from conventional family firms. As noted in Chapter 7 by Chen et al., for example, Taiwanese businesses in Vietnam have to forgo the adoption of any unified or standardized strategy and constantly restructure their management system and relations with network firms. As a result, the management and organizational structures tend to deviate from configurations commonly found in their home country.

Indeed, the organizational structures of many Chinese firms today are becoming increasingly similar to Western corporations (Wong 2004). This is particularly true for large conglomerates such as ESPRIT Holdings, Hutchison Whampoa, and Li & Fung that have a global reach. Many adopt explicit corporate governance structures to adequately protect the interests of major and minor shareholders, employees, customers, and other stakeholders. Such development in organizational restructuring is consistent with the "neo-institutional" argument that institutional isomorphism underscores the impetus for business transformations (DiMaggio and Powell 1983; Meyer and Rowan 1977; Powell and DiMaggio 1991). The relative success of these companies has further spawned the adoption of similar structures by other corporations, large and small.

In addition to these institutionally driven transformations, the challenge of rapidly changing demands from local consumers and global competitors also forces modern entrepreneurs to abandon the familial management structure. For instance, Chen et al. argue that the stronger the links the Chinese manufacturers have with Western multinational firms or trading companies in the global production network, the greater the pressures in adopting rational and efficient management structures. Traditional practices such as reserving senior executive positions to family members or close relatives can no longer provide the expected benefits of harmony and loyalty. In some cases, they may even be perceived as detrimental to growth and survival. Furthermore, aggressive entrepreneurs who aspire to become market leaders and innovators also tend to initiate organizational and management reforms. Although the success of such reforms in helping to seize market shares, increase profits, and consolidate consumer loyalty is by no means guaranteed, the projected payoffs still tempt many to jettison familism.

If the trend of changes in the organizational structure and management practices of Chinese firms is relatively clear, the underlying reasons and mechanisms of the changing demands of the economic environment that motivate such changes are subject to many interpretations. One factor often cited by authors here and elsewhere is the spread of globalization and global capitalism. Dicken (2003:14), for example, maintains that "we *are* witnessing the emergence of a new geo-economy that is *qualitatively different* from the past" (emphasis original). Up until the Second World War, the global economic map broadly resembled a core/periphery international division of labor as depicted by the world-systems theory (Wallerstein 1974). Production and trade were dominated by a few core economies in Europe and the United States, with, for instance, 71 percent of world manufacturing production concentrated in only four countries and 90 percent in only 11 countries in 1939. Two thirds of the core countries' manufactured exports were sold to the periphery and four fifths of the periphery's primary products made their way to the core (Dicken 2003:32). Since the mid-1970s, however, fundamental changes in the world economy, or *global shifts*, have occurred and accelerated. Today, the international division of labor organized along the structure of core, semi-periphery, and periphery no longer applies. In its place is a far more complex, multi-scalar structure where economic activities are now shaped by complex interaction between transnational corporations (TNCs) and nation-states set within the context of a volatile technological environment (Dicken 2003:81).

Other formulations of the changing economic environment call attention to the formation of a new regime of "flexible accumulation" that overcame the rigidities and inadequacies of Fordism (Harvey 1990). The new regime is characterized by flexibility in capital investment, production processes and consumption patterns, with new production sectors, mobile finances, and intensified rates of technological and organizational innovation. These new developments reflect a radical restructuring of the world economy through outsourcing and organized subcontracting that reaches beyond national boundaries. Affecting not only developing countries, the new global shift paradoxically also opens up opportunities for small businesses and the revival of "sweatshop" production in major urban cities within developed countries (Bonacich and Appelbaum 2000). According to Harvey (1990:159), modern capitalism is "becoming ever more tightly organized through dispersal, geographical mobility, and flexible responses in labor markets, labor processes, and consumer markets, all accompanied by hefty doses of institutional, product, and technological innovations."

The "flexible accumulation" thesis resonates with another account, the global commodity chain (GCC) approach advanced by Gary Gereffi and his associates. The GCC approach analyzes the organization and social processes of transnational production systems that sustain and reproduce the structures of the world economy. The organization of the global production of a commodity links manufacturers, technological inputs, raw material suppliers, traders, bankers, designers, and retailers in complex economic networks where the locus of profits and control is constantly shifting. These networks are situationally specific, socially constructed, and locally integrated, highlighting the social embeddedness of economic activities and organization. There are two dominant types of commodity chain. Producer-driven commodity chains are typified by the control of large, transnational corporations engaging in economy of scale production, whereas buyer-driven commodity chains are controlled by major retailers, brand-named merchandisers, and trading companies that are organized in highly decentralized production networks. With the increased industrial capacity of Third World countries, notably China in recent years, which provides a source of low-cost production, there is an important shift in global manufacturing from producer-driven to buyer-driven structures. Buyer-driven commodity chains emerged primarily during the mid-1970s and their structure allows for maximum organizational flexibility, reduced risks, and higher profitability. Unlike the producer-driven commodity chains that are still controlled by core firms at the point of production, control over buyer-driven commodity chains is exercised at the point of consumption (Gereffi et al. 1994). The ongoing process of globalization, according to Gereffi (1996), has eroded the traditional boundaries between nations, firms, and industries and opened up new capabilities for economic coordination and control. On this ground, the GCC approach provides both theoretical and methodological frameworks for a systematic understanding of the underlying micro and macro processes involved in the new economy. To its proponents, it offers a productive way of delineating the particular socioeconomic contexts in which contemporary entrepreneurs run their businesses.

There are yet other elaborations of global capitalism as a new and recent phenomenon. According to Sklair (1995; 1999), global capitalism exceeds the frame of reference in conventional nation-state analysis. An alternative model of understanding of the global system is based on the concepts of *transnational* practices, *transnational* capitalist class, and a *transnational* culture-ideology of consumerism that has a global reach of influence. Scholars who adopt this perspective tend to emphasize the importance of "transnational entrepreneurship" that differs from the conventional literature on local or immigrant entrepreneurship. As illustrated in Chapter 6 by Liu on transnational entrepreneurs in Singapore, this new breed of entrepreneurs does not have any fixed identities and/or residences. They are constantly on the move, speak multiple languages and dialects fluently, and immerse themselves in different cultures, tastes, and lifestyles. Thus, this perspective emphasizes the interplay between multiple identities, localities, and activities that constitute the changing and new environment. In sum, under the guise of globalization, the recent transformation underscores the significance of a new geographical division of labor, technological advancement, and transfer of knowledge and labor that is no longer restricted by national and geographical boundaries. The new breed of transnational Chinese entrepreneurs is a product of the "new economy."

Arguably, the globalization formulation is akin to the modernization thesis or its related thesis of industrialism (Kerr et al. 1960; Treiman 1970). Modernization theory postulates how the diffusion of technological innovations, Western lifestyles, individualism, and mass media exposure encourages a new 'state of mind' that would constitute an alternative way of life beyond the traditional outlook and be favorable to modernity or post-modernity (Lerner 1958; Rogers 1962; Schramm 1964). In other words, the spread of modernization alters not only technological adoption, but also the mentality, tastes, and aspirations of individuals. The process is largely facilitated through the role of education (the institutionalization of educational systems, curricula, and standardized testing in particular) and popular culture, as one can easily observe the dominance of Western, particularly American, culture – cultural icons such as McDonald's, Disney, Coca-Cola, and Hollywood movies – in many developing countries. In the case of East Asia, particularly Hong Kong and Singapore, the spread of Western management practices—American industrial management in the 1960s and Japanese retail management in the 1970s—is particularly noteworthy. In fact, it is also interesting to observe that those who subscribe to the importance of "Chinese culture" as an explanation for the prevalence of Chinese entrepreneurship either consciously or unconsciously downplay the encroaching influence of Western culture.

Besides the advancement of modernization and global capitalism, there are two important but often ignored factors that also contribute to the changing environment for Chinese entrepreneurship. These developments are not necessarily independent of, but rather interact intricately with globalization and modernization. The first one is the emergent and rapidly expanding domestic economy in China. According to official statistics, the Chinese economy currently ranks fourth in terms of absolute size and second in terms of purchasing power parity (Central Intelligence Agency

2007; International Monetary Fund 2007). Its meteoric rise and sheer size dwarf the economic achievement of any developing countries, including the Four Little Dragons and perhaps even Japan. By virtue of its sheer size, the Chinese economy has the potential to expand robustly without relying on rising exports once its internal growth engine or consumption shifts into high gear. There are already important early signs of such development.[2] The immense and rapidly expanding domestic economy has generated a wide range of economic activities of various scales, as well as significant market consolidations from mergers, acquisitions, and restructuring.

Furthermore, the Chinese government has played an active role in grooming conglomerates such as China Mobile, CNOOC, Bank of China, and China Life Insurance to gain market dominance in their respective sectors before opening up its domestic market as stipulated by the WTO agreements.[3] The Chinese government has been extremely careful not to pick one single winner, but rather multiple comparable competitors, within each industry or sector. The reshuffling and circulation of top managerial posts in the telecommunications industry, for example, is a good indication of this important state development strategy. Many of these companies now occupy important niches with sophisticated technological and regional dominance. Multinational corporations will find it difficult to overcome such market dominance when the market becomes open in the near future. Furthermore, these companies do not in any way resemble the so-called Chinese family firms as described in the existing literature. An interesting and significant question about the "new" development is whether these Chinese firms will further adopt Western models of multidivisional structures and administrative practices, or will return to or adapt some aspects of the management strategies of traditional "Chinese family firms" in the near future.

There are good reasons to expect the former rather than the latter. In order to strengthen and maintain market dominance and competitiveness, these Chinese conglomerates are likely to transform not only their organizational structures but also management practices. As they continue to shed the legacies of a state-run and collectivized economy and raise capital through the equity market locally and globally, the requisite corporate reforms in governance and shareholder accountability are likely to push their management structures toward greater transparency and further away from the characteristics of traditional family firms. If such corporate reforms eventuate, the Chinese experience could resemble the American transformation almost a century earlier. There is of course no guarantee for such developments, and much depends on the willingness of the Chinese government to relax state control and/or succumb to market forces.[4]

The factor of development in the Chinese domestic economy suggested here complements the argument advanced by Long and Han in Chapter 3, where they attempt to explain why Chinese entrepreneurs have yet to fully resemble their Western counterparts or behave similarly. Long and Han attribute the difference to a lack of well established institutional support to facilitate *socialized* transactions rather than purported cultural traits. Taking into account the lack of internal consumption engines will help us to further pinpoint internal structural limitations of the Chinese economy in the past that affected entrepreneurial practices. As the Chinese domestic market matures and a legal system is established to support socialized or institutionalized transactions, the importance of personalized transactions should decline accordingly (North 2000). The ability of overseas Chinese to take advantage of the growing Chinese market would further accelerate the pace and direction of corporate transformation as well. In fact, the continual development of the Chinese domestic economy is potentially a testing ground for evaluating whether Chinese cultural practices indeed inhibit corporate transformation and/or how structural contingencies limited the development of Chinese entrepreneurship in the past.

Finally, there is another more fundamental social process that has been in place for quite some time but is almost completely neglected in the business entrepreneur literature: the pure force of demography (but see Wong 2004). By this, I mean the changing composition of the population due to the cessation of migration flows from China and population growth via natural fertility, which has significant impacts on the composition of the labor force in general and the patterns of entrepreneurship in particular. China's closing of its border from the 1950s to the early 1970s, due to internal chaos and political instability, effectively curbed the large outflows of refugees from the mainland, although illegal immigration and smuggling into Hong Kong continued, though on a substantially reduced scale. A similar cessation of migration has occurred in many Southeast Asian countries such as Indonesia and Malaysia.

Given the well documented role immigrant Chinese entrepreneurs—particularly those coming from particular localities or regions of China, such as the Shanghainese in Hong Kong (Wong 1988) and Fujianese and Hakka immigrants throughout Southeast Asia (Brown 1994)—played in the early development of Asian economies, the cessation of Chinese migration is particularly significant. Interacting with globalization and modernization, the ensuing demographic changes arguably transformed the profiles and characteristics of Chinese entrepreneurship in some East and Southeast Asian countries. The composition of Chinese entrepreneurs in these countries today tends to differ significantly from the past. According to official statistics analyzed by Wong in Chapter 4, for example, the proportion of immigrant entrepreneurs (self-employed and employers) in Hong Kong dwindled dramatically from 85 percent in 1971 to less than 45 percent in 2001. No longer locked up in immigrant mentality (*luoye guigen*), an indigenization of Chinese entrepreneurs (*luodi shenggen*) raises the issue of the role of Western socialization, culture, lifestyles, and consumption in the formation of local particularities and ethnic integration in addition to a modern outlook. Furthermore, with indigenization, the "Chinese" entrepreneurs' level of attachment to traditional

Chinese practices (social, cultural, and economic) should no longer be assumed but has to be examined empirically. Having had an improved education and training, the young generation of entrepreneurs now engages in a wide repertoire of economic activities and its knowledge of and probable affinity to Western organizational and management practices help to enhance its ability to compete and adapt in the rapidly changing environment. Corresponding changes in business practices can then be expected, rendering the identification of a "new breed of Chinese entrepreneurs" more plausible and credible. Wong in Chapter 9 presents some supportive evidence in the case of Hong Kong entrepreneurs in the late 1990s.

Further evidence of such a generational shift and the development of local identity and gradual erosion of ethnic divisions can also be found in Gomez's chapter on business ties in contemporary Malaysia (Chapter 5), where intra-ethnic business relationships are slowly transformed into inter-ethnic ones. Unlike the ill formed 'Ali-Baba' alliances earlier, these new inter-ethnic relationships involve equal competency of partners, with both contributing to the productive development of the firm. Although Gomez is skeptical about the effectiveness of the Malaysian government's affirmative action policies in the past, it remains interesting to explore if they might nonetheless have contributed to the rise of a more confident Bumiputera middle class and a more integrative Chinese community. Under a long period of stable population growth without any massive influx of immigrants, a new generation of Malay Chinese, embracing Malaysia as their homeland, has emerged. The entrepreneurial practices of this young generation will have much to instruct us on the subject of a "new breed of Chinese entrepreneurs." As an interesting contrast, the booming Chinese economy and its relatively open immigration policy since the 1980s have created a new class of transnational Chinese entrepreneurs inside and outside China, as shown in Chapters 6 and 8. They are either immigrants themselves or returnees holding foreign degrees, credentials, or even passports. These new immigrant entrepreneurs differ significantly from their predecessors and add a new complexity and rich resources for exploring the question of the rise of a new breed of Chinese entrepreneurs.

In sum, various interactive factors, including globalization and local institutional and demographic changes, shape the contemporary contexts in which Chinese entrepreneurs operate. Whether these lead to significant departures from the profiles and business practices of Chinese entrepreneurs established in past studies which warrant the identification of a new breed of Chinese entrepreneurs remains to be seen. More systematic research that gauges the extent of transformation and its implications for future development, such as the studies collected in this volume, is needed. In any case, it is clear that, rather than the cultural argument underlying previous understandings and characterizations of Chinese entrepreneurs, sociological enquiries into the structural arrangements in which contemporary Chinese entrepreneurs are located will be particularly illuminating.

The state of East Asian economies

To better contextualize changes in Chinese entrepreneurship, it is useful to have a general picture of the East Asian economies in which many Chinese entrepreneurs operate, and to establish particularly whether the 1997 Asian economic crisis had any significant long-term effects on the growth and performance of the East Asian economies. Cumulative data show that despite drastic immediate impact, the crisis had little lasting effects on economic growth in the region. Furthermore, though many of the countries spun quickly into recessions, experienced currency devaluation, and encountered deflationary pressures, much of the poor performance in the following years might have more to do with the aftermath of the global meltdown of the Internet and Communication Technology bubble (or the ICT bubble in short) in 2000/01 than the 1997 crisis itself.[5] More importantly, the temporarily slowed-down economic growth did not impede the growing integration of East Asian economies and their deepening relationship with global capitalism.

If many of the East Asian economies faced stagnation or contraction in nominal terms after the crisis, growth in terms of constant prices after adjustment to price deflation gives a somewhat different picture. After accounting for the adjustments (for example, in constant US$ terms), the values of per capita GDP and annual growth rates in the East Asian economies all indicate significant rebounds from their lows in 1998 (see Figures 1.1 and 1.2 for details). The only exception is the Hong Kong economy, where its recession ended only after 2003 (Census and Statistics Department 2006). The inept handling of the crisis by the newly formed HKSAR government amidst an accelerated economic restructuring from manufacturing to service economy arguably accounts for this exceptionally slow recovery. As a group, the East Asian economies continued to achieve growth rates that were substantially better than many advanced, developed economies such as the United States and the European Union. Such stellar performance is, of course, related to the booming Chinese economy, as China turned into a *de facto* global factory. In fact, relative to the heights in the early 1990s, the rate of expansion of the Chinese economy has already dropped somewhat after 1997, though it still boasted an enviable rate of 7–9 percent per annum between 1998 and 2003.

Beneath the steady economic performance of the East Asian countries lies another important development—increasing investment activities *within* the region. Until the 1980s, foreign direct investment (FDI) in the Asia-Pacific region tended to come from former colonial powers, especially Great Britain and the United States. In the 1970s, the share gradually shifted to Japan as Japanese firms scouted around for better investment and production opportunities in East and Southeast Asia (Blomqvist 1993; Lobanov 1995). The amount of FDI in the region remained high in the 1980s, except that it was now the Four Little Dragons actively taking the lead, particu-

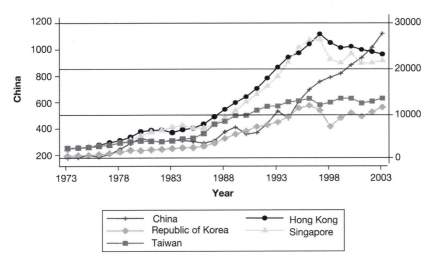

Figure 1.1 Per capita GDP in constant US$.

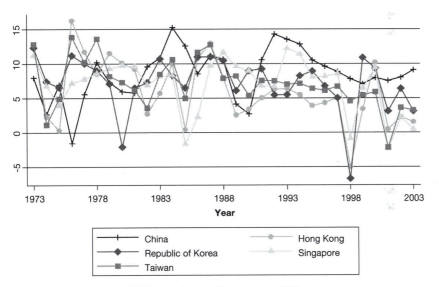

Figure 1.2 Per capita GDP growth rates in constant US$.

larly with investments in mainland China. The Little Dragons' engagement
in foreign investment was driven by complex reasons. These include chronic
internal labor shortages, huge accumulation of foreign reserves, economic
restructuring, and changing comparative advantages of neighboring countries. Together, these factors prompted the Little Dragons to search for
more advantageous production locations in China, Indonesia, Malaysia,
Thailand, and Vietnam. According to UNCTAD statistics, about 80 percent

of FDI that originates from developing countries come from just seven countries; six of them are East Asian NICs. Furthermore, Hong Kong alone accounts for about two thirds of the total among the group of seven (Dicken 2003:56–57). Besides changes in the sources of foreign investment, the nature of FDI in the region has also changed. Beginning with investment in the extraction of raw materials in the immediate postwar period, it shifted to manufacturing in the 1960s, and finally to services in the past two decades. As illustrated in various chapters in this volume and elsewhere, the development has resulted in a complex network of transnational firms in the Asia-Pacific region, where complementary units are often dispersed in multiple countries.

Cross-border investments by East Asian companies tend to concentrate geographically around the source country. This pattern is consistent with theoretical arguments about the significance of psychic distance or economic horizon in economic calculation, which postulate that the perceived advantages of specific locations are related to differences in business culture and judicial and government systems (Aitken 1973). This is especially true for small and medium-sized companies with limited resources when they are forced to relocate to other production sites. The experiences of Hong Kong entrepreneurs in China and Taiwan businesses in Southeast Asia certainly corroborate such considerations, as the discussions in chapters by Wong and Chen, Jou, and Hsiao indicate.

A significant by-product of cross-border investments is the triggering or acceleration of lasting structural changes in the East Asian economy, with rising intra-regional trade and economic interdependency and the evolvement of an integrated regional economic system. The empirical evidence presented below further suggests that the degree of internal integration has accelerated after the 1997 crisis (Isogai et al. 2002; Kamada et al. 2002). The East Asian economies have shown two remarkable developments since the 1980s; namely, (a) total exports and imports grew at faster rates than total production; and (b) intra-regional trade in East Asia grew more rapidly than total trade (Kamada et al. 2002:3). While the former indicates greater interconnectedness with the global economy, the latter reflects accelerated internal integration. As a result, the share of intra-regional trade in East Asia increased from 20 percent in 1980 to 36 percent in 2000, excluding Japan.[6] The increase is equally impressive when Japan is included, from 33 to 46 percent over the same period (Kamada et al. 2002).

The growth of intra-regional trade over time is presented graphically in Figure 1.3, adopted from Isogai et al. (2002). Both seasonally unadjusted and adjusted (not shown) figures clearly indicate that although intra-regional trade dropped temporarily soon after the 1997 crisis, both its volume and pace of growth rebounded quickly to surpass earlier records. However, the crisis had virtually no effects on exports from East Asia to the United States. They continued to grow unabated until the burst of the ICT bubble in 2000/01, which resulted in a slowdown in global demand. Thus, not only

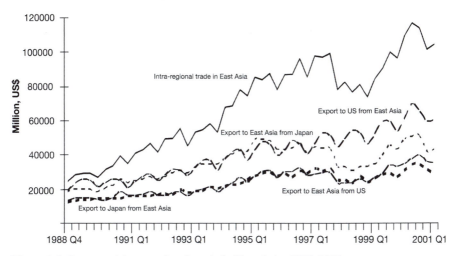

Figure 1.3 Intra- and inter-regional trade in East Asia, 1988–2001.

did the larger Asia-Pacific region become increasingly integrated with the global economy, but the degree of economic integration within the region also continued to grow significantly.

The growing interdependence of East Asian economies is evident in another emerging phenomenon – business cycle synchronization in East Asia (Moneta and Rüffer 2006). These economies now share significant common growth dynamics and they tend to grow and contract at similar paces. Such co-movement is, of course, directly related to their common export-oriented activities. Using statistics from the *Trade Development Report 2005* (UNCTAD 2005), Figure 1.4 presents recent trends in annual rates of growth in exports from a selective group of East Asian countries, while Table 1.1 reports the origins and destinations of world merchandise trade over the past several decades.

The degree of co-movement in exports in the six economies was high throughout the 1990s. While such synchronization is to be expected among the Four Little Dragons, Japan's inclusion is surprising. At first glance, China seems to be somewhat detached from the pack, though its average correlation of 0.79 with others is still substantial. Since 1999, the average correlation among all six countries increases dramatically to 0.97, indicating almost *full* synchronization. The emergence of an integrated export system is manifested through the triangular trade pattern, with Hong Kong and Singapore acting as trans-shipment hubs. Of course, this strong inter-dependency within the region is driven to a large extent by developments outside the region, that is, economic demands from the United States and the European Union. Nonetheless, short of a global recession, the future development of these economies as a system remains promising, especially since the Chinese domestic market is expected to grow rapidly in the near future.

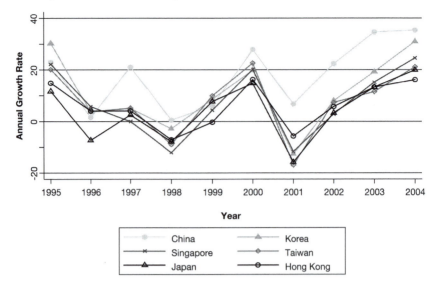

Figure 1.4 Export growth in East Asia, 1995–2004.

In terms of both export volumes and growth, the statistics in Table 1.1 confirm the rising importance of export and import activities from developing countries between 1970 and 2003. However, a detailed examination of the breakdown by region indicates that much of the growth is derived from East Asia. For instance, the share of exports from East Asia was 21.9 percent in 1970 and it has increased exponentially since then, to 24.1 percent in 1980, 49.4 percent in 1990, and 60.4 percent in 2003. As expected, the rise is particularly strong in China (from 3.6 percent in 1970 to 18.1 percent in 2003), featuring a fivefold increment. The Four Little Dragons' rise in share was relatively milder but still substantial (from 10.4 percent to 29.3 percent over the same period, indicating an almost threefold increment). In other words, economic growth in the developing world remains highly skewed and the rise of East Asia appears to be at the expense of other developing countries, notably countries in the African continent. Despite the hype about globalization and its associated positive changes, if East Asia is excluded, there has been virtually no change in world merchandise trade among the developing world in the past few decades. There is, however, some suggestive evidence that the recent expansion of intra-regional trade among East Asian countries has some spillover effects into other developing countries. The UNCTAD labels the new geography of international trade as "South-South trade." South-South exports increased from 25.1 percent in 1965 to 26.9 percent in 1985 and 43.4 percent in 2003 (UNCTAD 2005).

The data analyzed above clearly belie the bleak scenarios predicted by mass media pundits during the crisis. Contrary to expectations, the East Asian economies experienced robust growth again soon after suffering from

Table 1.1 Origins and destinations of merchandise trade, 1970–2003

	World market share					Average annual growth in value			
	1970	1980	1990	2000	2003	70–80	80–90	90–00	00–03
A. World merchandise exports									
Developed countries	75.0	65.3	72.0	65.7	64.8	18.8	7.3	5.9	4.6
Developing countries	19.2	29.5	24.3	31.6	32.1	25.6	3.1	8.9	5.8
Latin America	5.5	5.5	4.1	5.5	5.0	20.8	1.7	10.3	1.6
Developing Asia	8.5	18.0	16.9	23.8	24.7	29.6	4.6	9.5	6.7
South Asia	1.1	0.7	0.8	1.0	1.1	16.1	6.9	9.1	8.6
(India)	0.6	0.4	0.5	0.7	0.8	17.3	7.3	9.5	10.7
East Asia	4.2	7.1	12.0	18.6	19.4	26.6	11.7	10.4	6.9
(1st-Tier NIEs)	2.0	3.8	7.6	10.3	9.4	28.2	14.4	8.8	2.6
(China)	0.7	0.9	1.8	3.9	5.8	20.0	12.8	14.5	20.8
West Asia	3.1	9.9	3.9	4.1	4.1	34.5	-6.3	5.8	5.2
Africa	5.0	5.9	3.2	2.3	2.4	21.6	-1.2	2.8	6.9
Developing countries, excluding E. Asia	16.5	24.8	14.8	17.5	16.8	25.5	-0.9	8.1	3.8

continued on next page

Table 1.1 (continued)

	World market share					Average annual growth in value			
	1970	1980	1990	2000	2003	70–80	80–90	90–00	00–03
B. World Merchandise Imports									
Developed countries	75.6	70.8	73.1	69.5	68.4	19.4	6.9	6.2	4.3
Developing countries	18.8	24.0	22.5	28.7	29.0	23.6	4.0	8.3	5.4
Latin America	5.7	6.1	3.7	5.9	4.8	20.6	0.0	11.5	-2.5
Developing Asia	8.4	13.1	15.8	20.8	21.9	26.6	6.5	8.2	7.1
South Asia	1.3	1.3	1.1	1.2	1.4	20.0	3.7	8.6	9.2
(India)	0.6	0.7	0.7	0.8	0.9	20.7	4.2	10.1	11.5
East Asia	*5.1*	*7.2*	*11.7*	*16.7*	*17.6*	*24.4*	*10.9*	*8.9*	*7.0*
(1st-Tier NIEs)	*2.7*	*4.3*	*7.4*	*9.8*	*8.7*	*25.7*	*11.9*	*8.1*	*1.2*
(China)	*0.7*	*1.0*	*1.5*	*3.4*	*5.4*	*23.7*	*13.5*	*13.0*	*22.3*
West Asia	2.0	4.6	2.6	2.8	2.9	33.6	-2.4	5.2	7.1
Africa	4.4	4.6	2.9	2.0	2.2	21.0	-0.2	3.5	8.8
Developing countries, excluding East Asia	15.4	18.8	13.6	15.5	15.0	23.2	0.7	7.7	3.5

Source: Table 4.2 in Trade Development Report 2005 (UNCTAD 2005).

Note:
First-tier NIEs include Hong Kong, the Republic of Korea, Singapore, and Taiwan. The shares of Southeast Europe and the Commonwealth of Independent States (CIS) are not included in this table, which explains why the shares do not add up to 100.

a temporary setback. Riding this growth trend, Chinese entrepreneurs in the region continued to expand their influence. For instance, ethnic Chinese entrepreneurs in Malaysia have grown considerably stronger over time while the Bumiputeras suffered most of the adverse effects of the crisis. According to Gomez, the share of Chinese equity floated in the Malaysian stock market doubled from 22.8 percent in 1969 to 45.5 percent in 1999, despite decades of affirmative action policies by the Malaysian government to strengthen the Bumiputeras and undermine ethnic Chinese entrepreneurs. Taking the crisis in stride, Malaysian Chinese capitalists were able to take advantage of the situation to further consolidate their influence in the Malaysian economy. While such ability could conceivably be attributed to the Chinese cultural heritage, it is perhaps more illuminating to focus on their high rates of savings to weather the storm and their willingness to take risks in buying failing businesses at the expense of Bumiputeras and even their own co-ethnics. Of course, these economic activities remain profitable, particularly among the new class of transnational entrepreneurs, because of their expanding trade partnership with China. Similar developments can also be observed in Indonesia and Thailand, as the latter became integrated into the economic system of the Asia-Pacific region.

In sum, the Asia-Pacific economic region shows consistent growth despite a brief break in the 1997 crisis, and the increasing interdependency within the region further indicates the emergence of an integrated regional economic system. Therefore, rather than reflecting inherent deficiencies in the so-called Chinese (Confucian) culture, the crisis should best be seen as a normal corrective economic cycle, just like the ICT bubble in 2000–01, to wring out previous excesses in economic activities such as speculations in property and equity markets. If the 1973 world economic crisis can be seen retrospectively as triggering or accelerating the transformation of Western capitalism into global capitalism, the 1997 Asian economic crisis may similarly be regarded as the catalyst to transform East Asian economies into active participants in the evolving global system. One important implication of this development is the heightened economic activities and cooperation between managers of global corporations, transnational entrepreneurs, and local entrepreneurs, who may all be some form of reincarnation of "Chinese entrepreneurs." In this light, the transformation of Chinese entrepreneurship is clearly an ongoing business; it is still too early to perceive its final destination.

Evolving "Chinese" entrepreneurs

Whether or not the twenty-first century will indeed be the "Chinese century" as some predicted, it is clear that Chinese entrepreneurs will play significant roles in global economic development in the new millennium. The interesting question is not whether Chinese entrepreneurs will be able to gain greater economic power globally but, rather, whether their development will follow or resemble the trajectories of their Western business counter-parts. In other words, it remains to be seen whether the so-called Chinese cultural characteristics will lead entrepreneurs to develop alternative business organizational structure and management practices as they become more integrated into the global capitalist economic system. Will Chinese entrepreneurs adopt established Western corporate practices and openly embrace a more institutionalized and socialized environment for economic (and social) transactions? Or will they try to adapt (some of) the practices of Chinese family firms in order to operate in the changed global economic environment?

To ask such a question is to take the subject of Chinese entrepreneurship beyond the national/ethnic cultural framework that has shaped past studies. This shift has already taken place in recent scholarship. Instead of treating Chinese culture as some encompassing entity defining an essential identity for Chinese entrepreneurs, studies of Chinese entrepreneurship and business practices have increasingly focused attention on a more sociological concept – the prevalence of social networks in business. Social networks can be based on family and kinship ties, friendship relationships, and/or strategic alliances. The shift directs our attention from individual or cultural parti-cularities to resource mobilization and utilization, that is, the maximization of available resources given existing structural constraints. This approach is productively adopted in the chapters by Liu, Chen et al., and Bian, which powerfully demonstrate Chinese entrepreneurs' utilization of social networks to further their business. There is, however, still the danger of seeing social networks as some form of particular Chinese national/ethnic cultural characteristics. It needs to be stressed that the utilization of family and friends is just one kind of skillful manipulation and exploitation of available resources by entrepreneurs (Yao 2002). Indeed, social networking is now considered prevalent and operational not only among Chinese but throughout the business world (Burt 1992; Portes 1998; Uzzi 1996). To explore the *particularities* of business networks among Chinese entrepreneurs, then, we need to examine whether/how Chinese business networks differ in terms of structures and processes from other business networks. Until particular differences are persuasively demonstrated, it is more reasonable and fruitful to interpret the utilization of ethnic networks by Chinese entrepreneurs as strategic and skillful risk management, and allow for changes over time in the nature, extent, and usefulness of such resources.

The East Asian economies and the environment for Chinese entrepreneurship have clearly changed considerably in the past few decades. These changes are the outcomes of multitudinous factors, including globalization, technological innovations, diffusion of Western values and lifestyles, changes in demographic composition, and institutionalization. Given the emphasis of global capitalism on flexibility and mobility, more and perhaps even faster changes are expected as the new generation of Chinese entrepreneurs seeks ways to maximize business opportunities in diverse and changing economic environments. Such development is in line with the nature of entrepreneurship, the essential elements of which are change and adaptation, with individual entrepreneurs acting as "the agent of change" who responds creatively to incentives embedded in different institutional frameworks (North 1990:83). Thus, the study of entrepreneurship, Chinese or otherwise, should attend to social relations—both relations within the enterprise and its embedded relationships with the immediate surroundings (Swedberg 2000:35). Along this line, the studies collected here situate Chinese entrepreneurs in various national, social, and institutional settings, to offer diverse interpretations of the meaning and social construction of Chinese entrepreneurship in contemporary Asia. Without offering a definitive view on what constitutes Chinese entrepreneurship today and whether there is indeed a new breed of Chinese entrepreneurs, they provide rich analyses and discussions that enable further exploration of an evolving phenomenon.

Notes

1 According to statistics reported by the Hong Kong Exchanges and Clearing Limited, the total value of IPO has increased exponentially in recent years (from US$8.3 billion in 2001 to US$38.6 billion in 2005). The 2006 figure is expected to exceed previous records again. Although it is widely anticipated that Hong Kong would not be able to sustain the same level of offerings in 2007, many mainland Chinese companies understand the importance of raising equity through the Hong Kong capital market and have plans to do so in the near future.
2 According to official reports, over 70 percent of China's economy now depends on foreign trade, which has been growing at an annual rate of over 30 percent for years (*People's Daily* 2005).
3 As stipulated in the WTO agreements, China has to eliminate all trade barriers and expand market access to goods from foreign countries no later than 2010.
4 How extensive the Chinese corporate reform can go is of course an open question. Corruption, embezzlement, and mismanagement by corporate officials are still commonplace, and the interests of shareholders are not yet fully protected and guaranteed. The grip of the Communist Party and the central government is still strong and should not be ignored.
5 Tellingly, there is no attempt to link the irrational exuberance of Western investors to their salutary Christian or Anglo-Saxon culture. Again, the parallel behaviors of Western and Chinese investors indicate clearly that there is nothing intrinsically right or wrong in their respective culture or cultural practices.
6 Their definition of East Asia includes NIEs (South Korea, Hong Kong, Singapore), the ASEAN (Thailand, the Philippines, Indonesia, and Malaysia), and China.

References

Aitken, N. D. (1973) "The Effect of the EEC and EFTA on European Trade: A Temporal Cross-sectional Analysis," *American Economic Review* 63:881–92.
Aldrich, H. (1999) *Organizations Evolving*, London: Sage.
Berger, P. L. and Luckmann, T. (1966) *The Social Construction of Reality: A Treatise in the Sociology of Knowledge*, New York: Anchor Books.

Blomqvist, H. C. (1993) *Intra-Region Foreign Investment in East Asia*, Swedish School of Economics and Business Administration Working Paper no. 264.

Bonacich, E. and Appelbaum, R. (2000) *Behind the Label: Inequality in the Los Angeles Apparel Industry*, Berkeley, CA: University of California Press.

Brown, R. A. (1994) *Capital and Entrepreneurship in South-East Asia*, New York: St. Martin's Press.

Burt, R. S. (1992) *Structural Holes: The Social Structure of Competition*, Cambridge, MA: Harvard University Press.

Census and Statistics Department (2006) *Hong Kong Statistics*, Hong Kong: Census and Statistics Department.

Central Intelligence Agency (2007) *The World Factbook 2007*, Washington, DC: Central Intelligence Agency.

Committee on the Promotion of Civic Education (2005) *Biennial Opinion Survey on Civic Education 2004*, Hong Kong: Committee on the Promotion of Civic Education.

Dicken, P. (2003) *Global Shift: Reshaping the Global Economic Map in the 21st Century*, Fourth Edition, New York: Guilford Press.

DiMaggio, P. J. and Powell, W. W. (1983) "The Iron Cage Revisited: Institutional Isomorphism and Collective Rationality in Organizational Fields," *American Sociological Review* 48:147–60.

Dirlik, A. (1995) "Confucius in the Borderlands: Global Capitalism and the Reinvention of Confucianism," *boundary 2* 22:229–73.

Harvey, D. (1990) *The Condition of Postmodernity: An Enquiry into the Origins of Cultural Change*, Cambridge, MA: Blackwell.

Gereffi, G. (1996) "Global Commodity Chains: New Forms of Coordination and Control Among Nations and Firms in International Industries," *Competition and Change* 1:427–39.

Gereffi, G, Korzeniewicz, R. P., and Korzeniewicz, M. (1994) "Introduction: Global Commodity Chains," in G. Gereffi and M. Korzeniewicz (eds.) *Commodity Chains and Global Capitalism*, Westport, CT: Praeger.

Granovetter, M. (1985) "Economic Action and Social Structure: The Problem of Embeddedness," *American Journal of Sociology* 91:481–510.

International Monetary Fund (2007) *World Economic Outlook Database*, April.

Isogai, T., Morishita, H., and Rüffer, R. (2002) *Analysis of Intra- and Interregional Trade in East Asia: Comparative Advantage Structure and Dynamic Interdependence in Trade Flows*, Discussion Paper 02-E-1, International Department, Bank of Japan.

Kamada, K., Nakayama, K., and Takagawa, I. (2002) *Deepening Interdependence in the Asia-Pacific Region: An Empirical Study Using a Macro-econometric Model*, Working Paper 02–09, Research and Statistics Department, Bank of Japan.

Kerr, C., Dunlop, J. T., Harbinson, F. H., and Myers, C. A. (1960) *Industrialism and Industrial Man: The Problems of Labor and Management in Economic Growth*, Cambridge, MA: Harvard University Press.

Lerner, D. (1958) *The Passing of Traditional Society: Modernizing the Middle East*, Glencoe, IL: The Free Press.

Lobanov, S. S. (1995) *Japan's Foreign Direct Investment and Financing of Affiliates in East Asia*, International Economic Conflict Discussion Paper no. 85, Economic Research Center, School of Economics, Nagoya University, Japan.

Moneta, F. and Rüffer, R. (2006) *Business Cycle Synchronisation in East Asia*, European Central Bank (ECB) Working Paper no. 671, European Central Bank.

Meyer, J. W. and Rowan, B. (1977) "Institutionalized Organizations: Formal-Structure as Myth and Ceremony," *American Journal of Sociology* 83:340–63.

North, D. (1990) *Institutions, Institutional Change and Economic Performance*, Cambridge: Cambridge University Press.

——(2000) "Big-bang Transformations of Economic Systems: An Introductory Note," *Journal of Institutional and Theoretical Economics* 156:3–8.

People's Daily (2005) "China's Dependence upon Overseas, Domestic Demand Severely Imbalanced," November 20, 2005.

Portes, A. (1998) "Social Capital: Its Origins and Applications in Modern Sociology," *Annual Review of Sociology* 24:1–24.

Portes, A., Guarnizo, L. E., and Landolt, P. (1999)"The Study of Transnationalism: Pitfalls and Promise of an Emergent Research Field," *Ethnic and Racial Studies* 22:217–37.

——(2002) "Transnational Entrepreneurs: An Alternative Form of Immigrant Economic Adaptation," *American Sociological Review* 67:278–98.

Powell, W. W. and DiMaggio, P. J. (eds.) (1991) *The New Institutionalism in Organizational Analysis*, Chicago, IL: University of Chicago Press.

Rogers, E. M. (1962) *The Diffusion of Innovations*, Glencoe, IL: The Free Press.

Schramm, W. (1964) *Mass Media and National Development: The Role of Information in Developing Countries*, Urbana, IL: University of Illinois Press.

Sklair, L. (1995) *Sociology of the Global System*, Baltimore, MD: Johns Hopkins University Press.

——(1999) "Competing Concepts of Globalization," *Journal of World-Systems Research* 5:143–64.

Swedberg, R. (2000) "The Social Science View of Entrepreneurship: Introduction and Practical Applications," in R. Swedberg (ed.) *Entrepreneurship: The Social Science View*, Oxford: Oxford University Press.

Treiman, D. J. (1970) "Industrialization and Social Stratification," in E. Lauman (ed.) *Social Stratification: Research and Theory for the 1970s*, Indianapolis, IN: Bobbs-Merrill.

UNCTAD (United Nations Conference on Trade and Development (2005) *Trade Development Report 2005*, New York: United Nations.

Uzzi, B. (1996) "The Sources and Consequences of Embeddedness for the Economic Performance of Organizations: The Network Effect," *American Sociological Review* 61:674–98.

Wallerstein, I. (1974) *The Modern World-System*, New York: Academic Press.

Wong, R. S. K. (2004) "Chinese Business Firms and Business Entrepreneurs in Hong Kong," in E. T. Gomez and H. H. M. Hsiao (eds.) *De-essentializing Capitalism: Chinese Enterprise, Transnationalism, and Identity*, London: RoutledgeCurzon.

Wong, S. L. (1988) *Emigrant Entrepreneurs: Shanghai Industrialists in Hong Kong*, New York: Oxford University Press.

Yao, S. C. (2002) *Confucian Capitalism: Discourse, Practice and the Myth of Chinese Enterprise*, London: RoutledgeCurzon.

Part II

Theoretical and empirical concerns

2 Hybrid capitalism

A new breed of Chinese entrepreneurship in a global era

Henry Wai-chung Yeung

Introduction[1]

For several centuries, tens of millions of ethnic Chinese people in East and Southeast Asia have engaged in a distinctive form of economic organization through which an informal array of Chinese entrepreneurs, traders, financiers and their closely knit networks of family members and friends came to dominate the economic sphere of the very host economies they later considered "home."[2] While deeply rooted in the cultural norms and social values of the traditional Chinese society in mainland China, this form of economic organization has evolved and adapted to dramatically different institutional contexts and political-economic conditions in the host Asian economies. In this chapter, I use the term *Chinese capitalism* as a heuristic device to describe this historically and geographically specific form of economic organization that refers to the social organization and political economy of the so-called "overseas Chinese"[3] living outside mainland China, particularly in East and Southeast Asia (i.e. Hong Kong, Macau, Taiwan, Singapore, Indonesia, Malaysia, the Philippines, Thailand and Vietnam).[4] Chinese capitalism is a dominant mode of economic organization in East and Southeast Asia because of not only its economic significance in the host economies, but also its complex and, yet, intricate social organization and authority systems. The sheer diversity and prowess of economic activities controlled and coordinated by these ethnic Chinese has enabled some of them to become the very foundations of the Asian economies in which they primarily reside and operate.

Skeptics, nevertheless, may question the independent existence and coherence of this phenomenon known as "Chinese capitalism." Building on the important contributions of Redding (1990), Hamilton (1991; 1996a; 1999a; 2004), Whitley (1992; 1999) and others, I believe that there is a concrete phenomenon—known as Chinese capitalism—to be described and explained. As this chapter will demonstrate, while this form of capitalist economic organization is changing in a global era, it is logical and reasonable to start an enquiry into Chinese capitalism by assuming it to be a relatively distinct and coherent phenomenon. This is indeed the underlying logic of Redding's (1990:9) seminal work *The Spirit of Chinese Capitalism* in which he "begins with an assumption that there is a distinct and bounded phenomenon to be explained, that it is the culmination of a set of processes which need to be seen historically, and that the beliefs and values of businessmen have a part to play in the understanding of it." In fact, such an assumption about capitalism's distinctiveness and coherence has been made ever since Max Weber's (1992) controversial treatise on the spirit of modern capitalism. In his 1920 introduction to the work, Weber (1992:xxxiv) argued that "in modern times the Occident has developed, in addition to this [political capitalism through wars and acquisitions], a very different form of capitalism which has appeared nowhere else: the rational capitalistic organization of (formally) free labour. Only suggestions of it are found elsewhere." Instead of subscribing to Karl Marx's view of capitalism as the valorization of capital through the exploitation of labor on a contractual basis (see also Screpanti, 2001), Weber (1983:41) believed that "[w]here we find that property is an object of trade and is utilised by individuals for profit-making enterprise in a market economy, there we have capitalism." He went on to describe and explain this distinct form of modern capitalism in the Occident in relation to a peculiar ethos of accumulating wealth continually for its own sake, the rational utilization of labour and the rise of modern rational organizations (see also Andreski, 1983; Berger, 1986; Saunders, 1995; Silk and Silk, 1996). The spirit of modern industrial capitalism that Weber (1992:27, 31) described refers to "that attitude which seeks profit rationally and systematically ... Where it appears and is able to work itself out, it produces its own capital and monetary supplies as the means to its ends."

What then distinguishes Chinese capitalism from other forms of economic organization at the turn of the twenty-first century? My interest does not rest with comparing the success and failure of different varieties of capitalism—a difficult question to which not many scholars other than Max Weber can at least provide some tentative answers. Rather, I seek to theorize in this chapter the *changing dynamics* of Chinese capitalism in relation to globalization tendencies, and how these changes and transformations have led to the emergence of Chinese capitalism as a form of hybrid capitalism and a new breed of Chinese entrepreneurs (see Yeung, 2004 for detail empirical data and analysis). To conduct such a dynamic analysis, however, I need to start with at least a distinct "template" of what Chinese capitalism might be, as we have known it today. This is an equally difficult task because Chinese capitalism, if it exists at all, is embedded within particular political and socioeconomic contexts that cannot be easily isolated. As Berger (1986:16) cautioned in his influential account of the "capitalist revolution," "it is not easy to excise the capitalist phenomenon from this wider context and look at it [capitalism], as if holding it with pincers under a lens, in any kind of 'pure' form." As such, I do not assume the existence of a "pure" form of capitalism—whether in its Anglo-American, German and Japanese genres—with which Chinese capitalism can be compared and contrasted. I also recognize the continuously evolving character and transformative power of these diverse genres of modern capitalism. To distinguish Chinese capitalism as a distinct mode of economic organization in East and Southeast Asia in the late twentieth century, it is thus reasonable to identify it with a set of common denominators so that subsequent changes and transformations can be discerned. As pointed out by Block (2002:224), "[i]t is not enough to say that capitalism is a constructed system. The task is to illuminate how it is constructed; to see how a diverse and often contradictory set of practices are welded together to produce something that has the appearance of being a natural and unified entity."

Conventional definitions of Chinese capitalism: four key attributes

Broadly speaking then, Chinese capitalism has four key defining attributes that, taken together, might satisfy the simple definition of capitalism as "production for a market by enterprising individuals or combines with the purpose of making a profit" (Berger 1986:19, emphasis omitted). First, Chinese capitalism refers to an institutionalized mode of economic organization that, until recent decades, operated largely outside mainland China. It is rationalized and represented by a particular kind of economic institution— *the Chinese family firm*. This predominance of the family firm, however, is clearly not unique to Chinese capitalism. In fact, more than 75 percent of all registered companies in the industrialized economies today remain family businesses, and a third of listed companies in the Fortune 500 have families at their helm (Becht et al. 2003). Forty-three of Italy's top 100 companies are family-owned and 26 of France's and 15 of Germany's are also family-owned. In the U.K., where ownership is rapidly dispersed throughout the twentieth century, Franks et al. (2003) found that founding families retained board control well beyond the sale of their ownership stake (see also Chandler 1990). According to a recent study of corporate ownership around the world, La Porta et al. (1999:481) even classified Microsoft Corporation as a family-owned firm as 23.7 per cent of the stock is still controlled by its founder, Bill Gates.

In Chinese capitalism, the family firm serves as the key organizational platform or "mode of organizing," in the words of Hamilton (2000), for the continuous accumulation of wealth by ethnic Chinese families that in turn defines the rationality of Chinese capitalism, albeit in culturally specific ways. As Weber (1992:xxxi–xxxii, italics original) reminded us, "[modern] capitalism is identical with the pursuit of profit, and forever *renewed* profit, by means of continuous, rational, capitalistic enterprise." While historically such "rational" capitalistic enterprises might not have been developed in mainland China, Chinese capitalism—as I define it here—is organized around a particular social system of economic action and business activities that manifests itself through complex webs of family networks and personal relationships. It is embedded in a peculiar form of political economy in which the ethnic Chinese rule the "host" economy and leave the political sphere to the reign of indigenous ethnic groups or colonial masters. Chinese capitalism is thus organized and coordinated via neither market relations nor hierarchies of "rational" firms (cf. Williamson 1975; 1985; Powell 1990). Rather, it encompasses both markets and hierarchies and configures these capitalist institutions through an informal system of social relationships and family obligations (see Hamilton 2000). Redding (1990:3), a leading proponent of Chinese capitalism, thus observed that:

> the Overseas Chinese [*sic*] have developed one particular form of organization—the family business—and kept to it. Admittedly there are refinements to it, a wide range of sizes and technologies in use, a great variety of products, services, and markets, and an adventurous set of new variations on how to spin it out to larger and larger size, but certain common denominators seem never to be departed from. It remains in essence a family fortress, and at the same time an instrument for the accumulation of wealth by a very specific set of people. It is guarded against incursions from outside influence, and its workings are not publicly known. It is usually run nepotistically, with a benevolent paternalism throughout. Much of its effectiveness derives from intense managerial dedication, much of its efficiency from creating a working environment which matches the expectations of employees from the same culture. It is, in a very real sense, a cultural artifact.

Similarly, Brown (2000:6) concurred that "[t]he major institution within Chinese business has been the family. The family was the source of funds, contacts and managers. The primacy of the family has been maintained in recent decades, despite rapid diversification and international expansion. In many cases, the Chinese firm had no distinct existence outside the family."

Second, Chinese capitalism is not a mode of economic organization bound within specific territorial boundaries of nation-states. It is indeed a *"stretchable"* form of capitalism that is embedded, but not limited by, the institutional contexts of the "home" economies. As noted by Hamilton (1996b:337), "Chinese capitalism is not confined to a political space the way many other forms of capitalism have been. Rather, Chinese capitalism fills an economic space." He further argued that "instead of equating it with national economies, capitalism is best conceptualized in terms of the organized economic activities and institutional conditions that constitute it, and countries are best conceptualized as locations where specific activities occur" (Hamilton 1999b:4). Brown (2000:171) also recognized that "the rapidly changing economic and geographical expansion of Chinese firms in Southeast Asia means that a description of Chinese capitalism must jump between different countries, as Chinese businesses jumped." Defined as such, Chinese capitalism has no clear-cut political boundaries. Rather, it can only be delimited by the geographic extent and spread of its economic activities. This attribute poses a peculiar problem to the analysis of comparative capitalism and business systems in economic sociology and international political economy, because most studies in these two fields tend to focus on the development and institutionalization of different "varieties" of capitalism in distinctive *national* contexts (e.g. the U.S.A. and the U.K. vs. Germany and Japan). As such, Chinese capitalism should be conceived as a *supra-national* form of economic organization. This flexible territoriality of Chinese capitalism partly explains why several leading sociologists of Chinese capitalism (e.g. Wong 1988; Redding 1990; Whitley 1992; 1999; Hamilton 1996a; 1999a; 1999c; Orrù et al. 1997) tend to focus on Hong Kong and Taiwan (instead of Southeast Asian countries) as their primary geographical "target" of analysis because ethnic homogeneity in these two economies tends to facilitate the analysis of the emergence of a distinctive business system and economic organization of capitalism. Even in these two ethnic Chinese economies, however, the issues of national sovereignty and territorial boundedness remain highly contested and questionable. Examining the impact of cultural globalization in Taiwan, Hsiao (2002) recently observed that a distinctively Taiwanese business system is infused with influences from all sorts of management styles and practices.

Despite the globalizing of Taiwan's economy and its businesses over the past few decades, it is clear that neither American nor Japanese management models have supplanted Taiwan's indigenous business practices. Instead, there is significant fusion of management styles in many of the multinationals operating in Taiwan as well as in many of the local companies that compete in world markets. As a result, there is no pure American, European, Japanese, or Taiwanese-Chinese management model that can best characterize the actual business culture of today's Taiwan (Hsiao 2002:52).

Third, Chinese capitalism has achieved some degree of structural coherence and rationality—or "spirit" in the words of Weber (1992)—through centuries of distinctive cultural practices and social organization originating from then imperial China. This identifiable association of the *geographical origin* of cultural practices in Chinese capitalism with China as the Middle Kingdom in its historical times differentiates Chinese capitalism from the economic organization of other diaspora groups such as the Jews. As noted by Hwang (1987:968),

> Historically and, to an extent, even in modern contexts, many Chinese have lived in encapsulated communities that are hierarchically organized, with major economic and other resources controlled by a few power figures who could arbitrarily allocate resources. In these settings, it has been imperative to be sensitive to one's social position and to the kinds of resources that one could elicit and be forced to give up through obligations incurred over long periods of time.

These cultural practices serve as the underlying logic for distinctive economic behavior and social action among ethnic Chinese. In many ways, most ethnic Chinese identify with this structural coherence and rationality that in turn legitimizes their very socioeconomic behavior. In short, there is a kind of "economic culture"—defined by Berger (1986:24) as "structures of consciousness"—that constitutes Chinese capitalism. Put in another way, this cultural coherence and legitimation in Chinese capitalism is akin to Storper and Salais' (1997) idea of the economy as a hybrid object constituted through a diversity of conventions and worlds of production in which actors organize and legitimize their action and behavior.

> The processes by which actors interpret their situations and then enter into pragmatic forms of coordination with other actors constitute the work of constructing the economy. Actors select and build meaningful courses of action in production by engendering routinized, largely implicit forms of coordination, which we call conventions. It is in generating conventions, and then drawing on them in practical activity, that the creative, out-of-equilibrium pathways of development are constructed. There is a great diversity of possible conventions for organizing productive activity, and also a great diversity of possible, conventionally agreed-upon economic tests of whether an activity is economically viable or 'efficient' (Storper and Salais 1997:18).

The world of conventions in which Chinese capitalism is situated can be best described as "the interpersonal world" whereby economic activities are conducted and legitimized via interpersonal relationships and networks.

Fourth, unlike its Anglo-American counterpart analyzed in the "new institutionalism" literature (DiMaggio and Powell 1991; Orrù et al. 1997; cf. Whitley 1999; Guillén 2001), Chinese capitalism is *actor-centered* rather than institution-specific. Whitley (1999: 25) argued that "units of economic decision-making and control vary considerably in their constitution and organization across capitalist economies ... 'Firms' are by no means the same sorts of economic actors in different economies." In the absence of formal legal structures and political systems that are unique to ethnic Chinese outside mainland China, social actors such as families and their business groups have become the primary driving force in Chinese capitalism. To a certain extent, this actor-specific constitution of Chinese capitalism is related to the "geopolitical anxiety" of ethnic Chinese in East and Southeast Asia.[5] Their geographical dispersal during the past two centuries and their lack of political power in the host economies of Southeast Asia have greatly increased their geopolitical anxiety that in turn legitimizes their reliance on family-based actors rather than host country institutions to coordinate their social and economic activities. While these actors are influenced by the formal rules and regulations of their host economies (e.g. property rights and ownership requirements), their capacity to transcend territorial boundaries enables them to exploit inherent advantages embedded in different formalized regulatory systems throughout East and Southeast Asian economies. While Hong Kong and Singapore no doubt have very similar historical legacies and geographical advantages, their political economies differ very significantly (laissez-faire vs. developmental state), and yet Chinese family firms from both economies operate in broadly similar ways (Yeung 2002a). This observation of *realized* similarities in Chinese family firms from two contrasting economies characterized by distinctive political-economic structures thus runs contrary to Whitley's (1999:44) qualification that:

> Even where norms and values are reproduced by families and ethnic communities which are both subnational and international, as in the case of the overseas Chinese [*sic*] and many migrant communities, the significance of these informal social organizations for systems of economic organization remains dependent on the structures and policies of states and political economies more generally.

This contradiction in the lack of dependence of Chinese capitalism on state structures and policies is largely explained by the key role of social actors rather than institutional structures in coordinating the economic organization of Chinese capitalism.

The rise of hybrid capitalism: Chinese entrepreneurship in a global era

While Chinese capitalism continues to evolve in East and Southeast Asia, however, there is much misunderstanding and mystification of Chinese capitalism in the popular literature and mass media. Before the onset of the 1997/98 Asian economic crisis, much of the literature and media reports tended to perpetuate an *essentialist reading* of Chinese capitalism. The popularity and prominence of such optimistic characterization of Chinese capitalism as "bamboo networks" (Weidenbaum and Hughes 1996), "*guanxi* capitalism," the "Chinese commonwealth" (Kao 1993), and the "Chinese global tribe" (Kotkin 1992) had contributed significantly to the emergence of an essentialist idea that all ethnic Chinese in East and Southeast Asia hold similar worldviews bounded within their traditional social and cultural values. In what Ong (1997:195) referred to as a process of "self-orientalization," Chinese capitalism was seen as static and self-contained within peculiar social and political contexts in East and Southeast Asia. During and after the crisis, this misreading of Chinese capitalism and its social practices contributed to the widely circulated "crony capitalism" argument that guided much of the rescue efforts by international organizations such as the World Bank and the International Monetary Fund. It is therefore timely to revisit and demystify the nature and dynamics of Chinese capitalism in East and Southeast Asia.

In his polemical *Harvard Business Review* article published over a decade ago, John Kao (1993) concluded that Chinese capitalism and its "worldwide web" will become a major force in the global economy of the twenty-first century. In another popular book *Tribes*, Joel Kotkin (1992:9) was seemingly pushing for a similar appraisal of Chinese capitalism by noting that "the Chinese global tribe likely will rank with the British-Americans and the Japanese as a driving force in transnational commerce." Despite the 1997/98 Asian economic crisis, it appears that current thinking in international political economy reveals a serious reappraisal of the economic potential of Chinese capitalism and its associated organizations and institutions. Once established in their host economies, ethnic Chinese and their business firms begin to extend their operations and networks across borders to form increasingly seamless webs of Chinese capitalism on a regional and, sometimes, global scale. No longer bounded by what Hwang (1987:968) called "encapsulated communities that are hierarchically organized," the participation of these firms and actors in the wider globalization processes has led to some fundamental changes in the ways in which they organize entrepreneurial activities and social life. These emergent developments thus underscore the significance of a relatively recent phenomenon in Chinese capitalism—the gradual transformations in the *modus operandi* and economic institutions of Chinese capitalism towards a more open and flexible form of capitalism. I refer to this reshaped form of Chinese capitalism as *hybrid capitalism* that is defined by its incomplete, partial and contingent transformations toward an evolving set of capitalist norms, institutions and structures. My argument on Chinese capitalism thus complements Hamilton's (1999b:4) idea that "capitalism is not a stable and readily identifiable configuration that, like a flower, suddenly bursts forth in bloom. Instead, capitalism is merely a term that covers an extremely wide range of diverse economic activities organized in the context of competitive markets and whose institutional conditions include private ownership and non-state decision making."

The rise of this peculiar mode of hybrid capitalism is characterized by the infusion of a variety of *disembedded* economic logics and social organizations that defy easy identification and simple analysis. As argued by Gibson-Graham (1996:15–16), "a capitalist site (a firm, industry or economy) or a capitalist practice (exploitation of wage labor, distribution of surplus value) cannot appear as the concrete embodiment of an abstract capitalist essence. It has no invariant 'inside' but is constituted by its continually changing and contradictory 'outsides.'" The very transformative nature of hybrid capitalism also implies that there is no definite end-state and form because political and economic outcomes of transition depend very much on complex interactions among social actors and their embedded institutions. The unboundedness of Chinese capitalism within distinctive national economies also contributes to its emergent hybridity because multiple forces and conditioning factors shaping its structures and trajectories are at work. The key attributes of Chinese capitalism identified earlier are more prone to changes and transformations than those embedded in distinctively national business systems (e.g. American, British, German, and Japanese). Nonini and Ong (1997:20) called this hybridized Chinese capitalism "ungrounded empires" that refer to "the new deterritorialized and protean structures of domination that span the Asia Pacific and within which diaspora Chinese act—empires that constantly change shape, being constituted by Chinese transnational practices in the ether of airspaces, international time-zones, migrant labor contracts, mass media images, virtual companies, and electronic transactions, and operating across all recognized borderlines." To fully understand this new hybrid system, we should focus our analytical attention on its dynamics of transformation, not its equilibrium features and structures. The concept of culture in Chinese capitalism, for example, needs to be reconceptualized as a repertoire of historically contingent and geographically specific practices that respond and adapt to changing local, regional, and global circumstances rather than as permanently fixed mental and organizational structures that resist challenges and pressures to change (see also Hwang 1987; Yang 2002). This perspective on Chinese capitalism as hybrid capitalism is particularly relevant as Chinese capitalism undergoes dynamic transformations and increases in its economic and organizational complexity throughout different East and Southeast Asian economies.

It is common for researchers in international political economy to argue that there are distinctive ways of organizing economic institutions in different parts of the world. This stability in capitalist organizations and patterns of economic relationships often persists in the face of rapid political-economic change external to the societies concerned. Together, these patterns of social and organizational structuring form different business systems that refer to a phenomenon of relatively stable and enduring patterns of business practices in specific localities and societies. Once established in particular institutional contexts, these business systems may develop considerable cohesion and become resistant to major changes. Even such powerful changes as internationalization and globalization are deemed to have only limited effects on the nature of business systems (Whitley 1994; 1998; 1999). Even after they are transformed, these distinctive systems of economic organization would "bear the marks of conflicts between opposing conceptions of capitalism and their allied institutional arrangements and interest groups" (Whitley 1998:447). Their evolutionary trajectories are seen as dependent on pre-existing configurations of domestic social, economic, and political institutions (see also Whitley and Kristensen 1996; 1997; Grabher and Stark 1997; Guillén 2001; Hall and Soskice 2001a). As noted earlier, this business systems perspective is particularly relevant in analyzing the political economies of the Asia-Pacific region where business systems are socially and institutionally embedded. In the words of Backman (1999:365), "[o]ld habits are hard to break" in the context of opaque and corrupted business systems in some Asian economies. To some observers, these business systems in Asia are characterized by the differentiated role of inward-looking inter-firm networks, excessive reliance on personal relationships in business transactions, and the strong intervention of the state in business and economy. These qualitative differences in business systems constitute a mosaic of distinct political economies in Asia.

The central question here is whether Chinese capitalism and its allegedly distinctive business systems can be as stable and enduring in today's context of accelerated globalization. Taking a transformative view of globalization similar to that of Held et al. (1999) and Dicken (2003), globalization is defined as a set of dialectical processes that simultaneously create a functionally interdependent world economy and accentuate the importance of all kinds of differences in societies and space (see also Yeung 1998b; 2002b). These processes include global flows of materials (e.g. people, goods) and intangibles (e.g. capital, technology, information and services). My core argument is that in assessing the impact of globalization tendencies, it is important to distinguish between business systems as enduring *structures* of capitalism, and key social actors in these systems as *agents* of change. The lack of explicit attention to actors and their strategies/behavior as agents of organizational and system change is a major lacuna in the business systems perspective and related approaches in studies of comparative capitalism (Hall and Soskice 2001a; cf. Clegg and Redding 1990). Indeed, Whitley (1996:414) offered an auto-critique that his perspective "tends to downplay the significance of particular firms' actions in favor of the more general logic of particular institutional systems ... [It] has not paid a great deal of attention to international forms of economic organization, or how the growing cross-national interdependence of some firms and markets has affected national business systems." He further suggested that future studies should address the ways in which "the growing internationalization of economic activities has affected interdependencies between firms and their domestic business environments" and the mechanisms by which the roles of economic actors "become institutionalized and reproduced ... as well as the circumstances in which they are liable to change" (Whitley 1996:423). Sharing the same vision for organization studies, Gereffi (1996:437) concluded that "traditional boundaries between nations, firms, and industries are being reconfigured, and organization theory as well as development theory need to find ways of encompassing all the relevant actors within a single framework."

Thus, it is important to theorize how globalization tendencies can transform the dynamics of Chinese capitalism and, subsequently, its nature and organization. While such transformations are brought about by these globalization tendencies, I do not propose that a new cross-national form of economic organization will replace existing configurations in Chinese capitalism by virtue of its superior efficiency and that radical changes in Chinese capitalism will occur rapidly and in a single direction. In this sense,

I share Whitley's (1999:118) caveat that globalization's "significance and consequences for the different varieties of capitalism ... remain to be clarified. In particular, the conditions under which these changes are likely to result in a qualitative transformation of distinctive forms of economic organization require more detailed specification" (see also Redding 2000). To specify these conditions of transforming Chinese capitalism in a global era, I argue that the dialectical tendencies of globalization toward homogenization and differentiation have differential impact on the configurations and dynamics of Chinese capitalism and its constituents. The organizing framework of analysis can be summarized in Figure 2.1.

While the existing literature on Chinese capitalism has examined the imprinting effects of culture and the structuring effects of institutional conditions on the nature and organization of Chinese capitalism, our knowledge about how actor-specific processes in an era of globalization have contributed to the emergence of a hybrid form of Chinese capitalism remains limited. Here, I argue that globalization tendencies are undermining certain social and institutional foundations of Chinese capitalism and accentuating the need for transformations in its traditional dimensions. Today, key actors in Chinese capitalism increasingly face the dilemma of succumbing to the pressures of transparency in order to secure global finance while preserving their traditional practices of network reliance and complex family ownership and/or control. In this context, there are less competitive advantages derived from the reliance on personal relationships on the basis of intra-regional business networks. Instead, the spatiality of business networks has been promoted from the intra-regional scale to the global scale. Global actor-networks are increasingly influencing the nature and organization of Chinese capitalism. Globalization has made possible the complex interpenetration of global actor-networks into Chinese capitalism. Consequently, globalization tendencies intensify local differences in business conduct and discursive practices. This tendency toward local differentiation facilitates the process of creating and reforming the hierarchies and structures of national economies, though local embeddedness of Chinese business firms remains a key source of competitive advantage. This localization process enables Chinese capitalism to retain certain core attributes, thus contributing to its growing hybridity in form and organization. The dynamics of Chinese capitalism depend critically on globalization tendencies as a major transformational force.

Contrary to the argument that Chinese capitalism tends to be relatively enduring over time because of historical legacies and institutional embeddedness, key actors and their business firms emerging from this distinctive mode of economic organization may be much more susceptible to changes brought about by globalization tendencies. This is because key actors in these ethnic Chinese firms are increasingly participating and enrolled into global actor-networks that, in turn, reshape how these actors conceive and operate their own business firms/networks (see Figure 2.1). Although Chinese capitalism

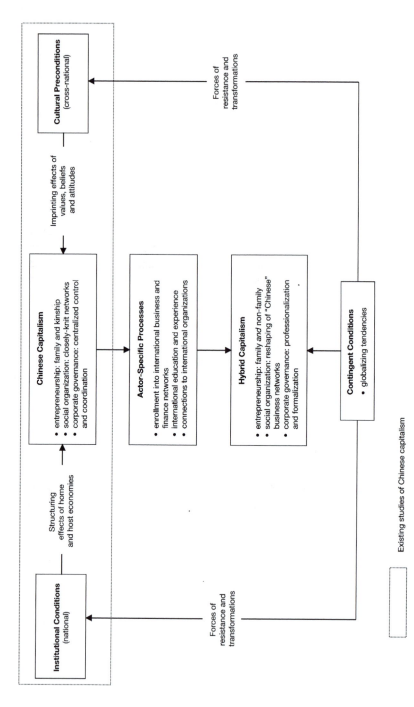

Figure 2.1 The hybridization of Chinese capitalism in a global era.

Cultural Preconditions
(cross-national)

Imprinting effects of
values, beliefs
and attitudes

Chinese Capitalism
- entrepreneurship: family and kinship
- social organization: closely-knit networks
- corporate governance: centralized control and coordination

Actor-Specific Processes
- enrollment into international business and finance networks
- international education and experience
- connections to international organizations

Hybrid Capitalism
- entrepreneurship: family *and* non-family
- social organization: reshaping of "Chinese" business networks
- corporate governance: professionalization and formalization

Contingent Conditions
- globalizing tendencies

Institutional Conditions
(national)

Structuring
effects of home
and host economies

Forces of
resistance and
transformations

Forces of
resistance and
transformations

Existing studies of Chinese capitalism

is structurally embedded in specific national social organization and political-economic institutions, its key actors are significantly more mobile and receptive to change. It is possible that globalization has only limited effects on Chinese capitalism at the structural level and, yet, significant transformative impact on its key organizational entities—ethnic Chinese and their business firms—at the level of key actors. The nature and degree of enrollment by key ethnic Chinese actors in the global economy therefore explains the dynamics of Chinese capitalism and its differential impact on specific actors and their embedded business systems. Facilitated by globalization, this enrollment process enables actors to experience different organizational behavior and business practices worldwide. It also allows these actors to transform their own business firms and networks, subject to some binding effects of their own distinctive business systems. When these dynamic changes occur collectively among ethnic Chinese firms in a clearly defined business system, fundamental institutional changes may be forthcoming, resulting in significant changes in the dominant forms and organization of Chinese capitalism itself. Chinese capitalism must be conceived as an "open" system and subject to dynamic changes from within, i.e. at the level of actors themselves. Interestingly, Whitley (1992; 1999) has pre-empted this argument:

> the open nature of social systems means that markets and firms can change as the result of learning and altered perceptions thus modifying the efficacy of previously successful structures and practices ... Social systems are open because they can develop emergent properties and powers as a result of reinterpretations of social and material realities which alter the nature of the social world. The meaningful and concept-dependent nature of social relations and institutions means that *internal* learning and changing perceptions as a result of *external* events can alter significantly and system outcomes become quite different. Thus, when enough people in an organization change their perception of what is going on and redefine its nature, its structure and procedures will alter (Whitley 1992:5–6, my emphasis).

But his distinction between internal learning and external events is not really meaningful in the analysis of how key actors in Chinese capitalism enroll and participate in global actor-networks. Also, Whitley has not pursued the argument further in his empirical analysis of business systems in East Asia. Elsewhere, in Olds and Yeung (1999) and Yeung (2000a; 2004), I elaborate in greater depth these complex interactions between actor-networks in Chinese capitalism and dynamic business systems in the context of contemporary globalization. Working from the varieties of capitalism perspective similar to Whitley's business systems approach, Hall and Soskice (2001b:5) argued that such strategic interaction is "central to economic and political outcomes, the most important institutions distinguishing one political economy from another will be those conditioning such interaction, and it is these that we seek to capture in this analysis." They proposed "a firm-centered political economy that regards companies as the crucial actors in a capitalist economy. They are the key agents of adjustment in the face of technological change or international competition whose activities aggregate into overall levels of economic performance" (Hall and Soskice 2001b:6).

The focus on ethnic Chinese actors and their enrollment into global networks at different spatial scales is highly important for at least three reasons. First, this bottom-up approach examines the dynamics of globalization and Chinese capitalism that operate at the level of actor-networks. This contrasts with and, yet, complements the top-down approach in much of the literature on globalization and the political economy of business systems (cf. Mittelman 2000). Second, whereas business firms and their strategies may be conceived as agents of economic change at the structural level, it is clear that these firms are controlled and managed by specific social actors (see also Yeung 1998a; 2002a). By focusing on the action and behavior of these social actors, we are better able to unpack the monolithic view of the firm as a coherent and stable feature of capitalist economies. This actor-network perspective helps us to appreciate the differentiated strategies and behavior of business firms as *deliberate responses* by social actors to the changing contexts of globalization and dynamic processes in business systems (see also Gomez's chapter in this volume). Third, while my analysis is rooted in the historical evolution of Chinese capitalism, it pays serious analytical attention to more recent trends and events in the global economy. The dynamics of the global economy, particularly those encapsulated in globalization tendencies, are conceived as critical to the changing nature and transformations in Chinese capitalism. In this sense, time—expressed through changing contexts—does play a major role here, albeit not in a linear and unidirectional manner. On this issue of time, I beg to differ from Redding's (1990:4) argument that:

> The Chinese family business has had plenty of time to develop new forms. Sophisticated Chinese organizations have flourished both in and out of China for as long as Western organizations, perhaps longer. They have interacted with powerful markets for just as long and have been accessible to modern managerial technology had they wished. The fact remains that a traditional form of control is retained, and a particular form of legitimacy seen as appropriate.

Redding's view is predicated on the Chinese family business in mainland China before the communist takeover in 1949, where the institutional structuring of norms and cultural practices was highly powerful in its historical context. It does not take into account the more recent changing contexts and circumstances with which Chinese family firms *outside* mainland China are confronted (cf. Wong 2000; Hong, Chapter 6, this volume).

After all, these firms in East and Southeast Asian economies have been relatively recent in their origin and formation since the 1950s and the 1960s. They have *not* had the luxury of "plenty of time" to develop their organizational forms because they have been preoccupied with either surviving hostile host economies (e.g. Indonesia and Malaysia) or participating in nation-building processes (e.g. Taiwan and Singapore). While they have carried with them distinctive cultural norms of control and forms of legitimacy from mainland China—centripetal authority exercised through the family—these Chinese family firms are by no means cultural artifacts resistant to changes and transformations in view of new competitive contexts arising from globalization tendencies. In fact, one might argue that the recent rediscovery of network forms of organizations in advanced industrialized economies has had a lot to do with the changing competitive context in the global economy. As DiMaggio (2001:23, my emphasis) explained in his introduction to *The Twenty-First-Century Firm,*

> [j]ust as Western observers first found the Japanese employment system exotic, but then, once they adjusted their conceptual lenses to take account of what they observed, began to perceive elements of it in their own societies, so the discovery of complex interfirm alliances in Japan and the "little tigers" of East Asia led Westerners to perceive *for the first time* the presence of *networks* in their own economies.

In this sense, changing contexts matter a great deal to our understanding (and rediscovery) of key elements of capitalist economic organizations across different economies and societies.

Conceived as such, Chinese capitalism has a certain degree of systemic endurance and, yet, is subject to dynamic transformations over time through its agents of change. I argue that such a gradual process of transition and transformation leads to a form of *hybrid capitalism* that is open and fluid in nature (see Figure 2.1). Through this process of hybridization, Chinese capitalism simultaneously converges toward certain norms and rules in Anglo-American capitalism—the dominant form of global capitalism today (itself changing of course) and, yet, diverges from its key institutions and structures, reflecting context-specific dynamics and the uneven impact of global flows of capital, information, discourses and technologies. At any given time, this hybrid form of capitalism evolves through the strategic interactions of key actors with globalizing forces—its hybridity represents the outcomes of these complex interactions in globalizing actor-networks. My conception of hybrid capitalism implicitly recognizes variety and divergence, and yet does not preclude the possibility of some degree of convergence. The notion also allows for dynamic and open analysis. It acknowledges diversity in the face of globalization tendencies and yet conceptualizes these changes as transitory and hybrid. This approach to the hybridization of Chinese capitalism is thus characterized by its non-essentialist view of capitalism (cf.

the debate on "Chineseness"), its non-static view of capitalist economic organization (cf. Chinese capitalism as a "cultural artifact") and its recognition of the co-existence of some elements of the past and new entities brought about through changes and transformations.[6] As Berger (2002:10) has recently commented on the rapid transformation of Chinese capitalism, hybridization represents a "deliberate effort to synthesize foreign and native cultural traits ... The development of an overseas Chinese [*sic*] business culture, combining the most modern business techniques with traditional Chinese personalism, is a very important case of this [hybridization], given the great economic success of the Chinese diaspora throughout the world" (see also Redding, 2000).

Conclusion

Taken together, this chapter illustrates how globalization tendencies have transformed the nature and organization of Chinese capitalism toward a form of hybrid capitalism. Contrary to many previous studies of Chinese capitalism, I am less interested in describing and explaining certain essentialized attributes (or "spirit") of Chinese capitalism as if they were permanent fixtures. Instead, I theorize how (Chinese) capitalism is a dynamic set of norms, beliefs, and institutions that simultaneously structure economy and society and is transformed by these changing economic and societal trends. For example, instead of asking *why* the 1997/98 Asian economic crisis has happened in Asia, it is much more useful to explain how the crisis has influenced and speeded up the ongoing development of the future trajectories of Chinese capitalism in East and Southeast Asia.

In developing a research agenda for future studies of Chinese capitalism, I focus on four major dimensions of this emerging hybridity of Chinese capitalism in a global era (see Figure 2.1): (1) the internationalization of actor-networks, (2) transnational entrepreneurship, (3) transformations in social organization, and (4) changing corporate governance and strategic management. To begin, dynamic transformations in the dominant form of Chinese capitalism cannot take place without some degree of *external* influence and pressure on institutionalized business practices and social action. These influences and pressures are unlikely to be found within domestic operating contexts precisely because the institutionalization of capitalist structures often takes place within these domestic contexts and political economies. Such external influence is likely to emerge when key actors in Chinese capitalism experience differential norms and rules in contrasting operating contexts during their *internationalization* processes. Through internationalization, these key actors are also more likely to develop new linkages and to enroll in actor-networks elsewhere. The ways in which these key actors in Chinese capitalism (i.e. leading business firms) participate in globalization processes are in turn explained by internal conditions (home/host economy) and external/global factors that contribute to the global reach of Chinese capitalism (see Yeung 1999a; 1999b; Yeung and Olds 2000; Mathews 2002; Hamilton et al. 2004).

Another dimension of the hybridization of Chinese capitalism refers to the changing nature of entrepreneurship that operates across borders. Ever since Schumpeter's (1934) seminal work, entrepreneurship is virtually synonymous with capitalist economic development. As the invisible force behind the Schumpeterian notion of "creative destruction," entrepreneurship is what drives the capitalist system via new firm formation and/or sustainable development of existing business organizations. By inference, entrepreneurship is also what changes and transforms capitalism. Within institutionalized business systems, it is not surprising to expect a certain pre-configured and relatively stable set of entrepreneurial traits. As described elsewhere (Yeung and Olds 2000; Yeung 2004), much research on Chinese capitalism has focused on its entrepreneurial tendencies within hostile domestic environments in Southeast Asia. A major missing link in this research into Chinese capitalism is the question of how key actors in Chinese capitalism develop and exhibit different repertoires of entrepreneurial tendencies and practices when they internationalize into different host economies. Focusing on this notion of *transnational entrepreneurship* among ethnic Chinese actors, specific actors in Chinese capitalism have not only internationalized their activities, but also brought about dynamic changes to Chinese capitalism. More empirical studies are needed to examine how their social and business practices have transcended traditional practices identified in the literature on Chinese capitalism (see Menkhoff and Gerke 2002; Yeung 2002a; Liu Hong, Chapter 6 in this volume).

Hybrid capitalism is also shaped by transformations in the *social organization* of economic activities. This dimension of Chinese capitalism, however, is particularly difficult to be reconfigured because of its embeddedness in particularized cultural norms and belief systems. As described earlier in this chapter, Chinese capitalism tends to be socially organized around the family firm, *guanxi* relationships and business networks. These attributes of social organization provide the institutional foundation on which Chinese capitalism crystallizes. What then happens to this foundation when key actors in Chinese capitalism are increasingly engaged with actor-networks on a global scale? Are globalization tendencies sufficiently powerful to "shake it up", so to speak? In this era of global business and finance, what will remain in the reconfigured and hybridized form of Chinese capitalism? While the "bamboo network" may no longer be exclusively based on *guanxi* relationships among ethnic Chinese in East and Southeast Asia, we need empirical studies to show how the social organization of Chinese capitalism is changing in the context of globalizing tendencies (e.g. Yeung 2000b; 2006; Gomez 2004; Wong 2004; Gomez, Chapter 5, this volume). More non-Chinese and non-family actors are now enrolled in "Chinese" business networks that were previously described as inward looking, closely knit, and based on family ties. We must specify empirically the main mechanisms through which these transformations in the social organization of Chinese capitalism are brought about.

The final, but perhaps most important, dimension of Chinese capitalism is the changing pattern of *corporate governance* and *strategic management* among its leading firms. Defined as the ownership structures and management control systems that arbitrate capital, production, and market exchanges, corporate governance represents the *genius loci* of any form of modern capitalism, irrespective of whether they are liberal market economies or coordinated market economies (see Shleifer and Vishny 1997; La Porta et al. 1999; Franks et al. 2003). In short, it is concerned with "the exercise of power over the direction of the enterprise, the supervision of executive actions, the acceptance of a duty to be accountable and the regulation of the corporation within the jurisdiction of the states in which it operates" (Tricker 1990:188). In fact, Chandler's (1977; 1990) work has clearly shown the emergence of managerial capitalism in the United States through the separation between ownership and management control of modern corporations. Earlier research on Chinese capitalism, particularly in the culturalist school, has pointed to the existence of a distinctive set of authority structures and coordination systems based on the integration of ownership and management control within the Chinese family firm. While I accept the predominance and continual significance of small family firms among ethnic Chinese in East and Southeast Asia, large business conglomerates controlled by ethnic Chinese are increasingly broadening their corporate governance structures to meet the competitive challenges of globalization. If globalization tendencies can exert a major impact on the transformation of Chinese capitalism, such impact is most likely to be evident in the changing corporate governance among Chinese business firms (e.g. Claessens et al. 2000; Carney and Gedajlovic 2002; Yeung 2003; Ahlstrom et al. 2004). As such, the hybridization of Chinese capitalism can be characterized by both the continual existence of Chinese family firms and the growing professionalization of management and governance structures in large Chinese business groups. Corporate governance among Chinese business firms, particularly those family-owned ones, is converging to a certain extent toward the Anglo-American model of managerial capitalism. Although this convergence process is neither complete nor fully accepted internally among actors in Chinese capitalism, there is strong evidence that the process has already started and is unlikely to be reversible in the near future.

Notes

1 This is a revised version of an earlier paper presented at the University of California Pacific Rim Research Conference on "A New Breed of Chinese Entrepreneurs? Culture, Organizational Imperatives, and Globalization," Hong Kong University of Science and Technology, May 21–22, 2004. I would like to thank Raymond Wong for kindly inviting me to participate in the conference. Yanjie Bian, Edmund Terence Gomez and Tony Tam also offered some very useful comments. I am solely responsible for all errors and misinterpretations.

2 I use "home" in inverted commas throughout because many East and Southeast Asian economies might not be the birthplace for the first and, sometimes, second generation of many ethnic Chinese people. Unless otherwise specified, the term "economies" is used throughout this chapter in lieu of "countries" because while economies like Hong Kong and Taiwan are populated by the largest concentration of ethnic Chinese outside mainland China, it is hotly debatable whether they can be known as "countries" in their own right.

3 The term "overseas Chinese" may be contentious for some scholars of ethnic Chinese who are living outside mainland China. The term is related to the Chinese term *huaqiao* (Chinese national abroad) that has been sharply criticized in Southeast Asia for its implications that Chinese born abroad with status as a citizen in another nation are still Chinese in essence. *Huaren* (ethnic Chinese) has become more politically acceptable. In English, "overseas Chinese" is usually used to include *huaqiao*, *huaren*, and residents of Taiwan, Hong Kong and Macau (*tong bao*) who are considered to be compatriots living in parts of the territory of China temporarily outside mainland Chinese control. See Wang (1991; 1999), Bolt (2000) and Ma (2003) for the origin and status of ethnic Chinese living outside mainland China. Throughout this chapter, I will refer to "ethnic Chinese" or to specific groups (e.g. Hong Kong entrepreneurs) rather than "overseas Chinese" in my discussions of research materials. But references to the literature sometimes require the term "overseas Chinese" to be clear. In such cases, I will use inverted commas to illustrate my discomfort with the term.

4 The term "mainland China" will be used throughout this chapter to denote the People's Republic of China. Despite the claim of "red capitalism" in post-reform mainland China (Lin 1997), the PRC is excluded from this chapter's analysis mainly because private ownership and individual control of business firms is indeed a very recent phenomenon in mainland China. To date, state-owned enterprises (SOEs) and town and village enterprises (TVEs) remain as the organizational backbone of China's transitional economy. The International Finance Corporation (2000:18) estimated that in 1998, the share of GDP generated by the officially registered self-employed and private businesses amounted to 13 percent. Another 13 percent might be added if we make some allowance for enterprises registered as collectives but run as de facto private businesses (see also Tang and Ward 2003:107). Taken together, private businesses controlled by individual Chinese contributed to roughly one quarter of China's GDP in 1998. My exclusion of mainland China from the analysis of Chinese capitalism thus follows Redding's (1990:3) delimitation:

> It is however important to draw a line and make clear that this chapter is not about China now, and will only make passing reference to what is happening there. There will be more substantial consideration, at the end, of possible implications for, even possibly strong influence on, a notional future China, but our agenda here is the Chinese as capitalists, not as communists or socialists.

5 I would like to thank David Ley at the University of British Columbia for the origin of this idea.

6 My argument finds its support in other excellent studies of the emerging hybrid forms of economic organization in transitional economies in mainland China (Nee 1992; Guthrie 1999; 2000) and Eastern Europe (Stark 1996; Grabher and Stark 1997; Stark and Bruszt 1998; 2001). Reviewing the diverse pathways to post-socialist capitalism in Eastern Europe, Stark and Bruszt (2001:1130) argued that

> the new hybrid game was played with institutions cobbled together partly from remnants of the past that, by limiting some moves and facilitating

other strategies, gave rise to a bricolage of multiple social logics. If from these coexisting and overlapping principles they are building a distinctively post-socialist capitalism, they share with all modern societies a common feature that the social fabric is woven with multiple, discrepant systems of value.

In a similar study of China's transitional economy, Guthrie (1999:6) contended that "[c]hanges in [mainland] Chinese organizations are part of a unique Chinese transitional path that will lead to an organizational configuration and market economic system at the end of transition that is distinctively Chinese."

References

Ahlstrom, D., Young, M. N., Chan, E. S., and Bruton, G. D. (2004) "Facing Constraints to Growth? Overseas Chinese Entrepreneurs and Traditional Business Practices in East Asia," *Asia Pacific Journal of Management* 21:263–85.

Andreski, S. (ed.) (1983) *Max Weber on Capitalism, Bureaucracy and Religion: A Selection of Texts*, London: Allen & Unwin.

Backman, M. (1999) *Asian Eclipse*, Singapore: John Wiley.

Becht, M., Betts, P., and Morck, R. (2003) "The Complex Evolution of Family Affairs," *Financial Times*, 2 February.

Berger, P. L. (1986) *The Capitalist Revolution*, New York: Basic Books.

——(2002) "Introduction," in P. L. Berger and S. P. Huntington (eds.) *Many Globalizations*, Oxford: Oxford University Press.

Block, F. (2002) "Rethinking Capitalism," in N. W. Biggart (ed.) *Readings in Economic Sociology*, Oxford: Blackwell.

Bolt, P. J. (2000) *China and Southeast Asia's Ethnic Chinese*, New York: Praeger.

Brown, R. A. (2000) *Chinese Big Business and the Wealth of Asian Nations*, London: Palgrave.

Carney, M. and Gedajlovic, E. (2002) "The Coupling of Ownership and Control and the Allocation of Financial Resources," *Journal of Management Studies* 39:123–46.

Chandler, A. D. Jr. (1977) *The Visible Hand*, Cambridge, MA: Harvard University Press.

——(1990) *Scale and Scope*, Cambridge, MA: Harvard University Press.

Claessens, S., Djankov, S., and Lang, L. H. P. (2000) "The Separation of Ownership and Control in East Asian Corporations," *Journal of Financial Economics* 58:81–112.

Clegg, S. R. and Redding, S. G. (eds.) (1990) *Capitalism in Contrasting Cultures*, Berlin: de Gruyter.

Dicken, P. (2003) *Global Shift*, 4th edition, London: Sage.

DiMaggio, P. J. (2001) "Introduction," in P. J. DiMaggio (ed.) *The Twenty-First-Century Firm*, Princeton, NJ: Princeton University Press.

DiMaggio, P. J. and Powell, W. W. (eds.) (1991) *The New Institutionalism in Organizational Analysis*, Chicago: University of Chicago Press.

Franks, J., Mayer, C., and Rossi, S. (2003) *The Origination and Evolution of Ownership and Control*, ECGI Working Papers no. 09/203, Brussels: European Corporate Governance Institute.

Gereffi, G. (1996) "Global Commodity Chains," *Competition and Change* 1:427–39.

Gibson-Graham, J. K. (1996) *The End of Capitalism*, Oxford: Blackwell.

Gomez, E. T. (2004) "Intra-Ethnic Cooperation in Transnational Perspective: Malaysian Chinese Investments in the United Kingdom," in E. T. Gomez and

H. H. M. Hsiao (eds.) *Chinese Enterprise, Transnationalism, and Identity*, London: RoutledgeCurzon.

Grabher, G. and Stark, D. (eds.) (1997) *Restructuring Networks in Post-Socialist Societies*, Oxford: Oxford University Press.

Guillén, M. F. (2001) *The Limits of Convergence*, Princeton, NJ: Princeton University Press.

Guthrie, D. (1999) *Dragon in a Three-Piece Suit: The Emergence of Capitalism in China*, Princeton, NJ: Princeton University Press.

——(2000) "Understanding China's Transition to Capitalism," *Sociological Forum* 15:727–49.

Hall, P. A. and Soskice, D. (eds.) (2001a) *Varieties of Capitalism: The Institutional Foundations of Comparative Advantage*, Oxford: Oxford University Press.

——(2001b) "An Introduction to Varieties of Capitalism.," in P. A. Hall and D. Soskice (eds.) *Varieties of Capitalism*, Oxford: Oxford University Press.

Hamilton, G. G. (1996b) "Overseas Chinese Capitalism," in W. M. Tu (ed.) *Confucian Traditions in East Asian Modernity*, Cambridge, MA: Harvard University Press.

——(1999b) "Introduction," in G. G. Hamilton (ed.) *Cosmopolitan Capitalists*, Seattle, WA: University of Washington Press.

——(1999c) "Hong Kong and the Rise of Capitalism in Asia," in G. G. Hamilton (ed.) *Cosmopolitan Capitalists*, Seattle, WA: University of Washington Press.

——(2000) "Reciprocity and Control," in H. W. C. Yeung and K. Olds (eds.) *Globalization of Chinese Business Firms*, New York: Macmillan.

——(2004) *Commerce and Capitalism in Chinese Societies*, London: RoutledgeCurzon.

Hamilton, G. G. (ed.) (1991) *Business Networks and Economic Development in East and South East Asia*, Hong Kong: Centre of Asian Studies, University of Hong Kong.

——(1996a) *Asian Business Networks*, Berlin: de Gruyter.

——(1999a) *Cosmopolitan Capitalists*, Seattle, WA: University of Washington Press.

Hamilton, G. G., Biggart, N. W., and Feenstra, R. (2004) *Comparing Business Networks in East Asia*, Cambridge: Cambridge University Press.

Held, D., McGrew, A., Goldblatt, D., and Perraton, J. (1999) *Global Transformations*, Cambridge: Polity.

Hsiao, H. H. M. (2002) "Coexistence and Synthesis: Cultural Globalization and Localization in Contemporary Taiwan," in P. L. Berger and S. Huntington (eds.) *Many Globalizations*, Oxford: Oxford University Press.

Hwang, K. K. (1987) "Face and Favour: The Chinese Power Game," *American Journal of Sociology* 92:944–74.

International Finance Corporation (2000) *China's Emerging Private Enterprises*, Washington, DC: IFC.

Kao, J. (1993) "The Worldwide Web of Chinese Business," *Harvard Business Review* March-April, 24–36.

Kotkin, J. (1992) *Tribes*, New York: Random House.

La Porta, R, Lopez-de-Silanes, F.. and Shleifer, A. (1999) "Corporate Ownership Around the World," *Journal of Finance* 54:471–517.

Lin, G. C. S. (1997) *Red Capitalism in South China*, Vancouver: University of British Columbia Press.

Ma, L. J. C. (2003) "Space, Place and Transnationalism in the Chinese Diaspora," in L. C. Ma and C. Cartier (eds.) *The Chinese Diaspora*, Boulder, CO: Rowman and Littlefield.

Mathews, J. A. (2002) *Dragon Multinational: A New Model for Global Growth*, Oxford: Oxford University Press.

Menkhoff, T. and Gerke, S. (eds.) (2002) *Chinese Entrepreneurship and Asian Business Networks*, Surrey, U.K.: Curzon.

Mittelman, J. H. (2000) *The Globalization Syndrome*, Princeton, NJ: Princeton University Press.

Nee, V. (1992) "Organizational Dynamics of Market Transition: Hybrid Forms, Property Rights and Mixed Economy in China," *Administrative Science Quarterly* 37:1–27.

Nonini, D. M. and Ong, A. (1997) "Chinese Transnationalism as an Alternative Modernity," in A. H. Ong and D. M. Nonini (eds.) *Ungrounded Empires: The Cultural Politics of Modern Chinese Transnationalism*, London: Routledge.

Olds, K. and Yeung, H. W. C. (1999) "(Re)shaping 'Chinese' Business Networks in a Globalising Era," *Environment and Planning D: Society and Space* 17:535–55.

Ong, A. (1997) "Chinese Modernities: Narratives of Nation and of Capitalism" in A. H. Ong and D. M. Nonini (eds.) *Ungrounded Empires*, London: Routledge.

Orrù, M., Biggart, N. and Hamilton, G. G. (1997) *The Economic Organization of East Asian Capitalism*, London: Sage.

Powell, W. W. (1990) "Neither Market nor Hierarchy: Network Forms of Organization," *Research in Organizational Behaviour* 12:295–336.

Redding, S. G. (1990) *The Spirit of Chinese Capitalism*, Berlin: De Gruyter.

——(2000) "What is Chinese about Chinese Family Business?" in H. W. C. Yeung and K. Olds (eds.) *Globalization of Chinese Business Firms*, New York: Macmillan.

Saunders, P. (1995) *Capitalism*, Minneapolis, MN: University of Minnesota Press.

Schumpeter, J. A. (1934) *The Theory of Economic Development*, Cambridge, MA: Harvard University Press.

Screpanti, E. (2001) *The Fundamental Institutions of Capitalism*, London: Routledge.

Shleifer, A. and Vishny, R. W. (1997) "A Survey of Corporate Governance," *Journal of Finance* 52:737–83.

Silk, L. and Silk, M. (1996) *Making Capitalism Work*, New York: New York University Press.

Stark, D. (1996) "Recombinant Property in East European Capitalism," *American Journal of Sociology* 101:993–1027.

Stark, D. and Bruszt, L. (1998) *Postsocialist Pathways: Transforming Politics and Property in East Central Europe*, Cambridge: Cambridge University Press.

——(2001) "One Way or Multiple Paths: For a Comparative Sociology of East European Capitalism," *American Journal of Sociology* 106:1129–37.

Storper, M. and Salais, R. (1997) *Worlds of Production*, Cambridge, MA: Harvard University Press.

Tang, J. and Ward, A. (2003) *The Changing Face of Chinese Management*, London: Routledge.

Tricker, R. I. (1990) "Corporate Governance: A Ripple on the Cultural Reflection," in S. R. Clegg and S. G. Redding (eds.) *Capitalism in Contrasting Cultures*, Berlin: de Gruyter.

Wang, G. W. (1991) *China and the Chinese Overseas*, Singapore: Times Academic Press.

——(1999) "Chineseness: The Dilemmas of Place and Practice," in G. G. Hamilton (ed.) *Cosmopolitan Capitalists*, Seattle, WA: University of Washington Press.

Weber, M. (1983) "The Failure of Capitalism in the Ancient World," in S. Andreski (ed.) *Max Weber on Capitalism, Bureaucracy and Religion: A Selection of Texts*, London: Allen & Unwin.

——(1992) *The Protestant Ethic and the Spirit of Capitalism*, translated by Talcott Parsons, London: Routledge.

Weidenbaum, M. and Hughes, S. (1996) *The Bamboo Network: How Expatriate Chinese Entrepreneurs Are Creating a New Economic Superpower in Asia*, New York: The Free Press.

Whitley, R. (1992) *Business Systems in East Asia*, London: Sage.

——(1994) "The Internationalization of Firms and Markets," *Organization* 1:101–24.

——(1996) "Business Systems and Global Commodity Chains," *Competition and Change* 1:411–25.

——(1998) "Internationalization and Varieties of Capitalism," *Review of International Political Economy* 5:445–81.

——(1999) *Divergent Capitalisms*, New York: Oxford University Press.

Whitley, R. and Kristensen, P. H. (eds.) (1996) *The Changing European Firm*, London: Routledge.

——(1997) *Governance at Work*, Oxford: Oxford University Press.

Williamson, O. E. (1975) *Markets and Hierarchies*, New York: The Free Press.

——(1985) *The Economic Institution of Capitalism*, New York: The Free Press.

Wong, R. S. K. (2004) "Chinese Business Firms and Entrepreneurs in Hong Kong," in E.T. Gomez and H. H. M. Hsiao (eds.) *Chinese Enterprise, Transnationalism, and Identity*, London: RoutledgeCurzon.

Wong, S. L. (1988) *Emigrant Entreprenerus*, Hong Kong: Oxford University Press.

——(2000) "Transplanting Enterprises in Hong Kong," in H. W. C. Yeung and K. Olds (eds) *Globalization of Chinese Business Firms*, New York: Macmillan.

Yang, M. M. H. (2002) "The Resilience of *Guanxi* and its New Deployments," *The China Quarterly* 170:459–76.

Yeung, H. W. C. (1998a) *Transnational Corporations and Business Networks*, London: Routledge.

——(1998b) "Capital, State and Space," *Transactions of the Institute of British Geographers* 23:291–309.

——(1999a) "Under Siege? Economic Globalisation and Chinese Business in Southeast Asia," *Economy and Society* 28:1–29.

——(1999b) "The Internationalization of Ethnic Chinese Business Firms from Southeast Asia," *International Journal of Urban and Regional Research* 23:103–27.

——(2000a) "The Dynamics of Asian Business Systems in a Globalising Era," *Review of International Political Economy* 7:399–433.

——(2000b) "Economic Globalisation, Crisis, and the Emergence of Chinese Business Communities in Southeast Asia," *International Sociology* 15:269–90.

——(2002a) *Entrepreneurship and the Internationalisation of Asian Firms*, Cheltenham, U.K.: Edward Elgar.

——(2002b) "The Limits to Globalization Theory," *Economic Geography* 78:285–305.

——(2003) "Financing Chinese Capitalism," paper presented at the conference on "Cultural Approaches to Asian Financial Markets," Cornell Law School, Ithaca NY, U.S.A, April 26, 2003.

——(2004) *Chinese Capitalism in a Global Era: Towards Hybrid Capitalism*, London: Routledge.

——(2006) "Change and Continuity in Southeast Asian Business," *Asia Pacific Journal of Management* 23:229–54.

Yeung, H. W. C. and Olds, K. (eds.) (2000) *Globalization of Chinese Business Firms*, New York: Macmillan.

3 Beyond culture

Economic analysis of the characteristics of overseas Chinese business

Denggao Long and Qiming Han

Introduction

It has been argued that no matter where they live, should it be in mainland China, Hong Kong, Taiwan, Southeast Asia, or America, ethnic Chinese have always demonstrated a stronger desire to become their own bosses or business owners than people from other countries and areas. Such a widespread phenomenon has been conventionally and conveniently attributed to the unique Chinese culture or cultural tradition. Overseas Chinese[1] (sometimes also known as ethnic Chinese, diaspora Chinese, Chinese overseas, and Chinese abroad) build family-run enterprises with capital raised largely from clans or pan-families and establish complex and intricate social networks that are based on pan-family ties of bloodline and locality. According to this line of reasoning, the utilization of family/ethnic clans and social networks is a reflection of Chinese culture in general and diaspora culture in particular. Furthermore, these Chinese business entrepreneurs are shrewd in exploring new and existing opportunities to make profits, even though they do not possess strong brand names and advanced technology as most of their Western counterparts do.

Similarly, when people talk about distinctive and unique characteristics of Chinese business practices, they tend to attribute such phenomena to the *unique* Chinese cultural influences. As Hodder (1996:187) summarized, "it is commonly believed that the most important determinant [in shaping Chinese business practices] is [their] culture." Yao (2002) further pointed out that the concept of Confucian capitalism has been crucial in shaping our understanding of the economic success of the Chinese diaspora. The most influential argument has been summarized in Gordon Redding's (1993) work about the spirit of Chinese capitalism. Together, these scholars espoused the importance of "Confucianism" or Chineseness as the major source of unique Chinese business management and operation style.

Although this line of reasoning may seem logical and reasonable, some scholars argue that it is not sufficient to draw the above conclusions about the origins of overseas Chinese business management practices. While some critics argue that the influence of Chinese culture has probably been exaggerated

(Li 2001) or misinterpreted and misunderstood (Chan 1998), others even argue that many of the so-called unique characteristics may never have existed. Although these criticisms cast some doubts or even reject outright the view of cultural determinism, their narrow and delimited inquiries *within* the cultural context are certainly restrictive and unfortunate. For example, most previous studies ignore similarities between Chinese and non-Chinese business practices. Hodder's (1996) study of overseas Chinese business is probably an exception, and he investigates cultural factors as well as economic, sociological, and psychological forces. In particular, he found that the success of overseas Chinese is not an outcome of Chineseness, but rather of "multidimensional values, institutions, and actions which have been consciously manipulated by the Chinese and 'turned' towards the extension and institutionalization of trade" (Hodder 1996:xi).

The purpose of this chapter is to extend this particular line of reasoning further to explain Chinese business characteristics from an economic perspective. It is our contention that the characteristics of Chinese business entrepreneurship, if not all but surely a large majority, should be viewed as one form or another of *personalized transactions* that can be accounted for under the institutional economics theory. According to Douglas North (2000), one of the most important economic transformations under a modern economy is the gradual replacement of personalized transactions by non-personalized transactions. Personalized transactions are often based on personal ties such as bloodline (consanguinity), common locality, common unit and organization, friendship, and classmates. Non-personalized transactions, on the other hand, refer to socialized or institutionalized transactions that are frequently based on modern institutions and laws.

In the non-personal environment, the principal-agent plays an important role in the conduct of business. For example, a public company has shares of its stock distributed among many owners who do not take active part in the daily management of company. Instead they entrust professional managers to be their agents to direct and administer company resources. The principal-agent also represents legal ties or basic elements of financial instruments, such as security markets, mutual funds, and pension funds. With the help of the principal-agent, companies and financial markets are able to rapidly raise capital and human resources anywhere, without geographic or other restrictions. Inevitably, this arrangement costs businesses huge sums of money for the professional services of agent organizations such as accounting and legal firms. In return, these companies are able to raise capital effectively and efficiently in the market and enjoy higher liquidity and better performance of their stocks.

On the other hand, personalized transactions, which are based on special personal ties without relying on the services of principal-agents, incur much less cost. At the same time, personalized transactions have little effects beyond their personal ties and cannot reach outside of their personal networks to raise capital, human resources, and management skills. Under such a non-institutional environment, the ability to raise large capital and human resources for expansion is extremely limited and prohibitively expensive. It is under this institutional economic framework that this chapter will try to (re)interpret the origins of overseas Chinese enterprise management style, as well as investigate how factors such as the local and global economic context influence the way overseas Chinese entrepreneurs operate their businesses.

Chinese culture and Chinese business

As noted earlier, a number of scholars claim that the fact that many Chinese prefer to be their own boss and operate their own business is an outcome that is directly or indirectly influenced by Chinese culture. Can "Chinese culture" really lead many Chinese at home or abroad to become business owners? Our response below will first begin with the experience of China and then proceed with a discussion of other countries.

Indeed, there are many small business owners in mainland China today. Since China's economy is still at an early stage of economic development with rapid growth and the transition from a planned/command economy to a market-oriented economy, there are numerous and increasing opportunities for people to set up small enterprises. In fact, we would argue that it probably is easier for small business owners to make good profits in such a burgeoning environment than for large corporations. However, as the scales of economy and efficiency weigh more and more in conducting business in China, the opportunities and space for people to become business owners should become less in the future, similar to the experiences of the United States and other developed countries in the past century.

What about Chinese businesses in Hong Kong, Taiwan, and Southeast Asia? They all experienced rapid economic growth during the past several decades and the role of small-scale enterprises seemed to dominate in major industries and fields. To keep things in proper perspective, however, it is important to consider significant differences between these economies and the mainland Chinese economy. Most of these countries and regions have small economies with limited internal consumer demand and market. They are driven largely by export industries, with brands and technologies supplied by Western multinational corporations. Many Chinese enterprises are manufacturing factories in the putting-out system of multinational corporations and occupy middling positions in the production/supply chain of the global economy. Although the export industry also constitutes an important component in the Chinese economy, its level of dependency is much lower and the potential for expansion in the internal market is significantly greater.

While it is probably true that the prevalence of entrepreneurship and small businesses among ethnic Chinese in Southeast Asia and China is higher than in Europe and America, it probably reflects more about the economic conditions under which overseas Chinese operate their businesses rather than inherent cultural influences. Undoubtedly, the Western economy is at a higher and mature stage of market development and technology advancement, where many industries have undergone repeated industrial integrations and consolidations. As a result, a few corporate giants dominate in their respective businesses with unsurpassed economies of scale and high value-added products and/or services. They create significant barriers and thresholds for new enterprises to cross and enter. For instance, giant supermarket chains such as Wal-Mart, Shaws, and Walgreens in the United States all seized sizable shares in their respective sectors at the national level, making it extremely difficult for small, independent supermarkets and grocery stores to compete directly. In the manufacturing industry, big corporations generate large profits by relying on strong brand names and core technology with high value-added products and services. Some industries, especially those with low value-added products and services, have increasingly moved their operations to developing countries and areas such as China and Southeast Asia. As a result, with the exception of a few "new" markets, it has become harder and harder for Americans with small means to start their own businesses as well.

Paradoxically, these "sunset" industries with low value-added products and services and low thresholds to enter represent ample business opportunities for Chinese entrepreneurs. They provide a large, private market space and opportunities for Chinese to operate their own businesses throughout Southeast Asia and China. Under this new arrangement, Americans (and Europeans) still have their chances to carry out the dreams of investment. Even though they may not be able to become their own bosses directly, they can share corporate profits via the securities market, which is already fully developed in the West. Furthermore, because wages are higher in Western countries than in Southeast Asia and China, the start-up cost is higher in the former whereas the incentives to operate their own businesses are higher in the latter.

While there are more business owners of Chinese descent than local natives and other ethnic groups in a number of Southeast Asian countries, this can be partly attributed to their historical intermediary or go-between status in their adopted countries. Chinese merchants had served as the middlemen between the then-developed China and underdeveloped Southeast Asia long before the arrival of Westerners who built the colonial commercial systems. Later, Chinese merchants became intermediaries between local natives and Western colonists during their long period of mutual interactions, when most natives continued to make their living in agriculture (Long 2002).

It is our contention that the lack of development of an economy of scale in these countries contributes to the encouragement of ethnic Chinese to be their own boss either in China or abroad. Closely related is our further argument that there has been a lack of principal-agents based on modern institutions in these places. With the exception of Hong Kong, Singapore, and Taiwan, there has been relatively weak development of the principal-agent in Southeast Asia and China in the past two decades. Given existing constraints, a full development of such a system to help the expansion of enterprises in China and Southeast Asia may not be forthcoming in the foreseeable future. Without the institution-based principal-agents, entrepreneurs have limited ways to raise capital beyond their immediately controlled enterprise(s) or to entrust professional managers to help manage their businesses. This is in sharp contrast with the myriad financial instruments that American and European companies can utilize to raise capital from security markets, mutual and pension funds, trusts and foundations, and venture capital.

Our discussion so far has focused on why Chinese businesses tend to differ from Western businesses in operation in China and Southeast Asia. What about their operations in North America and Western Europe? In those places, many Chinese immigrants have become small grocery store and restaurant owners, while a few, mostly from Hong Kong, Taiwan, and Southeast Asia, venture outside and engage in other business endeavors. The explanations here only differ slightly from the discussion earlier. First, like most other immigrants, many Chinese feel less competitive in the American labor market as they might not be proficient at the English language, their skills and professional/academic credentials from their home country may not be recognized, and/or they are not familiar with the local culture. The existence of an invisible "glass ceiling" in the corporate hierarchy and obstacles in upward mobility for ethnic minorities certainly encourage many to seek alternative routes to economic success (Saxenian et al. 2002; Wong 2004). Their route to ownership usually begins as workers in Chinatowns or Chinese restaurants somewhere in the country. Eventually, after accumulating sufficient capital, they then strike out on their own, opening their own grocery stores and restaurants. Most owner-operators, together with their employees, work 12 hours a day and 7 days a week, a working condition that the average American does not like or even cannot endure. The situation, however, is not unique but very common in other ethnic businesses as well.

Many are able to establish niche markets within the Chinese American communities and fill the void in the supply of certain services. The intercity bus services between Chinatowns in New York, Boston, Philadelphia, and Washington DC offers a perfect example. These inter-Chinatown buses are operated mainly by Chinese immigrants. The fares are extremely cheap, costing only a fraction of those of its national competitor, Greyhound. These intercity bus services are not only able to take advantage of the frequent movement of the Chinese population among the nation's major metropolitan areas, but their successful operations have also attracted non-Chinese travelers.

Recently, because of a booming Chinese economy and its related trade opportunities, a number of first and second generation immigrant entrepreneurs have used their connections in China and knowledge of Asian markets to conduct business between Asia and America, thus transcending the traditional local boundary limitations. They fly frequently across the Pacific to conduct business and maintain multiple residences and personal identities (see Chapter 6 of this volume on transnational entrepreneurs for further examples).[2]

Chinese business entrepreneurs in America used to pursue opportunities in marginal areas outside of the mainstream economy; these included laundries, restaurants, and grocery stores. It is only in the past two decades that they have turned their attention to a few forefront and nascent technology areas. The most notable example, of course, is the activities of some high-caliber business entrepreneurs, including new immigrants, and their venture companies in Silicon Valley (see Table 3.1). Several important characteristics of this "new" form of investment strategy are that the technology is relatively new, rapidly evolving, knowledge-based, and no one can hold absolute monopoly power. The development of a "new economy" (driven largely by information technology and biotechnology) of the 1990s provided many new opportunities for Chinese entrepreneurs (and others) to forge ahead into some important areas of American mainstream industry. According to one calculation, the number of Chinese who have occupations in the high-technology industries located in Silicon Valley more than doubled in less than ten years, from 19,218 in 1990 to 41,684 in 1998 (Saxenian 1999).[3] Many of them were employed or directly engaged in new start-up activities. Start-up firms are important sources of new ideas and innovations. They have advantages over larger established firms in emerging areas where the new technology has yet to be worked out and the demand patterns are unclear and risky. By assuming higher risks, these entrepreneurs, if successful, can receive handsome rewards as well. It is therefore of little surprise that ethnic minorities who possess technical skills and training find the "new economy" particularly attractive. In fact, the proportional share of start-up firms by ethnic Chinese in the Silicon Valley skyrocketed from 9 percent in 1980–84 to about 20 percent in 1995–98. The increased share of ethnic Indians was equally impressive, from 3 percent to 9 percent over the same period (Saxenian 1999).

Family firms and social networks

It is widely held that family operations and extensive business networks among overseas Chinese are the most visible and, perhaps, defining characteristics of Chinese business enterprises. Their origins are believed to derive from Chinese culture, particularly Confucianism. In reality, family-run firms are common everywhere in the world and are not restricted to Chinese per se (Gersick et al. 1997). For instance, family-run businesses account for more than 85 percent of all firms in OECD countries and approximately 30 to 40 percent of the Fortune 500 companies in the United States (OECD 2002).

Table 3.1 Sales and employment of Silicon Valley high-technology Chinese firms in 1998

	Number of firms	Total sales ($m)	Total employment
Number of Chinese	2,001	13,237	41,684
Share of Silicon Valley high-tech firms	17.3%	13.4%	10%

Source: Dun & Bradstreet database, 1998.

Note:
Statistics are for firms started by Chinese between 1980 and 1998.

Similarly, the prevalence of business connections and networks is not just widespread among overseas Chinese, but is also equally common among other diaspora groups such as Jews and overseas Indians. For instance, through intricate and diverse merchant networks, capital, goods, and human flows originating from the Indian subcontinent are linked to other countries of the world. Indian merchants who need help at every step can find contacts and services provided by these networks (Markovits 1999). Many of the overseas Chinese business networks were formed in their respective host countries rather than originating in China. In fact, we would further argue that the development of an elaborate and sophisticated business network is only a recent one, a reflection of the changing business and economic environment rather than some stable cultural disposition.

In sum, both business networks and family operations are not just confined among overseas Chinese groups but are characteristics of diasporas. They represent necessary and conscious choices made by different ethnic groups in order to survive in the host economy. These relatively weak ethnic groups face significant barriers and obstacles in language, culture, and skills for economic advancement and therefore are more prone to seek resources internally. The only difference is that in Southeast Asia, the capital market is either undeveloped or underdeveloped and the protection of legal institutions is rather limited whereas in North America and Europe, the opportunity structure and capital markets are more structured and matured.

It should be noted that some family enterprises, particularly those in developed countries and in Hong Kong, Singapore, and Taiwan, gradually transformed into companies with share capital and managed by professional managers. These companies frequently acquired capital and management talents outside the family and clan networks. In places like Southeast Asia where the capital markets are still underdeveloped, however, similar transformation proves to be rather difficult. Of course, this is not to deny the possibility of a few successful companies. Rather, it points out that the general conditions and environment slow down the transformation process. Without an encouraging environment and suitable conditions, Chinese family enterprises may hesitate to break up family ownership, install professional management, and tap outside capital even though the owners themselves fully understand that this would contribute to the long-term vitality and viability of their businesses.

On the other hand, it will be difficult for enterprises to expand if they continue to restrict their options exclusively among their own family or clan. Non-personal relations come into existence in modern society through the establishment of law and order. Unfortunately, the relative paucity of capital and management resources in Southeast Asia imposes severe constraints in the use of such non-personal, institutional means. The available options are rather limited locally. This helps to explain why a number of Southeast Asian Chinese entrepreneurs gradually shifted some, if not a significant proportion, of their capital to places like Singapore and Hong Kong where the supply of qualified managerial personnel is abundant and capital markets are well established and institutionalized. In sum, the lack of an adequate legal system in many Southeastern Asian countries contributes to the importance of personal factors in resource distribution and allocation. Trust in business transactions is still based on personal relationships (Menkhoff 1994) or personal trust (Long 2003), as opposed to institutional trust that is based on contractual and legal agreement. Of course, the fact that the Chinese population has been singled out as a target for discrimination by the indigenous majority group further limits their willingness to enlarge their trust beyond their ethnicity (but note the latest development in Malaysia as documented by Gomez in Chapter 5 of this volume). Finally, it should be noted that the exclusion of Chinese immigrants also occurred in North America, Australia, and elsewhere (Chirot and Reid 1997). The extent of such barriers is today much narrower and subtle and has been reduced over time, though they never completely disappear.

Why do Chinese choose to operate family-run business and utilize personal social networks in business? Our tentative answers above outline two interrelated factors: the lack of institutions and the early stages of economic development. The former implies a general lack of principal-agency whereas the latter implies the lack of an economy of scale. They both explain why existing Chinese family enterprises tend to be of small scale. More importantly, they also point to the limits to further growth of Chinese enterprises unless these constraints can be transformed and lifted.

Characteristics of Chinese entrepreneurs

Overseas Chinese business entrepreneurs are often characterized as bold and good at taking risks in rapidly changing markets. They venture into emerging markets with significant risks of failure, though the promises of rewards are high as well. Can one really relate such opportunistic moves to the influence of Chinese culture? Are Chinese entrepreneurs culturally more endowed to spot new business opportunities? To answer these questions, perhaps we may also want to step back and consider different but related questions: if culture is really the key, is there anything *inherent* in Chinese culture that would make Chinese entrepreneurs lag behind their Western counterparts in technology and brand-name creation? Or, why do they concentrate on specific service sectors and continually strive to diversify their portfolios into related or unrelated businesses?

Indeed, many overseas Chinese entrepreneurs are able to reap handsome profits from taking substantial risks in entering and opening up new and emerging markets. These represent markets that many multinational corporations (MNCs) initially tried to avoid either because of perceived high risk or unstable markets with weak demand. For instance, overseas Chinese were the first to enter untested new markets in Southeast Asia, and in China's eastern coastal areas in the 1980s, and then recently moved inland to central and western China, Vietnam, and Burma (Long 2003). Western multinational corporations soon followed suit, but only when these markets showed enduring signs of success and stability, long after the pioneering work of overseas Chinese entrepreneurs. Similar situations can be observed in the once red-hot but highly risky information technology (IT) industry in Silicon Valley during the 1990s. During that period, many Chinese and Indian venture capitalists took great risks investing in nascent technologies. Many of these small venture firms were later merged with or bought out by big corporations, though a substantial number failed miserably as well.

With the exception of the Silicon Valley case, however, most Chinese entrepreneurs rely on low cost factors to make their firms competitive and reap profits through sales volume rather than upon brand names and advanced technology. While it proves to be advantageous in numerous situations, the strategy of reliance or over-reliance upon low cost factors also represents a major weaknesses of Chinese businesses and hinders their future expansion (Yoshihara 1988). Although these observations have been echoed in a number of theoretical and empirical works, it would be inappropriate and mistaken to conclude that the development is inherent in or attributable to Chinese culture.

In order to be successful, many Chinese entrepreneurs, just like their counterparts elsewhere, understand the importance of technology in economic activities. Yet, the core technology has been tightly controlled or dominated by Western MNCs. These large corporations provide and control the necessary production facilities and installation services. They entrust only their production lines to certain companies, particularly those owned by Chinese entrepreneurs in East and Southeast Asia. Under such arrangements, Chinese manufacturing companies can only compete in the cost of production—an abundant supply of cheap labor and lands in underdeveloped areas, particularly within China—and search all over the world for cheap raw materials. From the perspective of MNCs, it is far more convenient and economical to outsource their production functions to the Chinese than to manufacture products themselves, particularly when they would be subjected to much more stringent labor regulations than their Chinese counterparts.

This division of labor works well for both sides, especially the latter, since the Chinese would not be able to manufacture these products without the technology transfer from their Western counterparts. Under existing arrangements, they would have to rely on the brand names of Western corporations to sell their products globally and locally. According to this interpretation, there is nothing inherent in Chinese culture that would imply that the Chinese are weak in technology. Rather, the outcome is due to their adopted economic role and conscious economic choices in a highly competitive global market. The phenomenon reflects the strategic division of labor and specialization in the global economy, given that the Chinese enterprises are still in a weak position and dependent on Western technologies. At the current stage, it is rational for Chinese entrepreneurs to pay little attention to technological innovations and instead devote their energies to reducing production costs and thus generate profits. As one Chinese Malaysian businessman once told the first author in Kuala Lumpur before the 1997 Asian economic crisis, "We need not promote technological skill with huge cost. We simply buy innovations from the West."

The perception that it is cheaper for Chinese entrepreneurs to buy innovations from the West rather than to conduct their own research and development is quite widespread. At the same time, an increasing number of Chinese entrepreneurs are realizing that they should change their dependent status or secondary role in the world economy and start investing more resources in research and development (R&D) to enhance their technological competitiveness in the future. Nonetheless, R&D requires an enormous amount of investment in capital, human talent, and other supporting resources. As one manager of a big television manufacturer in Jiangmeng, Guangdong, told the first author in 2000, individual corporations currently cannot directly challenge their Western counterparts in R&D spending because the latter continue to hold core technologies and have deep pockets. Instead, he suggested that the Chinese government should invest and coordinate manufacturers' efforts in R&D of core technology. This, of course, is not a far-fetched idea and follows the successful experiences of some Japanese and Korean companies in the past.

This point can be further illustrated by another example: the Tsann Kuen International Group. Tsann Kuen is a multinational enterprise based in Taiwan. It was once the model of an original equipment manufacturer (OEM) in the manufacturing of electrical appliances. Over time, the company grew and became an original design manufacturer (ODM) in Xiameng, China, and then started to develop and market its own brand-name products under the EUPA label. According to the Shanghai Economic Information Research Center, EUPA was the second best known household electrical appliances brand in Shanghai in 1996. In particular, EUPA's flat iron was the number one brand in China with an approximately 33 percent market share. Wu Tsann Kuen, the company owner, once hoped to capitalize on the brand's popularity and expand his company by using an aggressive brand-promotion strategy. However, after a careful study of the failed experience of some less successful Korean companies to gain world market share by drastically reducing prices and giving up profits, Mr. Wu hesitated to pursue such an expansion strategy. He recognized that it is extremely difficult to develop and promote *new* brand names to the world markets that have been traditionally dominated by the West, particularly the hegemonic American culture, in shaping consumer taste and demand worldwide. In the end, Tsann Kuen International decided to focus on the company's core competitiveness in the global chain of industrial production by utilizing cheap labor in China, low-cost raw materials from the world, and the higher selling price in Western markets. It was also practical to cooperate with Western corporations in design development that had already been outsourced to various design companies in Europe and America. This division of labor is now enabling Tsann Kuen International to catch up with the technological and market trends in Western countries while maintaining lower production costs and stable profit margins.

Overseas Chinese businesses are also good at service industries such as real estate, hotels, and financial services. These sectors share the following common characteristics: their prosperity is not determined by technology, the barrier of entrance is relatively low, and brand-name recognition is not critical. In addition, the performance of these industries is more likely to be decided by non-technical market factors such as price fluctuations and information availability. Redding (1993) has discussed the involvement of overseas Chinese in these industries, although he couches his explanations exclusively in cultural terms.

Another successful "trait" of overseas Chinese businessmen is that they are flexible in making constant adjustments according to the changing demand in the market. Their flexibility is reflected in the constant shift from one industry to another or an expansion from a single industry into multiple industries. This explains why many Chinese businesses eventually become diversified business groups. In Malaysia, for example, nine out of ten of the top tycoons are ethnic Chinese; they all own holding companies, with interests in real estate and infrastructure properties, hotels, recreation, and banking (Malaysian Business 2001). Similarly, Ling (2000) found that 27 business groups in Malaysia have a common characteristic of the investment holding company with diversified investment portfolios. Among the top 24 Chinese business groups in the Philippines, 20 are engaged in property, construction, and hotels either as their core businesses or as diversified subsidiaries, 16 in banking and financial services, and 14 in trading or retailing (Jiang 2000:120). Only a handful of them are in the manufacturing sector. Whereas Western business groups are more specialized in one or two industries and frequently dominate in their respective industry on the basis of their superior technology and strong brand names, Chinese business entrepreneurs opt for diversification with well mixed portfolios.

Again, the decision to adopt such an economic mode should be interpreted as a conscious economic choice in the rapidly changing global market, which may, on surface at least, make the Chinese practices seem unique and different from their Western counterparts. Such practices also reflect long historical adaptations from the precarious and sometimes volatile positions that the Chinese population occupied in these economies. Although they once led Asian trade until the 1800s, their role was relegated to becoming secondary to the Western colonial capitalists as middlemen and intermediaries, particularly in Southeast Asia. Today, they are becoming business partners in the global economy and may soon compete with Western multinationals (Long 2002). However, under existing global trade arrangements, the factors of production flow into different areas according to their capital priority. Through their domination of superior technological and business innovations, Western multinational corporations control and lead changes in the marketplace and will probably continue to do so in the near future. While these MNCs can extract huge profits by brand recognition and advanced technology, overseas Chinese entrepreneurs have to rely on unconventional but pragmatic ways to make their businesses competitive and successful.

Because of its relative success, it is understandable that "Chinese culture" leaves some marks on overseas Chinese business practices. But this shrewdness is the result of the conscious manipulation of existing constraints. The so-called unique Chinese business style is definitely not *determined* by Chinese culture in general or diaspora culture in particular. As illustrated above, overseas Chinese are highly flexible and adaptable people. In their business pursuits, they do what they see fit in the marketplace and in the local social, legal, economic, and cultural systems of their adopted countries. They will fully utilize their own advantages, cultural or non-cultural, and minimize their disadvantages to try to fit into the local and global business environment.

Conclusion

This chapter argues that many of the so-called characteristics of overseas Chinese entrepreneurs are rooted in economic considerations rather than cultural predispositions. First, most Chinese entrepreneurs, particularly those in Southeast Asia, conduct their business in an environment that is at a relatively lower stage of economic development. These businesses are predominantly small-scale, with no brand-name recognition or core technology. Second, without a well established principal-agent system that is based on modern legal and economic institutions and sophisticated financial instruments, Chinese entrepreneurs are trapped and cannot enlarge their scale, region, and field of economic activity. In a sense, they are obliged, either voluntarily or involuntarily, to rely on personal or family ties, which in turn impose limits on the size of their firms and operations. Third, Chinese-owned businesses currently occupy the lower rung (low-value links) of the commodity production/supply chains in the global economy. They are largely dependent on the multinational corporations in core technology. Finally, it is not because of cultural factors that American Chinese are engaged in marginal areas of the U.S. economy, or conversely, their recent participation in the frontiers of the "New Economy." In fact, they have long been interested in and will continue to search and develop niche markets within the local (Chinatown) economy. At the same time, they will also explore high-risk and high-reward opportunities in the new economy, just like any other entrepreneur would do.

Notes

1 This chapter focuses on the Chinese entrepreneurs in Southeast Asia, Hong Kong, and Taiwan. Sometimes it also touches upon the Chinese in America and Europe. Individual case studies are based on personal interviews and field investigations conducted by the first author.
2 These entrepreneurs are sometimes nicknamed "astronauts" by the Chinese media.
3 The number in 1990 is from the U.S. Census 1990 PUMS. The number in 1998 is from the Dun & Bradstreet database.

References

Brown, R. A. (2000) *Chinese Big Business and the Wealth of Asian Nations*, New York: Palgrave.
Chan, K. B. (1998) *The Chinese Diaspora*, World Diasporas series, London: Routledge.
Chirot, D. and Reid, R. (1997) *Essential Outsiders: Chinese and Jews in the Modern Transformation of Southeast Asia and Central Europe*, Seattle, WA: University of Washington Press.
Gersick, K. E., Davis, J. A., Hampton, M. M., and Lansberg, I. (1997) *Generation to Generation: Life Cycles of the Family Business*, Cambridge, MA: Harvard Business School Press.
Gomez, E. T. (1999) *Chinese Business in Malaysia: Accumulation, Ascendance, Accommodation*, London: Curzon Press.
Hamilton, G. G. (1999) *Cosmopolitan Capitalists: Hong Kong and the Chinese Diaspora at the End of the 20th Century*, Seattle, WA: University of Washington Press.
Hodder, R. (1996) *Merchant Princes of the East: Cultural Delusions, Economic Success and the Overseas Chinese in Southeast Asia*, Chichester, U.K.: John Wiley.
Ip, D., Lever-Tracy, C., and Tracy, N. (eds.) (2000) *Chinese Business and the Asian Crisis*, Aldershot, U.K.: Gower.
Jiang, X. D. (2000) "Philippians Chinese Economy" (in Chinese), in N. J. Zhou (ed.) *Encyclopedia of Overseas Chinese*, economy volume, Beijing: Press of Overseas Chinese.
Li, P. S. (2001) "Chinese Canadians in Business," *Asian and Pacific Migration Journal* 10:99–121.
Ling, W. G. (2000) "Public-Listed Chinese Company in Malaysia" (in Chinese), in N. J. Zhou (ed.) *Encyclopedia of Overseas Chinese*, economy volume, Beijing: Press of Overseas Chinese.
Long, D. G. (1998) "A Sociological Analysis of Overseas Chinese Businessmen of Operation and Management," *Sociological Research* 2:75–82.

——(2002) "Keynote Address: Overseas Chinese Businessmen in the History of Globalization," conference on Globalization and Overseas Chinese, Kobe, Japan.

——(2003) *On Overseas Chinese Business* (in Chinese), Hong Kong: Social Sciences Press.

Malaysian Business (2001) *Malaysian Business*, February, 2001.

Markovits, C. (1999) "Indian Merchant Networks Outside India in the Nineteenth and Twentieth Centuries: A Preliminary Survey," *Modern Asian Studies* 33:883–991.

Menkhoff, T. (1994) "Trade Routes, Trust and Tactics: Chinese Traders in Singapore," in H. D. Evers and H. Schrader (eds.) *The Moral Economy of Trade: Ethnicity and Developing Markets*, London: Routledge.

North, D. (2000) "Big-bang Transformations of Economic Systems: An Introductory Note," *Journal of Institutional and Theoretical Economics* 156:3–8.

OECD (2002) *OECD Observer*, no. 234, October.

Redding, S. G. (1993) *The Spirit of Chinese Capitalism*, New York: de Gruyter.

Saxenian, A. L. (1999) *Silicon Valley's New Immigrant Entrepreneurs*, San Francisco, CA: Public Policy Institute of California.

Saxenian, A. L., Motoyama, Y., and Quan X. H. (2002) *Local and Global Networks of Immigrant Professionals in Silicon Valley*, San Francisco, CA: Public Policy Institute of California.

Wong, B. P. (2004) "Culture and Work: The Chinese Professionals in Silicon Valley," paper presented at the 5th Conference of the International Society for the Study of Chinese Overseas, University of Copenhagen, May 10–14, 2004.

Yao, S. C. (2002) *Confucian Capitalism: Discourse, Practice and the Myth of Chinese Enterprise*, London: RoutledgeCurzon.

Yoshihara, K. (1988) *The Rise of Ersatz Capitalism in Southeast Asia*, Singapore: Oxford University Press.

4 Contemporary changes in Chinese entrepreneurship in Hong Kong[1]

Raymond Sin-Kwok Wong

Introduction

The magnitude and influence of Chinese entrepreneurial activities have been expanding at an astonishing pace since the end of World War II. Initially, Chinese entrepreneurial activities were most noticeable in a few countries in East Asia (Hong Kong, Singapore, and Taiwan) dominated by ethnic Chinese. After mainland China opened its economic door in 1978 and became "the global factory," the volume of economic activities by ethnic Chinese multiplied exponentially. Concomitantly, with the spread of global capitalism, Chinese entrepreneurial activities also flourished elsewhere in the Pacific Rim region, particularly in Southeast Asia. The range of their economic activities has also expanded from petty trading and low value-added products to include high-technology and high value-added products and services. A few Chinese-owned business firms have even become global conglomerates and play an important economic role in the Pacific Rim region and beyond.

Such flourishing activities have led to increasing interest in why and how ethnic Chinese from divergent political, economic, and social contexts come to similar entrepreneurial enthusiasm and achievement. The conventional understanding favors a culturalist explanation, attributing Chinese entrepreneurial vigor to (post-)Confucian ethics that stress the importance of family and kin-based networks (Berger and Hsiao 1988; Bond and Hofstede 1990; Hofstede 1980; Kahn 1979; Rozman 1991; Vogel 1991). It is commonly thought that unlike the Western Protestant ethic that emphasizes individualism, competitiveness, and maximization of self-interest, Confucian ethics stress the importance of interpersonal relatedness, harmony, and obligations/responsibility. Built on these ethics, Chinese business practices high light social embeddedness. Business ties are structured by pre-existing interpersonal ties, and these personalized networks (*quanxi*) are instrumental in facilitating and enhancing economic transactions (Chen 1986; Fukuyama 1995; Hamilton and Kao 1990; Huang 1988; Redding 1988). Thus, Chinese entrepreneurs generate a complex web of personalized networks linking the firms back to sources of supply and forward to consumers (Chan 1982; Omohundro 1981; Wong 1985). This *quanxi*-driven business practice is believed to be shared by ethnic Chinese all over the world, including communist China (Bian 1997; 1999; Walder 1986; Yang 1994; 2002).

Associated with traditional Chinese familism that stresses collectivism, obedience, and obligation, Chinese entrepreneurs are generally character- ized as predisposed to paternalistic management and their firms as small family entities that rely on family members for financial and labor support (Espy 1970; King and Man 1974; King and Leung 1975; Lau 1982; Redding 1980; 1990; Redding and Tam 1990; Redding and Wong 1986; Sit et al. 1979; Whitley 1991; Wong 1979; 1985; 1989). In sum, business organiza- tions operated by ethnic Chinese tend to be small, family-dominated, cen- tralized, informally but effectively coupled, paternalistically organized, and antithetical to professional management. There is a close overlap of owner- ship, control, and family (Redding 1990; Redding and Whitley 1990).

However, much of the literature on Chinese business culture and prac- tices, particularly those pertaining to the experience of Hong Kong entre- preneurs, is dated. It is based largely on work conducted in the 1960s and 1970s, and may be over-generalized, as little of it is based on comparative or temporal investigations. Furthermore, the findings are drawn exclusively from non-representative samples of entrepreneurs, say small industrial owners, rather than the entire population of business owners. With the importance of the manufacturing industry fading and that of the business and financial service industry rising rapidly, there is clearly a need for reas- sessment. In other words, any information about the social composition of industrial owners can hardly be representative of the entire population. Finally, with the adoption of advanced technology in production that is usually both capital and skill intensive, as well as the growing influence of conglomerates, the organization of production and business in con- temporary Hong Kong may be very different and render the reliance on personalized networks less effective and beneficial. Indeed, some recent studies cast doubts on the culturalist interpretation and suggest changed conditions in the contemporary economic setting for Chinese entrepreneurs.

In my earlier work on business organizations and business entrepreneurs in Hong Kong, I found several tendencies that contradict the conventional understanding (Wong 2004). First, the degree of organizational complexity of Hong Kong firms, in terms of number of vertical levels, formalization, decentralization, and departmentalization, has become remarkably similar to the national sample of firms in the United States. Second, contrary to the understanding of the typical Chinese firm as a family firm, no more than two thirds of the business establishments in Hong Kong satisfy at least one of three criteria in the classification scheme—having family members and relatives in the company; self-identification as a family firm; and the inten- tion to pass the business on to the next generation. While the figure may still seem high, it is by no means unique and is indeed comparable to figures found in Great Britain and Canada (Family Firm Institute 2000). Third, while some entrepreneurs still favor the hiring of family members and relatives, a large proportion, particularly those born in Hong Kong, view negatively such practices and Chinese family firms in general (see Chapter 9 for additional evidence regarding their management philosophies and practices). In sum, even if family firms were indeed the norm in the past, the current organizational environment is dramatically different and business entrepreneurs are more open to Western management and organizational strategies.

In this chapter, we seek to provide an historical understanding of the changes in the social composition of entrepreneurs in Hong Kong during the past 30 years. Owing to the lack of public data, our analysis is based on the one-percent sample of the decennial data in 1971, 1981, 1991, and 2001, provided by the Hong Kong Census and Statistics Department. Admittedly, the amount of information available from the decennial censuses is limited. On the other hand, the number of entrepreneurs included in each census is representative and large (ranging from 1,288 in 1971 to 3,426 in 2001). By restricting the analysis to those who are economically active, the distinction between workers, self-employed workers, and employers should provide a better understanding of characteristics associated with the social composition of entrepreneurs and their possible changes over time.

The distinction between self-employed workers and employers is an important one. First, they differ significantly in terms of the amount of human and financial capital involved. The entry barriers for self-employment usually range from weak to non-existent. Self-employment is financially attractive, particularly among those who lack sufficient human capital to advance in the corporate hierarchy. Second, there is a strong theoretical (neo-Marixan and neo-Weberian) tradition in the stratification literature to distinguish them (Erikson and Goldthorpe 1992; 1987; Wright 1985). Third, their motivations for entrepreneurship can be different. Self-employed workers may be drawn to entrepreneurship because of the promise of autonomy and independence, whereas financial success and the boss mentality are important attractions for employers. In fact, the figures reported in Table 4.1 indicate clearly that while the incidence rates for entrepreneurship have remained stable, there are significant internal changes as the rise in the proportion of employers is offset by the decline in self-employed workers.

The analysis reported in this chapter is restricted only to those who were aged between 15 and 70 and economically active in the non-farm sector. As Hong Kong society becomes increasingly urbanized, the proportion of workers in the agricultural sector is shrinking considerably. Our focus of investigation is individual employment status. For the sake of convenience, family members working with or without pay are classified under the worker category. Table 4.1 provides a detailed breakdown of the number of valid cases from the four censuses. Because each household can have more than one member active in the labor force, the data cannot be treated as if they were drawn from simple random sampling. In the multivariate analysis section, all statistical models are estimated with robust standard errors to correct for household clustering.

Table 4.1 Basic statistics from the one-percent 1971, 1981, 1991, and 2001 censuses

	1971	1981	1991	2001
Number of unique households	7,617	10,740	13,975	17,746
Total working individuals	13,952	21,400	26,258	32,153
Working members per household	1.83	1.99	1.88	1.81
Employment status				
Worker	12,644	19,442	23,485	28,737
Self-employed worker	905	1,170	1,232	1,315
Employer	383	788	1,541	2,101
Percentage of entrepreneurs	9.2%	10.1%	10.6%	10.6%
Self-employed	6.5%	5.5%	4.7%	4.1%
Employer	2.7%	4.6%	5.9%	6.5%

Industrial diversification and occupational upgrading

Hong Kong has undergone a phenomenal transformation since its beginnings as a small fishing port several centuries ago. Many of the changes, however, occurred after the end of the Second World War, culminating with the large influx of refugees and capitalists from socialist China, with ebbs and flows depending on the political conditions in the mainland. With the talent, skills, and capital from many fleeing Shanghainese industrialists and those from elsewhere, most of the economic activities between 1950s and early 1970s were concentrated in manufacturing, from basic processing of textiles and plastics to garments and electronics. Even the composition of the manufacturing industry changed rapidly as well, sometimes within a few years, such as wig production in the 1960s, responding rapidly to the changing demand in the global market.

As of 1971, more than half of the non-farm population was engaged in the manufacturing industry (see Table 4.2).[2] The proportionate share of jobs in the manufacturing industry probably peaked around the mid-1970s. But within just three short years since China opened her economic door to foreign investments, its share reduced drastically to 45 percent in 1981. As economic reform in China intensified, the trend became irreversible with more and more capitalists (big and small) moving their entire production operation to China, mostly to the nearby Shenzhen and the larger Pearl River Delta region. The proportion of manufacturing workers dropped to less than 29 percent in 1991 and slightly more than 12 percent in 2001.

The rate of decline of entrepreneurs working in the manufacturing industry, however, is far less dramatic. Much of the decline was among self-employed workers (from 31 to 7 percent between 1971 and 2001), whereas the decline among employers was still significant but subdued, from 36.6 to 20.5 percent. This is hardly surprising given that the decline of manufacturing jobs in Hong Kong does not equate with a decline in manufacturing activities; only the nature of the organization of production has

Table 4.2 Industrial diversification in Hong Kong, 1971–2001

Major industry	Worker	SE	Employer	Total
1971				
Mining and quarrying	0.003	0.003	0.000	0.003
Manufacturing	0.520	0.309	0.366	0.502
Electricity, gas, and water	0.006	0.002	0.003	0.006
Construction	0.058	0.011	0.016	0.054
Wholesale and retail	0.059	0.536	0.308	0.097
Import and export	0.032	0.012	0.112	0.033
Restaurant and hotel	0.051	0.010	0.042	0.049
Transport, storage, and communication	0.077	0.041	0.021	0.073
Finance, insurance, and real estate	0.019	0.003	0.013	0.018
Community, social, and personal service	0.174	0.072	0.120	0.166
Agriculture	0.001	0.000	0.000	0.001
1981				
Mining and quarrying	0.001	0.000	0.000	0.001
Manufacturing	0.447	0.127	0.268	0.423
Electricity, gas, and water	0.007	0.002	0.001	0.007
Construction	0.090	0.035	0.065	0.086
Wholesale and retail	0.065	0.519	0.338	0.100
Import and export	0.031	0.016	0.127	0.034
Restaurant and hotel	0.066	0.084	0.047	0.066
Transport, storage, and communication	0.078	0.129	0.055	0.080
Finance, insurance, and real estate	0.055	0.010	0.044	0.052
Community, social, and personal service	0.161	0.078	0.056	0.153
Agriculture	0.000	0.000	0.000	0.000
1991				
Mining and quarrying	0.001	0.000	0.000	0.001
Manufacturing	0.288	0.179	0.322	0.285
Electricity, gas, and water	0.007	0.002	0.001	0.006
Construction	0.073	0.033	0.073	0.071
Wholesale and retail	0.082	0.309	0.193	0.099
Import and export	0.039	0.062	0.115	0.044
Restaurant and hotel	0.084	0.029	0.055	0.080
Transport, storage and communication	0.097	0.167	0.056	0.098
Finance, insurance, and real estate	0.114	0.065	0.084	0.110
Community, social, and personal service	0.214	0.149	0.099	0.204
Agriculture	0.002	0.004	0.003	0.002
2001				
Mining and quarrying	0.000	0.000	0.001	0.000
Manufacturing	0.118	0.067	0.205	0.122
Electricity, gas, and water	0.006	0.000	0.001	0.005
Construction	0.075	0.069	0.077	0.075
Wholesale and retail	0.096	0.214	0.199	0.108
Import and export	0.069	0.082	0.158	0.076
Restaurant and hotel	0.086	0.018	0.059	0.082
Transport, storage and communication	0.108	0.274	0.087	0.113
Finance, insurance, and real estate	0.169	0.116	0.111	0.163
Community, social, and personal service	0.272	0.157	0.100	0.256
Agriculture	0.001	0.003	0.004	0.002

been transformed. Although the locations of industrial production were shifted to China and Southeast Asia, the coordination of manufacturing activities, such as order processing, research and development, production planning, and shipment, largely remained in Hong Kong. This "new division of labor" also resulted in flourishing entrepreneurial activities in the import and export trading sector. Together with the rise of the service economy, particularly in the financial, insurance, and real estate (FIRE) sector, the economic mix of Hong Kong society today is much more diversified. This industrial diversification has also resulted in a profound transformation of the occupational structure, as we shall see shortly.

Together, the two service industries (personal and social; and finance, insurance, and real estate) constituted less than 19 percent of the working population in 1971. By 2001, their share increased to 42 percent. More significantly, since 1991, no single industry had more than 30 percent of the working population—clearly another healthy sign of economic diversification. Generally speaking, the changes in the distributions of entrepreneurs over time mirror the trend of industrial diversification observed earlier. In 2001, slightly more than three quarters of employers were concentrated in five industries, namely manufacturing (20.5 percent), wholesale and retail (19.9 percent), import and export (15.8 percent), financial and business service (11.1 percent), and social and personal service (10.0 percent), whereas over four fifths of self-employed workers were concentrated in transport, storage, and communication (27.4 percent), wholesale and retail (21.4 percent), social and personal services (15.7 percent), financial, business, and real estate (11.6 percent), and import and export (8.2 percent). Changes in the composition of self-employed workers were particularly noticeable in the wholesale and retail industry, where roughly half of them were engaged in such activities in 1971 and 1981 and the proportion declined dramatically to only 20 percent in 2001. We believe that a significant proportion of them in the two earlier censuses were street hawkers instead. It is noteworthy that contrary to the conventional rhetoric of the important role of manufacturing in the Hong Kong economy, entrepreneurial activities were prominent in the wholesale and retail industry in the 1960s and 1970s. Ironically, it was during the 1980s and 1990s that the manufacturing industry had the highest proportion of employers (see Table 4.3).

In addition to industrial diversification, there is also a gradual trend in occupational upgrading in white-collar and professional occupations. As the proportion of professional and managerial workers doubled from 14 to 30 percent between 1971 and 2001, the share of manual workers declined precipitously from 67 percent to 20 percent over the same period. One can gauge a similar conclusion from two measures of occupational rankings: the international socioeconomic index (ISEI) and the standard international occupational prestige scale (SIOPS) (Ganzeboom et al. 1992; Ganzeboom and Treiman 1996; Treiman 1977).[3] The improvement in status or prestige rankings among self-employed workers mirrors that of the general population. There

Table 4.3 Occupational upgrading in Hong Kong, 1971–2001

Major occupations	Worker	SE	Employer	Total
1971				
Professional and managerial	0.116	0.232	0.729	0.140
Routine non-manual	0.171	0.460	0.042	0.186
Skilled manual and supervisors	0.377	0.202	0.144	0.359
Semi- and unskilled manual	0.337	0.106	0.086	0.315
Occupational status (ranking)	34.189	33.131	45.554	34.433
Occupational prestige(ranking)	34.336	32.203	44.963	34.489
1981				
Professional and managerial	0.105	0.139	0.709	0.129
Routine non-manual	0.188	0.514	0.047	0.201
Skilled manual and supervisors	0.246	0.121	0.112	0.234
Semi- and unskilled manual	0.461	0.226	0.132	0.436
Occupational status (ranking)	36.414	33.711	45.850	36.614
Occupational prestige(ranking)	35.275	31.071	44.279	35.376
1991				
Professional and managerial	0.185	0.356	0.720	0.225
Routine non-manual	0.471	0.371	0.144	0.447
Skilled manual and supervisors	0.104	0.076	0.048	0.010
Semi- and unskilled manual	0.240	0.197	0.088	0.229
Occupational status (ranking)	38.940	40.786	49.204	39.629
Occupational prestige (ranking)	36.281	38.390	46.663	36.989
2001				
Professional and managerial	0.269	0.310	0.689	0.299
Routine non-manual	0.538	0.322	0.173	0.505
Skilled manual and supervisors	0.061	0.056	0.041	0.059
Semi- and unskilled manual	0.132	0.312	0.097	0.137
Occupational status (ranking)	41.460	40.189	48.294	41.854
Occupational prestige (ranking)	37.495	38.019	45.515	38.041

is, however, some sign of polarization as recently as 2001, with a slightly greater representation in the semi- and unskilled categories as a result of the economic slowdown and record unemployment. On the other hand, the improvement among employers is marginal, as many of them were already occupying managerial positions.

The trend toward industrial diversification and occupational upgrading could have profound implications for entrepreneurship. Such transformations, for example, would transform and create new environments that demand different sets of skills and perhaps even styles and types of entrepreneurship. Most entrepreneurs in the finance, insurance, and real estate industry today, for instance, are professionals themselves, with relevant credentials, training, and experience. Paradoxically, an important consequence of occupational upgrading is the increasing returns to education. Increasing job security, pay, and promotion in an expanding economy, particularly during the 1980s and early 1990s, may inhibit entrepreneurship among those who are better equipped with human capital. The extent to which the social composition of entrepreneurs may have changed over time is the focus of the next section.

Changing demographic composition of entrepreneurs

Do entrepreneurs today differ from their counterparts in the 1970s and 1980s in any significant manner? In terms of education attainment, contemporary Hong Kong business entrepreneurs are definitely better educated, and this improvement mirrors that of the larger society. In 1971, an overwhelming majority of self-employed workers (80 percent) had primary or lower education, while only 2 percent had at least some form of tertiary training (see Table 4.4). By 2001, only slightly more than 20 percent had primary or lower education, but the proportion with at least some form of tertiary training increased six times to 12 percent. Despite such improvement, the road to self-employment remains attractive among those who lack proper credentials for upward mobility. Relative to the general population, a disproportionately large segment continues to be drawn from individuals with primary and lower secondary education. In an increasingly formalized labor market, self-employment nonetheless provides a viable alternative or channel for career advancement and economic success. On the other hand, employers were substantially better educated than anyone else, especially during the 1960s and 1970s, where the extent of over-representation of those who had some college or higher education was two to four times higher than the general population. This educational gap narrowed considerably in the 1980s and 1990s. By 2001, the two distributions had become virtually indistinguishable. One can draw a similar conclusion by also comparing the average number of years in education.

Similar to the experience of women in many countries, women's representation in entrepreneurship is relatively low. Even if they do go into business, they are more likely to become self-employed workers rather than employers, though the discrepancies between the two sexes has narrowed over time. The odds for women to become self-employed workers as opposed to employers were almost 3:1 in 1971. This figure declined to 2:1 in 1981 and became close to parity in 1991 and 2001. Although women have made significant inroads, entrepreneurship is still dominated by men. In 2001, there is still only one female entrepreneur to four male entrepreneurs.

Results from Table 4.4 also confirm previous findings that entrepreneurs in the 1960s, self-employed or not, were much more likely to be drawn from the immigrant population. On the other hand, more and more of them today are natives, mirroring the demographic experience of the larger population. In 1971, less than 15 percent of entrepreneurs were born in Hong Kong, relative to 36 percent among workers. The proportion increased to over 24 percent in 1981, but the proportion among workers increased to 49 percent. During the 1990s, an exclusive reliance of immigrant talents was no

Table 4.4 Changing demographic composition of the labor force in Hong Kong, 1971–
2001

Major occupations	Worker	SE	Employer	Total
1971				
Education (years)	6.238	4.534	8.146	6.182
Primary or less	0.638	0.798	0.444	0.643
Lower secondary (F1–F3)	0.132	0.084	0.141	0.129
Upper secondary (F4–F5)	0.176	0.097	0.266	0.173
Postsecondary (F6/F7)	–	–	–	–
Some college/non-B.A.	0.030	0.008	0.052	0.029
University or more	0.025	0.013	0.097	0.026
Female	0.341	0.229	0.081	0.326
Born in Hong Kong	0.357	0.148	0.149	0.338
Age	34.352	44.339	42.984	35.237
Labor force experience	18.712	29.021	26.569	19.597
Married	0.530	0.815	0.838	0.557
Speak English	0.297	0.114	0.392	0.287
1981				
Education (years)	7.534	5.605	8.976	7.481
Primary or less	0.461	0.681	0.382	0.470
Lower secondary (F1–F3)	0.202	0.169	0.154	0.199
Upper secondary (F4–F5)	0.229	0.096	0.230	0.222
Postsecondary (F6/F7)	0.043	0.012	0.056	0.041
Some college/non-B.A.	0.029	0.009	0.043	0.029
University or more	0.036	0.033	0.136	0.040
Female	0.380	0.189	0.100	0.359
Born in Hong Kong	0.490	0.239	0.266	0.468
Age	33.515	44.709	43.454	34.493
Labor force experience	17.521	29.214	26.628	18.496
Married	0.519	0.816	0.874	0.548
Speak English	–	–	–	–
1991				
Education (years)	9.247	8.450	9.949	9.251
Primary or less	0.278	0.364	0.238	0.280
Lower secondary (F1–F3)	0.205	0.221	0.203	0.206
Upper secondary (F4–F5)	0.316	0.258	0.317	0.313
Postsecondary (F6/F7)	0.085	0.054	0.064	0.083
Some college/non-B.A.	0.045	0.025	0.034	0.043
University or more	0.071	0.078	0.144	0.076
Female	0.403	0.209	0.182	0.381
Born in Hong Kong	0.587	0.429	0.472	0.573
Age	35.341	42.094	41.281	36.006
Labor force experience	18.661	25.734	24.220	19.319
Married	0.578	0.775	0.857	0.604
Speak English	0.424	0.308	0.468	0.421
2001				
Education (years)	10.540	9.606	10.692	10.512
Primary or less	0.173	0.229	0.154	0.174
Lower secondary (F1–F3)	0.192	0.265	0.219	0.197
Upper secondary (F4–F5)	0.336	0.292	0.319	0.333
Postsecondary (F6/F7)	0.098	0.094	0.101	0.098

Table 4.4 (*continued*)

Major occupations	Worker	SE	Employer	Total
Some college/non-B.A.	0.044	0.026	0.041	0.043
University or more	0.156	0.094	0.167	0.154
Female	0.471	0.252	0.221	0.446
Born in Hong Kong	0.626	0.579	0.548	0.619
Age	37.408	42.823	44.084	38.066
Labor force experience	19.977	26.063	26.647	20.662
Married	0.594	0.738	0.829	0.616
Speak English	0.538	0.434	0.527	0.533

longer the case and there is virtually no distinction between the pool of entrepreneurs and workers in 2001 by immigrant status. Together with the improvement in schooling, this indigenous growth of entrepreneurs implies that the new generation of owners has had greater exposure to, and has been influenced by, Western culture, practices, lifestyles, and philosophy and may adhere less to the so-called "traditional" Chinese cultures.

Generally speaking, business entrepreneurs tend to be older, have more experience,[4] and more likely to be married. Differences among self-employed workers and employers in these characteristics are minor. On the other hand, employers are much more likely to be able to speak English, though the difference between employers and workers becomes negligible in 2001.[5] Given that self-employed workers are more likely to be drawn from those with less than lower secondary education, it is not surprising to observe that few of them can speak or use English regularly. However, it is pertinent to recognize that the ability to speak English is not synonymous with educational attainment. There is a substantial overlap between them but they are not identical. In the next section, we will explore how each factor can exert an independent influence on employment status.

Correlates of employment status: multivariate analysis

While the above descriptions may be informative, they do not assess their relative importance, especially when the influences of other factors are examined simultaneously. The latter can only be achieved through multivariate analysis. Since the variable we are interested in, employment status, is categorical in nature, the multinomial logistic regression model offers the most appropriate statistical technique for further examination.[6] Two models are presented separately for each census year. Model 1 is the main effects model whereas model 2 includes interaction effects as well. In all four census years, the interaction model is preferred because it adds explanatory power to our understanding.

To aid the search for possible interactions, the following procedure has been adopted. First, only one interaction term, say, between female and industry or between born in Hong Kong and education, is added to the main effects model. Any interaction term that is statistically significant at the 0.10 level is retained. Second, all plausible interactions retained in the first step are added to the main effects model simultaneously. They are then deleted sequentially using the backward selection strategy. It should be noted this modeling exercise is exploratory, as the goal is not to establish causal relationships. Rather, we want to pinpoint significant factors or correlates that are associated with entrepreneurship.

Results from the 1971 census

Relative to workers, there is an over-representation of entrepreneurs (self-employed workers and employers) in manufacturing, wholesale, retail, import, and export, and service industries (see Table 4.5). However, women entrepreneurs were particularly disadvantaged in manufacturing and service industries. Among entrepreneurs themselves, there is a larger presence of male employers in manufacturing and restaurant and hotel industries than self-employed workers, whereas female employers outnumbered self-employed workers in the personal and social service industry. Although the reference category includes a number of residual industries, in terms of absolute size, it comprises largely of individuals in the construction and transport, storage, and communications industries.

Ceteris paribus, the role of education in the decision of self-employment is small and negligible. The only exception is that women with secondary education (form 1 to form 6) had much lower representation than their male counterparts. In particular, the odds for women with form 4 to form 6 education were only 0.13 times ($e^{-2.040}$) as that of men with identical background whereas women with form 1 to form 3 education fared slightly better, 0.34 times as likely as their male counterparts. Note that the influence of women is negative in the main effects model (model 1) but positive in the interaction model (model 2). It means that had we failed to consider gender interactions, we would have missed the important fact that less educated women were actually more likely to become self-employed than their male counterparts with a similar background. On the other hand, the coefficients of all educational dummies are positive for employers and their strengths increase as education rises. Given that their interactions with gender are not statistically significant, one can conclude that both male and female employers were much better educated than their counterparts in the worker category. For instance, the odds for university graduates to become employers are 5.5 times ($e^{1.699}$) as likely as those with primary or less education.

Although the ability to speak English is related to educational background, each exerts independent influence. Apparently, such an ability is not as critical as one would imagine in entrepreneurship during the 1960s. The coefficient for speaking English among employers is practically zero, whereas its relationship with self-employment is negative. Given the limited range of economic

Table 4.5 Multinomial logistic regression for entrepreneurship in Hong Kong, 1971

Variable	Model 1		Model 2	
	Self-employed	*Employer*	*Self-employed*	*Employer*
Intercept	−5.243***	−6.844***	−5.217***	−6.824***
Manufacturing	0.766***	1.545***	0.936***	1.586***
Wholesale/retail/import/ export	3.044***	2.977***	2.893***	2.897***
Restaurant/hotel	−0.659	1.284***	−0.818#	1.252***
Financial/insurance/ real estate	0.108	0.873	0.040	0.840
Service	0.422*	1.085***	0.820***	1.117***
Married	0.309*	0.634**	0.279*	0.628**
Experience	0.099***	0.079***	0.093***	0.077***
Experience squared ($\times 10^{-2}$)	−0.117***	−0.089*	−0.105***	−0.085*
Female	−0.391***	−1.399***	0.585***	−0.785*
Born in Hong Kong	−0.111	−0.437**	−0.117	−0.440**
Lower secondary (F1–F3)	−0.100	0.715***	−0.006	0.636***
Upper secondary (F4–F6)	−0.268	0.940***	−0.084	1.010***
Some college/non-B.A.	−0.648	1.257***	−0.688	1.240***
University or more	−0.257	1.702***	−0.266	1.699***
English	−0.798***	−0.052	−0.766***	−0.040
Female × manufacturing			−1.415***	−0.951*
Female × service			−2.617***	−0.669
Female × lower secondary (F1–F3)			−1.069*	0.803#
Female × upper secondary (F4–F6)			−2.040***	−1.380
Log-likelihood		−3953.54		−3901.72
Model chi-square		2251.37		2355.00
df		30		38
Pseudo R-squared		0.222		0.232

Notes:
***$p<0.001$, **$p<0.01$, *$p<0.05$, #$p<0.10$. The standard errors are robust standard errors after correction for clustering.

activities of self-employment (as street hawkers, for instance) at the time and its almost exclusive recruitment from individuals with primary education, the ability to speak English is immaterial. Those who were equipped with such a capability would have fared much better in the labor market. As we will see shortly, the effects of English speaking capability are not constant and change over time.

As expected, the relationship between labor force experience and entrepreneurship has an inverted U-shape, reaching maximum with 44 and 45 years of experience for self-employed workers and employers, respectively.

Table 4.6 Multinomial logistic regression for entrepreneurship in Hong Kong, 1981

Variable	Model 1		Model 2	
	Self-employed	Employer	Self-employed	Employer
Intercept	−4.570***	−6.487***	−4.544***	−6.520***
Manufacturing	−0.874***	0.354**	−0.614***	0.462***
Wholesale/retail/import/ export	2.069***	2.183***	1.916***	2.159***
Restaurant/hotel	0.347	0.362#	0.314*	0.283
Financial/insurance/ real estate	−0.660*	0.410#	−0.668*	0.330
Service	0.422**	−0.659***	−0.279*	−0.657***
Married	0.460***	0.932***	0.458***	0.935***
Experience	0.112***	0.137***	0.110***	0.138***
Experience squared ($\times 10^{-2}$)	−0.141***	−0.184***	−0.139***	−0.185***
Female	−0.697***	−1.455***	−0.497*	−0.646*
Born in Hong Kong	−0.078	−0.002	−0.159	0.071
Lower secondary (F1–F3)	−0.141	0.334**	−0.339**	0.295*
Upper secondary (F4–F5)	−0.868***	0.674***	−0.639***	0.652***
Postsecondary (F6/F7)	−0.951***	1.216***	−0.966***	1.211***
Some college/non-B.A.	−0.917**	1.336***	−0.895**	1.336***
University or more	−0.248	1.732***	−0.261	1.614***
Female × manufacturing			−1.534***	−1.410***
Female × W/R/I/E			0.545*	−0.586#
Female × services			−0.890*	−0.668
Female × born in Hong Kong			−0.146	−0.700*
Female × upper secondary			−1.363***	0.364
Female × university or more			0.083	1.008*
Born in HK × lower secondary			0.529**	0.059
Log-likelihood		−5982.37		−5919.65
Model chi-square		3770.73		3896.17
df		30		44
Pseudo R-squared		0.240		0.248

Notes:
***p<0.001, **p<0.01, *p<0.05, #p<0.10. The standard errors are robust standard errors after correction for clustering.

While the numbers may seem high by today's standards, it is important to recognize that most individuals at this time period began their working careers at a very young age. In fact, the number could have been even higher had we not set the minimum working age at 15 in constructing the variable. Finally, entrepreneurs are much more likely to be married than otherwise. It is difficult to gauge whether this is a cause or effect of entrepreneurship. But granted that most entrepreneurs tended to be older and had been in the labor force longer, the chances of them being married should be high as well.

Results from the 1981 census

In terms of industrial concentration, there is a dramatic turnaround from over-representation to under-representation for male self-employed workers in the manufacturing industry. The opening of the economic border in the north has proved to be disastrous for independent manufacturers, as they have to rely on orders from their larger counterparts. Although male employers were able to preserve their strong presence in manufacturing, the extent was much more subdued than an earlier period. For women entrepreneurs, their presence in the manufacturing industry was still meager (see Table 4.6).

The empirical evidence continues to support the notion that the decision to strike it out on their own as economically self-supporting was driven primarily by their lack of human capital. Better educated workers, especially women with upper secondary education, or those with at least some form of tertiary training, are far less likely to join the ranks of the self-employed. For instance, those individuals with college or higher education are only about 0.41 times as likely as those with primary or less education to engage in self-employment. Note that this is the period when the availability of higher education was still extremely limited and the economy was expanding rapidly. Viewed under such light, it is perhaps understandable why many well educated workers preferred not to take the plunge and trade job security and promotion chances for autonomy and independence.

For employers, the effect of education on entrepreneurship is exactly the opposite. While it was the less educated who joined the ranks of the self-employed, better educated men and women were more attracted to become employers. Among male employers, education continued to play an important role in facilitating successful entrepreneurship. Compared with their male counterparts with comparable education, only women with university training were particularly more successful (2.7 times) in becoming employers. Significant obstacles remained for those who were not better positioned educationally. Note again that the coefficient of women dropped precipitously from the main effects model to the interaction model. The latter model is preferred, as it provides insights and pinpoints the sources of under-representation of women in entrepreneurship.

Controlling for other effects, native-born men in 1981 were no longer under-represented in the employer category as in 1971, while native-born women continued to be disadvantaged. For the first time, we witness that native-born men and women with lower secondary education (that is, the first three years of secondary education) had greater likelihood in engaging in self-employment. The odds were 1.7 times higher than for those who were not born locally. The relationship between entrepreneurial activities, labor

force experience and marriage was similar to an earlier period. The likelihood of entrepreneurship increased with years of labor force, peaked at age
40 and 37 for self-employed workers and employers respectively, and then
declined thereafter. Finally, there is a far greater representation of married
entrepreneurs than married workers. Unfortunately, the variable that measures English language ability was not included in the 1981 census and it is
impossible to gauge its influence.

Results from the 1991 census

Results from the 1991 census indicate that after the manufacturing industry
began its wholesale relocation outside of Hong Kong in the 1980s, the
number of self-employed workers in this sector fell dramatically. On the
other hand, we find their presence in the wholesale, retail, import, and
export industry instead. While similar pressures of relocation are equally
applicable to employers, only the nature of production arrangements was
transformed. As a result, male employers continued to be over-represented
in the manufacturing industry. At the same time, it is important to recognize that their dominance in the wholesale, retail, import, and export
industries is substantially weaker than before.

The relationship between education and entrepreneurship changed again
in the 1980s. In the case of self-employment, the role of education was
negligible for men, though women with secondary education (form 1 to
form 5) were under-represented and those with higher education were over-
represented. However, the actual extent of over-representation is severely
curtailed because of the significant negative effect of gender. As a result, the
overall pattern of gender difference in the effect of education is quite different from 1981 but similar to 1971, discussed earlier. Because of the
interactive relationship between education and those who were born in
Hong Kong, the interpretation is further complicated. The relatively weak
influence of education refers mainly to self-employed workers who were
non-native-born. For the native-born, there is some slight disadvantage with
post-secondary education (form 6 and form 7 education). On the other
hand, women with some form of secondary education were under-represented
in self-employment but those with university education are more likely to
engage in self-employment than their male counterparts. The effect of education on employer status is generally positive. That is, the higher the education, the greater the likelihood of becoming an employer. Those native-
born with upper secondary and university education were less likely to become
employers. Similarly, women with upper secondary education are also slightly
penalized or under-represented (see Table 4.7).

Labor force experience again displays an inverted U-shape relationship
with entrepreneurship. For self-employment, the probability reaches a maximum of 38 years for men and 52 for women. In other words, the chance of
entrepreneurship pretty much increases with labor force experience until

Table 4.7 Multinomial logistic regression for entrepreneurship in Hong Kong, 1991

Variable	Model 1		Model 2	
	Self-employed	Employer	Self-employed	Employer
Intercept	−4.407***	−5.779***	−4.395***	−5.855***
Manufacturing	−0.404***	0.720***	−0.235*	0.800***
Wholesale/retail/import/ export	1.372***	1.568***	1.353***	1.543***
Restaurant/hotel	−1.013***	0.236	−1.087***	0.204
Financial/insurance/real estate	−0.282*	0.084	−0.262$^{\#}$	0.083
Service	−0.115	−0.248*	−0.191$^{\#}$	−0.301*
Married	0.247**	0.944***	0.293***	0.955***
Experience	0.102***	0.116***	0.097***	0.115***
Experience squared ($\times 10^{-2}$)	−0.130***	−0.163***	−0.127***	−0.159***
Female	−0.800***	−1.028***	−0.656***	−0.694***
Born in Hong Kong	−0.089	0.016	−0.019	0.161*
Lower secondary (F1–F3)	0.106	0.348***	0.162$^{\#}$	0.323***
Upper secondary (F4–F5)	0.143	0.587***	0.296*	0.793***
Postsecondary (F6/F7)	−0.008	0.356*	0.282	0.369$^{\#}$
Some college/non-B.A.	−0.086	0.434*	−0.045	0.820***
University or more	0.452**	1.193***	0.168	1.072***
English	−0.161$^{\#}$	0.428***	−0.120	0.454***
Female × manufacturing			−0.952***	−0.512***
Female × experience squared ($\times 10^{-2}$)			0.033**	−0.011
Female × lower secondary			−0.452*	−0.009
Female × upper secondary			−0.672***	−0.365*
Female × university or more			0.845***	0.368
Born in HK × upper secondary			−0.072	−0.320*
Born in HK × postsecondary (F6/F7)			−0.682*	−0.149
Born in HK × some college/non-BA			−0.197	−0.855**
Log-likelihood	−9413.00		−9359.11	
Model chi-square	2693.59		2801.37	
df	32		48	
Pseudo R-squared	0.125		0.130	

Notes:
***p<0.001, **p<0.01, *p<0.05, #p<0.10. The standard errors are robust standard errors after correction for clustering.

retirement. Among employers, the probability reaches a maximum at 36 years of labor force experience, disregarding their gender. Those who can speak English had a greater likelihood of becoming employers rather than workers (the odds are 1.6). Since the comparable effect was negligible in 1971 and the variable does not exist in the 1981 census, it is unclear when the fundamental shift actually occurred. Interestingly, the strong negative effect of English speaking ability in self-employment found in 1971 is no longer important in 1991. Perhaps, as the economy transformed from an industrial-based to a service-based one and with a steady educational upgrading of the population, the number of jobs that demand English speaking skills has increased for both workers and self-employed workers alike (take the case of accountants and lawyers, for instance). The ability to speak English therefore no longer represents a distinguishing factor for these two types of worker. On the other hand, the success of employers continues to depend heavily on their ability to maneuver complex transactions locally and globally. The ability to speak English constitutes an invaluable asset.

Results from the 2001 census

Comparing the 2001 results with previous years (see Table 4.8), changes in the concentration of male and female entrepreneurs in specific industries were even more dramatic and extensive. For instance, men were now under-represented as self-employed workers and employers in finance, insurance, and real estate and service industries, and over-represented in wholesale, retail, import, and export industry. Self-employed workers continued to be under-represented in manufacturing though significantly greater proportion of male employers was still engaging in manufacturing activities relative to their female counterparts. Women entrepreneurs, on the other hand, were over-represented in wholesale, retail, import, and export; finance, insurance, and real estate; and service industries as self-employed workers and under-represented in manufacturing; wholesale, retail, import, and export; finance, insurance, and real estate; and service industries as employers. It thus appears that male and female entrepreneurs have segmented participation in different types of economic activity and they do not share identical economic space. In other words, gender segregation in the workplace applies to workers and entrepreneurs alike (for similar observations for Western countries, note the works by Luber and Leicht 2000; Boden and Nucci 1997; and Mauser and Picot 1999).

The effect of education was once again relatively minor in the case of self-employment. In fact, the 2001 pattern is very similar to 1971, except that the incidence of self-employment was higher as more men and women from various educational backgrounds were seizing the opportunity to make it in the business world. For employers, the role of education is positive, with tremendous advantages conferred on those with post-secondary or higher education. At the same time, we should note that the effects of higher education (college or above) in 1991 and 2001 were significantly weaker than those observed in 1971 and 1981, probably because of the competition and reward in the salaried and waged sector. Despite persistent inequalities against women, better educated women with some college or higher education were able to circumvent some of these obstacles in entrepreneurship. At

Table 4.8 Multinomial logistic regression for entrepreneurship in Hong Kong, 2001

Variable	Model 1		Model 2	
	Self-employed	*Employer*	*Self-employed*	*Employer*
Intercept	−3.647***	−5.144***	−3.709***	−5.197***
Manufacturing	−1.044***	0.739***	−0.973***	0.814***
Wholesale/retail/import/ export	0.337***	1.210***	0.294***	1.275***
Restaurant/hotel	−1.939***	0.103	−1.932***	0.254*
Financial/insurance/ real estate	−0.669***	−0.184#	−0.870***	−0.262*
Service	−0.713***	−0.543***	−0.908***	−0.400***
Married	−0.005	0.426***	0.130	0.571***
Experience	0.073***	0.132***	0.067***	0.126***
Experience squared ($\times 10^{-2}$)	−0.064***	−0.154***	−0.058***	−0.153***
Female	−0.722***	−0.943***	−1.285***	−0.846***
Born in Hong Kong	0.014	−0.124*	0.147#	0.048
Lower secondary (F1–F3)	0.016	−0.022	0.036	−0.028
Upper secondary (F4–F5)	−0.125	0.146	0.085	0.285*
Postsecondary (F6/F7)	0.138	0.360**	0.135	0.370**
Some college/non-B.A.	−0.359#	0.317*	0.167	0.739***
University or more	−0.211	0.604***	0.138	0.593***
English	0.050	0.273***	0.057	0.291***
Female × manufacturing			0.101	−0.573**
Female × W/R/I/E			0.746**	−0.462*
Female × restaurant/hotel			0.584	−0.837**
Female × FIRE			1.329***	0.163
Female × service			1.029***	−0.726***
Female × married			−0.321*	−0.330*
Female × experience squared ($\times 10^{-2}$)			0.016	0.044***
Female × upper secondary			−0.294#	0.310*
Female × some college/ non-B.A.			−0.385	0.757**
Female × university or more			−0.023	0.703***
Born in HK × upper secondary			−0.179	−0.357**
Born in HK × some college/non-B.A.			−0.597	−0.962***
Born in HK × university or more			−0.581**	−0.306*
Log-likelihood	−11660.69		−11594.64	
Model chi-square	3004.80		3136.89	
df	32		58	
Pseudo R-squared	0.114		0.119	

Notes:
***p<0.001, **p<0.01, *p<0.05, #p<0.10. The standard errors are robust standard errors after correction for clustering.

the same time, native-born men and women with comparable education were expected to be under-represented. In fact, the model predicts that non-native-born individuals with a college education were more likely to become employers than the native-born.

Finally, consistent with findings from earlier years, the relationship between labor force experience and entrepreneurship has an inverted U-shape. Similar to the findings in 1991, the importance of English was only applicable to employers and had no effect on self-employment. The strength of relationship, however, is considerably weaker. Those who can speak English are 34 percent more likely than non-speakers to become employers, which is substantially smaller than the 57 percent found in 1991. Nonetheless, this does not necessarily indicate the declining significance of English among employers. Much of its influence is likely to be derived directly from education, as we have already noted the advantages conferred by tertiary education.

Conclusion

The nature of business entrepreneurship in Hong Kong has changed dramatically in the past three decades. Entrepreneurs today are no longer concentrated in one or two economic areas (such as manufacturing and wholesale, retail, and import and export industries in the 1960s and early 1970s) but are well diversified across the economic spectrum. Thus, Hong Kong Chinese entrepreneurs have satisfied the Schumpeterian definition of entrepreneurship; that is, it is inherently dynamic, and business entrepreneurs must be quick to switch from one economic activity to another when new opportunities arise.

Based on the results presented in this chapter, we can make the following observations about changes of entrepreneurship in Hong Kong. First, paralleling the experience of educational and occupational upgrading in the general population, contemporary entrepreneurs are better educated and well diversified. Individuals with a university education who are attracted to become employers represent an important development of the past ten years and may promise a new way to rejuvenate the stagnant economy. More importantly, their exposure to Western education can also open up the possibility of introducing Western philosophy and management practices into their organizational structure. We interpret the positive role of the ability to speak English among employers in 1991 and 2001 as corroborative support for this particular argument.

Historically, immigrants from mainland China formed an important pool of business entrepreneurs in Hong Kong. The empirical results from the two earlier censuses certainly lend strong support for this interpretation and validate findings from previous work. For instance, we find that non-Hong Kong born residents in 1971 were 55 percent more likely to become employers than native-born residents. However, that is only part of the story, as the social composition of entrepreneurs changes dramatically over time as well. By the late 1980s, this advantage has diminished significantly to only 17 percent. As the large and periodic influx of immigrants has been effectively curtailed since the mid-1970s and Hong Kong has attained a large and stable stock of local residents, more and more entrepreneurs (and residents as well) today are born and educated in Hong Kong, and the importance of the immigrant entrepreneur is declining. Although better educated native-born residents may prefer stable and secure employment to the risky business of striking out on their own, the new generation of Chinese entrepreneurs nonetheless will have had more exposure to Western ideas, tastes, and preferences than traditional Chinese cultural and business practitioners.

Generally speaking, entrepreneurial activities remain dominated by men. Although women had made some inroads into entrepreneurship, they still made up less than one quarter of entrepreneurs in 2001. It appears that the types of economic activity that male and female entrepreneurs are involved in are rather segregated. It also appears that only women with university or higher education are better positioned to circumvent persistent gender hurdles to have slightly better chances of entering entrepreneurship. Despite significant progress, gender inequality in entrepreneurship is certainly one area that needs improvement. Finally, the empirical findings discussed in this chapter clearly suggest that the distinction between self-employed workers and employers is a fruitful one. Not only do the two groups differ in terms of size and scale of business activity, their demographic composition differs rather dramatically, as do the changes in this demographic over time. Future research on entrepreneurship should continue to maintain a clear distinction between them.

Notes

1 An earlier version of this chapter was presented at the University of California Pacific Rim Research Conference on "The New Breed of Chinese Entrepreneurs: Globalization, Culture, and Organizational Imperatives" at the Hong Kong University of Science and Technology in May, 2004. The conference is co-sponsored by the Division of Social Sciences, Hong Kong University of Science and Technology.
2 To facilitate comparison over time, the classification of industries of each census is first mapped into the 1988 Standard Industrial Classification scheme developed by the International Labor Office (ILO 1989) and they are then aggregated to form major industries.
3 The occupational codes in each census are first coded into the 1988 International Standard Classification of Occupation (ISCO) codes. They are then mapped into the CASMIN class categories (Erikson and Goldthorpe 1992), status scores, and prestige scores.
4 Labor force experience is calculated by subtracting years of education and six from age and by setting the minimum working age to 15. This procedure can introduce errors for some who worked during early childhood, particularly in the 1971 and 1981 censuses. Since 1970, the official minimum working age has been 15.

5 The 1981 data do not contain information about the ability to speak English or other languages.

6 In all multinomial logistic models, workers are chosen as the reference category.

References

Berger, P. L. and Hsiao, H. H. M. (1988) *In Search of An East Asian Development Model*, New Brunswick, NJ: Transaction Books.

Bian, Y. J. (1997) "Bringing Strong Ties Back In: Indirect Ties, Network Bridges, and Job Searches in China," *American Sociological Review* 62:366–85.

——(1999) "Getting a Job through a Web of *Guanxi* in China," in B. Wellman (ed.) *Networks in the Global Village: Life in Contemporary Communities*, Boulder, CO: Westview.

Boden, R. J. and Nucci, A. R. (1997) "Counting the Self-Employed Using Household and Business Sample Data," *Small Business Economics* 9:427–36.

Bond, M. H. and Hofstede, G. (1990) "The Cash Value of Confucian Values," in S. R. Clegg and S. G. Redding (eds.) *Capitalism in Contrasting Cultures*, New York: de Gruyter.

Chan, W. K. K. 1982. "The Organizational Structure of the Traditional Chinese Firm and its Modern Reform," *Business History Review* 56:218–35.

Chang, L. Y. and Tam, T. (2004) "The Making of Chinese Business Culture: Quanxi versus Organizational Imperatives," in E. T. Gomez and H. H. M. Hsiao (eds.) *De-essentializing Capitalism: Chinese Enterprise, Transnationalism, and Identity*, London: RoutledgeCurzon.

Chen, C. N. (1986) "Traditional Family System and Business Organization," *Marriage, Familism and Society*, Taipei: Yun-Chen Publishing Company (in Chinese).

Erikson, R. and Goldthorpe, J. H. (1992) *The Constant Flux: A Study of Class Mobility in Industrial Societies*, Oxford: Clarendon Press.

Espy, J. L. (1970) "The Strategy of Chinese Industrial Enterprise in Hong Kong," unpublished dissertation, School of Business Administration, Harvard University.

Family Firm Institute (2000) *Facts on Family Businesses in the U.S., U.K., and Canada*, Boston, MA: Family Firm Institute (www.ffi.org/looking/factsfs.html).

Fukuyama, F. (1995) *Trust: The Social Virtues and the Creation of Prosperity*, New York: Free Press.

Ganzeboom, H. B. G., De Graaf, P. M., and Treiman, D. J. (1992) "A Standard International Socio-Economic Index of Occupational Status," *Social Science Research* 21:1–56.

Ganzeboom, H. B. G. and Treiman, D. J. (1996) "International Comparable Measures of Occupational Status for the 1988 International Standard Classification of Occupations," *Social Science Research* 25:201–39.

Goldthorpe, J. H. (1987) *Social Mobility and Class Structure in Modern Britain*, Oxford: Clarendon Press.

Hamilton, G. G. and Kao, C. S. (1990) "The Institutional Foundations of Chinese Business: The Family Firm in Taiwan," *Comparative Social Research* 12:135–57.

Hofstede, G. (1980) *Culture's Consequences*, London: Sage.

Huang, M. H. H. (1988) "An East Asian Development Model: Empirical Exploration," in P. L. Berger and M. H. H. Hsiao (eds.) *In Search of an East Asian Development Model*, New Brunswick, NJ: Transaction.

ILO (International Labour Organization) (1989) *International Standard Classification of Occupations 1988*, Geneva: ILO.

Kahn, H. (1979) *World Economic Development: 1979 and Beyond*, London: Croom Helm.

King, A. Y. C. and Man, P. J. L. (1974) *The Role of Small Factory in Economic Development: The Case of Hong Kong*, Social Science Research Centre, The Chinese University of Hong Kong.

King, A. Y. C. and Leung, D. S. K. (1975) *The Chinese Touch in Small Industrial Organizations*, Social Science Research Centre, The Chinese University of Hong Kong.

Lau, S. K. (1982) *Society and Politics in Hong Kong*, Hong Kong: The Chinese University Press.

Luber, S. and Leicht, R. (2000) "Growing Self-Employment in Western Europe: An Effect of Modernization?" *International Review of Sociology* 10:101–23.

Mauser, M. E. and Picot, G. (1999) "The Role of Self-Employment in U.S. and Canadian Job Growth," *Monthly Labor Review* 122:10–25.

Omohundro, J. T. (1981) *Chinese Merchant Families in Iloilo*, Athens, OH: Ohio University Press.

Redding, S. G. (1980) "Cognition as an Aspect of Culture and Its Relation to Management Processes: An Exploratory View of the Chinese Case," *Journal of Management Studies* 17:127–48.

——(1988) "The Role of the Entrepreneur in the New Asian Capitalism," in P. L. Berger and H. H. M. Hsiao (eds.) *In Search of An East Asian Development Model*, New Brunswick, NJ: Transaction.

——(1990) *The Spirit of Chinese Capitalism*, New York: de Gruyter.

Redding, S. G. and Tam, S. (1990) "Networks and Molecular Organizations: An Exploratory View of Chinese Firms in Hong Kong," *Proceedings: Inaugural Meeting of the Southeast Asian Region Academy of International Business*, Hong Kong: The Chinese University of Hong Kong.

Redding, S. G. and Whitley, R. D. (1990) "Beyond Bureaucracy: Towards a Comparative Analysis of Forms of Economic Resource Co-ordination and Control," in S. R. Clegg and S. G. Redding (eds.) *Capitalism in Contrasting Cultures*, New York: de Gruyter.

Redding, S. G. and Wong, G. Y. Y. (1986) "The Psychology of Chinese Organizational Behavior," in M. H. Bond (ed.) *The Psychology of the Chinese People*, Hong Kong: Oxford University Press.

Rozman, G. (1991) *The East Asian Region: Confucian Heritage and its Modern Adaptation*, Princeton, NJ: Princeton University Press.

Sit, V. F. S., Wong, S. L., and Kiang, T. S. (1979) *Small Scale Industry in a Laissez-Faire Economy: A Hong Kong Case Study*, Centre of Asian Studies Occasional Papers and Monographs, no. 30, University of Hong Kong.

Treiman, D. J. (1977) *Occupational Prestige in Comparative Perspective*, New York: Academic Press.

Uzzi, B. (1997) "Social Structure and Competition in Interfirm Networks: The Paradox of Embeddedness," *Administrative Science Quarterly* 42:35–67.

Vogel, E. F. (1991) *The Four Little Dragons: The Spread of Industrialization in East Asia*, Cambridge, MA: Harvard University Press.

Walder, A. (1986) *Communist Neo-Traditionalism: Work and Authority in Chinese Industry*, Berkeley, CA: University of California Press.

Whitley, R. D. (1991) "The Social Construction of Business Systems in East Asia," *Organization Studies* 12:1–28.

Wong, R. S. K. (2004) "Chinese Business Firms and Entrepreneurs in Hong Kong," in E. T. Gomez and H. H. M. Hsiao (eds.) *De-essentializing Capitalism: Chinese Enterprise, Transnationalism, and Identity*, London: RoutledgeCurzon.

Wong, S. L. (1979) "Industrial Entrepreneurship and Ethnicity: A Study of the Shanghainese Cotton Spinners in Hong Kong," unpublished Ph.D. dissertation, University of Oxford.

——(1985) "The Chinese Family Firm: A Model," *British Journal of Sociology* 36:58–72.

——(1989) "Modernization and Chinese Cultural Traditions in Hong Kong," in H. C. Tai (ed.) *Confucianism and Economic Development: An Oriental Alternative*, Washington, DC: Washington Institute Press.

Wright, E. O. (1985) *Classes*, London: Verso.

Yang, M. M. H. (1994) *Gifts, Favors, and Banquets: The Art of Social Relationships in China*, Ithaca, NY: Cornell University Press.

——(2002) "The Resilience of *Guanxi* and its New Deployments: A Critique of Some New *Guanxi* Scholarship," *The China Quarterly* 170:459–76.

Part III

Contemporary Chinese entrepreneurship in local settings

5 Enterprise development and inter-ethnic relations in Malaysia

Affirmative action, generational change, and business partnerships

Edmund Terence Gomez

Affirmative action and the NEP

Following the racial riots of May 13, 1969, the Malaysian government implemented an ambitious 20-year social engineering plan in 1971 to achieve national unity. This plan, the New Economic Policy (NEP), sought to attain national unity by eradicating poverty, irrespective of race, and restructuring society so as to achieve inter-ethnic economic parity between the predominantly Malay *Bumiputera* (or "sons of the soil") and the predominantly Chinese non-Bumiputera. The government hoped to increase Bumiputera corporate equity ownership to 30 percent and reduce the poverty level to 15 percent by 1990. With the end of the NEP, the National Development Policy (NDP), building on the objectives of its predecessor, was implemented between 1991 and 2000.

The implementation of NEP entailed partial abandonment of the laissez-faire style of economic management. It favored greater state intervention, particularly for ethnic affirmative action, including an accelerated expansion of the Malay middle class, capital accumulation on behalf of the Malays, and the creation of Malay capitalists. The measures used to achieve these goals included requiring companies to restructure their corporate holdings to ensure at least 30 percent Bumiputera ownership and allotting publicly listed shares at par value or only nominal premiums to Bumiputeras. The government would subsequently encourage inter-ethnic business partnerships, as a means to promote ethnic coexistence as well as help advance the involvement of Malays in business.

This chapter focuses on two key but related issues. First, it provides a brief theoretical discussion on the evolution of business partnerships. Second, through an analytical tracing of the historical evolution of inter-ethnic business relations in Malaysia, it offers some insights about the evolving nature of these inter-ethnic business ties, brought about through the implementation of NEP and NDP, in enterprise development, the newly emerged middle class, and "generational change" in Malaysia.

The main arguments can be briefly summarized as the following. First, although partnerships are common during business start-ups, they are not sustainable in the long run. In view of this, the Malaysian government's policy of encouraging inter-ethnic business ties through business partnerships is not a proper mechanism to promote national unity. Second, changes in the nature of business relationships indicate that identity transformations have occurred in Malaysia with the rise of the middle class and as new generations of Malaysians emerge.

Development of Malaysian enterprise

Malaysian corporate history is replete with cases of business partnerships (for example, see Puthucheary 1960; Tan 1982; Sieh-Lee 1982; Hara 1993; Brown 1994; Searle 1999; and Gomez 1999). This history also indicates that the nature of business relationships is constantly evolving. When the Chinese first migrated to Malaya during the pre-colonial and colonial periods, intra-ethnic partnerships were common during the formation of businesses. Migrants saw common ethnicity as a tool they could exploit to help them cope with their new environment. Once acclimatized, however, they no longer had the same need (Benton and Gomez 2001).

Inevitably, when independence was achieved in 1957, or even in 1970 when the NEP was introduced, no enterprises forged intra-ethnic partnerships among the leading publicly listed firms in Malaysia. The most prominent quoted companies during the early 1970s were all controlled by families or individuals, including Kuala Lumpur-Kepong Bhd (Lee Loy Seng), Federal Flour Bhd (Robert Kuok), Tan Chong Motors Bhd (Tan family), Empat Nombor Ekor Bhd (Lim family), and Manilal & Sons Bhd (Patel family) (Lim 1981:141–60). This pattern has not changed much over time. In fact, a study of ownership patterns of the long-established firms or the top 20 companies (in terms of capitalization) quoted on the Kuala Lumpur Stock Exchange (KLSE) in 2000 indicated that none of them are based on partnerships (see Appendix 5.1 for details). This raises an interesting question: are partnerships sustainable in Malaysia?

Business ownership patterns

Studies of enterprise development in Malaysia indicate that when partnerships break up, these companies tend to come under the control of one individual or family. In some cases, partners even become competitors within the same sector (Benton and Gomez 2001). This transition in business ownership patterns, however, is nothing unusual and is consistent with the theoretical literature on enterprise development (see, for example, Chandler 1962; 1977; Penrose 1980). Briefly, the stages of enterprise evolution in this literature are as follows:

Stage 1 partnerships
Stage 2 single owner/family business
Stage 3 managerial control

The transition period from Stage 1 to 2, that is from a partnership to a family-owned enterprise or single ownership, is quite fast, usually occurring within a number of years after the formation of a company. On the other hand, the transition from Stage 2 to 3, that is, from a family business to managerial control, would normally involve a generational change, sometimes two or more generations (Chandler 1962; 1977; Penrose 1980). In contemporary Malaysia, the change from a family business (Stage 2) to professional management (Stage 3) is not yet evident, primarily because most leading companies are still owned and controlled by either the founder or the second generation. In other words, they are still young firms.

Moreover, issues regarding succession and the division, dismantling, or even takeover of major firms continue to receive no or little academic and scholarly attention in the study of enterprise development in Malaysia (and Singapore). Yet, examples of the disintegration of family firms and family feuds among descendants of major entrepreneurs are legion. For instance, in Singapore, a number of major companies have been taken over because of differences among family members over ownership and management of these firms. Other cases that can be cited as evidence include the Malayan Credit, which was controlled by the Teo family, the Cycle & Carriage Group, controlled by the Chua family, the Yeo Hap Seng (YHS) Group, controlled by the Yeo family, and the Haw Par Group, controlled by Aw family.

The best examples of major family firms where disagreements or problems have occurred among the second generation are the Aw family's Haw Par Group and the Kwek family's Hong Leong Group. The rise of Aw Boon Hwa in the early 1920s was attributed to the popularity of his "Tiger" brand of medicinal products, especially the "Tiger Balm" ointment. By the 1950s, Aw had helped the establishment of the Chung Khiaw Bank in Singapore and emerged as a "press king," running more than a dozen newspapers throughout East and Southeast Asia, including the Singapore-based *Sin Chew Jit Poh*. Soon after Aw's death in 1954, intense family feuding eventually contributed to a takeover of the Haw Par Group in the early 1970s (Gill 1985; Lee and Chow 1997:1–2).

The late Kwek Hong P'ng, who, with three of his brothers, founded the Hong Leong Group in Singapore in 1941, provides further clues to the problem of succession and generational change. The Hong Leong Group is now divided between the branches in Singapore and Malaysia, and there has been competition and differences between the Kwek cousins. When Kwek Hong P'ng was asked about the problems that had emerged among the second generation of Kweks, his response was quite instructive: "it's not easy to pass down a Chinese-owned business from generation to generation. … The founders were fairer [in distributing benefits]. The older generation was more straightforward, and the elders looked after the younger ones. But the new generation mostly looks out for themselves" (quoted in *Asiaweek*, May 15, 1992).

Only in a smaller number of cases do we observe that some large firms have been subjected to management control. For instance, the large enterprises closely associated with Lee Kong Chian, including Lee Rubber Bhd and the Overseas-Chinese Banking Corporation (OCBC), are now professionally managed, though the ownership of these enterprises is still under his family. The situation is similar with the companies owned by the Malacca-based rubber magnate, Tan Cheng Lock, who was associated with the Pacific Bank Bhd and United Malacca Rubber Estates Bhd. Recent studies also indicate that when a new generation takes over an enterprise, the tendency is towards professional management and inter-ethnic business ties (Gomez 1999; Yeung 2002). Among the companies cited as examples include publicly listed YTL Corp. Bhd and the Hong Leong Group.[1]

From intra-ethnic to inter-ethnic business relationships

Inter-ethnic business ties during the NEP

During the colonial period, Malay involvement in the emerging capitalist economy was not encouraged by the British, who preferred the Malays to remain in food production, primarily that of fish and rice. When Malay peasants tried to venture into modern commercial sectors of the economy such as rubber production, the British blocked their efforts by imposing restrictive cultivation conditions on land. These early discriminatory policies in favor of British plantation interests severely limited the potential development of indigenous capital and shackled Malays to low-income economic activities. Since the British had hindered the development of Malay capital during the colonial period, this reason has been used to justify and rationalize why the post-1969 policies should positively discriminate for or benefit the Bumiputeras.

Another outcome of the 1969 riots was the formation of the *Barisan Nasional* (National Front), a multi-party coalition under the hegemony of the United Malays' National Organization (UMNO). The *Barisan Nasional* was comprised of the ethnically based Malaysian Chinese Association (MCA) and Malaysian Indian Congress (MIC), as well as a number of other parties in the Sabah and Sarawak peninsula. UMNO secured hegemony over the *Barisan Nasional* when it managed to reduce the MCA's influence with the incorporation of opposition parties that had Chinese support in the new coalition. The hegemony of UMNO in the coalition allowed the party to argue successfully for the need for selective patronage in favor of all Bumiputeras, though this eventually led to the creation of an effective system of patronage that enabled influential politicians to channel state concessions in various forms to well connected businessmen, most of whom were Malays.

Chinese capital, however, continued to grow during the NEP period, but there was an increasing need for it to come to accommodations with the state in order to continue to expand.[2] During the implementation of the

NEP, inter-ethnic relationships were common on three different levels. First, among the largest enterprises, prominent Malays with a background in politics or the civil service were appointed as company directors, mainly to serve as avenues to secure access to the state or bypass bureaucratic red-tape in government. During the NEP and NDP decades, prominent Malays who held executive and non-executive posts in Chinese-controlled companies included former cabinet ministers Musa Hitam, Mohd Khir Johari, and Aishah Ghani. Musa, who also served as deputy prime minister from 1981 to 1986, was a director of Lion Land Bhd, while Khir was a director of Leisure Management Bhd, Malayan United Industries (MUI) Bhd, and Magnum Corporation Bhd, and Aishah was a director of Metrojaya Bhd and Ganz Technologies Bhd. Former inspector general of police Haniff Omar was a director of General Corporation Bhd, Genting Bhd, and Resorts World Bhd, while the former lord president Hamid Omar was a director of Olympia Industries Bhd, Lien Hoe Corporation Bhd, and FACB Bhd (Gomez 1999:145–46). Most of these directors had equity ownership, but they were not actively involved in the management and development of these companies (Jesudason 1989).

Second, at the level of the small and medium-scale enterprises (SMEs), the "Ali-Baba" relationships were established, but there was an unequal relationship between the partners involved. In such ties, the Malay (sleeping) partner would be responsible for securing a contract or licence from the government, while the Chinese partner would implement the project. A large proportion of the companies that can be characterized as Ali-Baba firms during the NEP decades were involved in the construction and property development sectors. In many cases, these companies eventually would come under the control of the Chinese (Chin 2001).

Third, among a few Malaysian elites, business partnerships were forged on a more equal basis. Among the most prominent partnerships established in the early 1980s include those between the well connected lawyer, Ibrahim Mohamad, and Brian Chang in Promet Bhd, a construction, property development, and oil exploration firm. Unfortunately, the company disintegrated almost as rapidly as it emerged as a leading quoted enterprise because of a bitter dispute between the partners, which resulted in the expulsion of Ibrahim from Promet (Gill 1985; Yoshihara 1988). In another example, Eric Chia worked with ex-academic Mokhzani Abdul Rahim and former bureaucrat Shamsuddin Kadir in United Motor Works Bhd (UMW), the holder of the Toyota franchise and a distributor of heavy equipment. Later, Shamsuddin moved on to develop Sapura Holdings Sdn Bhd, an enterprise that thrived in the telecommunications industry (Yoshihara 1988:201–2; Gomez and Jomo 1999:72–74; Searle 1999). Mokhzani secured a major interest in the publicly listed Innovest Bhd, which once held the Kentucky Fried Chicken (KFC) franchise; he also served as director of Powertek Bhd, a power generation firm under the control of T. Ananda Krishnan. Another prominent company established through a partnership was the financial conglomerate, Rashid Hussain Bhd, established by Abdul Rashid Hussain and Chua Ma Yu. Overtime, Chua went on to develop his own business interests.

By 2000, none of the partnerships forged on an inter-ethnic level, either among elites or at the SME level, had emerged as major publicly listed enterprises (see Appendix 5.1 for details). RHB Capital Bhd, although listed among the top 20 firms quoted on the KLSE in 2000, was by then under the sole control of Rashid Hussain. Rashid would subsequently lose control of his financial conglomerate to another company owned by family members of the chief minister of Sarawak in 2002. Other companies listed in this top 20 under private ownership were controlled either by the founder—Genting and Resorts World (Lim Goh Tong) and Public Bank Bhd (Teh Hong Piow)—or by a family—YTL Corp. and YTL Power International Bhd (Yeoh family) and Kuala Lumpur Kepong (KLK) Bhd (the late Lee Loy Seng family)—or by a particular individual—Renong Bhd and its associate company, United Engineers Malaysia Bhd (UEM) (Halim Saad) and Berjaya Sports Toto Bhd (Vincent Tan Chee Yioun). Magnum Corp. Bhd, though long under the control of the T. K. Lim and his family had fallen into the hands of businessmen linked to former finance minister Daim Zainuddin.[3]

The Chinese

Since the early 1990s, most research on Chinese enterprise has focused on the supposed consolidation of companies owned by ethnic Chinese of the diaspora and of the form of their business networking (Redding 1990; Whitley 1992; Kao 1993; Kotkin 1993; East Asia Analytical Unit 1995; Weidenbaum and Hughes 1996; Hamilton 1996; Lever-Tracy et al. 1996; Yeung and Olds 2000). Many of them promote the Weberian view that the "spirit" of Chinese enterprise is founded in their belief systems. Co-ethnic-based networks have reputedly emerged as an avenue for the Chinese to cooperate in business for mutual benefit. These networks are especially important for ethnic Chinese who are minorities in a country where the state has been hostile to the development of their economic interests. Chinese capital is conceptualized primarily as intra-ethnic networks, based on cooperation and trust, to help reduce transaction costs (see Fukuyama 1995 for a different perspective on this discussion).

The proposition that ethnic identity and culture inspires the creation of intra-ethnic business networks has, however, been challenged with the publication of detailed case studies of the development of Chinese-owned firms, concentrating on the context under which these enterprises operated (Gomez 1999; Chan 2000; Gomez and Hsiao 2001; Chin 2001; Menkhoff and Gerke 2002). Intra-ethnic business cooperation has not been a factor in the development of Chinese capital in Malaysia, though this contention can be questioned because, in spite of the NEP, Chinese equity had doubled from 22.8 percent in 1969 to 45.5 percent in 1999 (see Table 5.1 below).

During the NEP decades, a number of new Chinese capitalists had emerged; among them including Vincent Tan Chee Yioun, Khoo Kay Peng, William Cheng Heng Jem, Tong Kooi Ong, Teh Soon Seng, T. K. Lim, and Ting Pek Khiing. By the beginning of 2001, according to one study, of the twenty wealthiest business people in Malaysia, apart from one ethnic Indian, T. Ananda Krishnan, the remaining top 10 wealthiest corporate figures were all ethnic Chinese (*Malyasian Business*, February 1, 2001). No Malay could figure prominently among the richest, according to the total value of corporate assets that they owned. Of the 20 wealthiest businessmen in the country, only four were non-ethnic Chinese—Ananda, Abdul Rashid Hussain, Azman Hashim, and Shamsuddin Kadir.[4] In reality, the most common feature among Chinese enterprises during the NEP period was that of extensive and intensive competition for limited resources between them rather than intra-ethnic cooperation (Benton and Gomez 2001).[5] This lack of cooperation among Chinese business people was also obvious during the promotion of the "corporatization movement."

From the early 1970s, in order to fulfill the NEP objectives, the government had increased public sector expenditure to fund trust agencies and the growing number of government-owned enterprises participating in business activities on behalf of the Bumiputeras. With increased government funding, public enterprises and trust agencies went on an acquisition binge. This acquisition drive was further aided by a 1975 government ruling that each public-listed company had to ensure that a minimum 30 percent of its equity was allocated to Bumiputera agencies or individuals.[6] Apart from this, public enterprises incorporated wholly owned firms to venture into most areas of business and established joint ventures with Bumiputera, non-Bumiputera, and foreign companies. Inevitably, affirmative action endeavors soon aroused non-Bumiputera dissatisfaction with the NEP. These fears were exacerbated when public enterprises began encroaching into economic sectors in which the Chinese had been prominent, particularly banking, property, construction, and manufacturing.[7]

As Chinese concern increased over the hegemony of UMNO and the implementation of NEP, the MCA promoted an alternative "corporatization movement" to secure mass Chinese support to protect the community's economic interests. The movement was presented as an attempt to get Chinese firms to overlook narrow clan divisions and cooperate in business in the face of growing state capitalism. The movement also involved structural reforms to small-scale businesses and a modernization of their family-run management techniques. However, owners of large-scale Chinese firms became extremely wary of the corporatization movement, especially when the MCA incorporated a holding company called Multi-Purpose Holdings Bhd (MPHB) to pool Chinese resources, ostensibly to venture into all key sectors of the economy. This project was quite successful initially. The MCA even managed to obtain, for the first time, the support of working-class Chinese who were won over by the argument that the company was a means to develop Chinese economic interests (Gale 1985; Yeoh 1987; Gomez 1994:189–226). MPHB, however, led by MCA politicians, was soon mired in allegations of corruption and conflicts of interest, and burdened with huge debts from the massive acquisition binge, including of firms linked to the MCA president, Tan Koon Swan. In the event, Tan and other prominent party leaders were sentenced to jail on various charges of corruption, while MPHB was taken over by Kamunting Bhd, a relatively obscure but quoted construction firm owned by the Lim family, who had close business ties with prominent UMNO leaders, specifically to the finance minister Daim. The manner of the demise of the corporatization movement put the Chinese off ethnically backed institutions, especially if they had links with politicians.

Following the demise of the corporatization movement, Chinese capitalists in control of large firms did not try and coalesce their enterprises or cooperate in business ventures in spite of UMNO's growing hegemony, which was used to rapidly promote Malay businessmen closely aligned with party leaders. In fact, because of UMNO's growing hegemony, leading Chinese capitalists stepped up efforts to establish links with the Malay political elite, thus undermining even further the MCA's influence among these businessmen.

After the severe mid-1980s recession, the importance of Chinese—and foreign—capital to further promote industrialization and sustain economic growth in Malaysia became evident to the government in the 1990s. Prime Minister Mahathir Mohamad's desire to industrialize Malaysia, and his recognition of the potential Chinese contribution to these goals, led to economic liberalization and the inclusion of Chinese capital into his development aspirations, albeit they had to be defined on his own terms. Moreover, the prime minister saw the opening up of China's economy as offering potentially lucrative business ventures for Malaysian capital. These factors appear to have encouraged Mahathir's call for greater business cooperation between Chinese and Malays. At the 1996 Second Fujianese World Chinese

Table 5.1 Malaysia: ownership of share capital (at par value) of limited companies, 1969–99 (%)

	1969	1970	1975	1980	1985	1990	1995	1999
Bumiputera individuals and trust agencies	1.5	2.4	9.2	12.5	19.1	19.2	20.6	19.1
Chinese	22.8	27.2	n.a.	n.a.	33.4	45.5	40.9	37.9
Indians	0.9	1.1	n.a.	n.a.	1.2	1.0	1.5	1.5
Others	–	–	–	–	–	–	–	0.9
Nominee companies	2.1	6.0	n.a.	n.a.	1.3	8.5	8.3	7.9
Locally controlled firms	10.1	–	–	–	7.2	0.3	1.0	–
Foreigners	62.1	63.4	53.3	42.9	26.0	25.4	27.7	32.7

Sources: Seventh Malaysia Plan, 1996–2000; Eighth Malaysia Plan, 2001–2005.

Note:
n.a. = not available.

Entrepreneurs Convention held in Malaysia in 1996, Mahathir said, "Malaysian Fujianese's close connections with their fellow-provincials in different corners of the world will help promote the business and investment opportunities in Malaysia" (quoted in Liu 1998). These factors have influenced the nature of inter-ethnic business cooperation, suggesting a more level playing field between the two communities, even though this may not necessarily be the case in reality.

The shareholding pattern among Chinese-owned firms in 2000 indicates that they tend to function rather independently of one another. In fact, an in-depth study of the largest Chinese-owned firms in Malaysia revealed that these enterprises have not attempted to cooperate in business, either domestically or abroad, in spite of the state's failure to support their interests (Gomez 1999). Chinese SMEs have similarly shown scant inclination to cooperate with other ethnic Chinese (Chin 2001). The owners of a number of the largest quoted Chinese enterprises, including Lim Goh Tong's Genting Group, Vincent Tan's Berjaya Group, Franics Yeoh's YTL Corp. Group, and even Quek Leng Chan's Hong Leong, long reputed to be independent of political ties, have attempted to establish inter-ethnic ties, especially with politically influential Bumiputeras, to help them protect and expand their interests (Gomez 1999). While most studies tend to attribute the dynamism of Chinese enterprises to intra-ethnic business cooperation (Redding 1990; East Asia Analytical Unit 1995), the Malaysian case indicates that in spite of polices that discriminate against them, there has been little collaboration among business people of this community. In most cases, an independent entrepreneurial zeal appears to have contributed to significant competition, forcing the Chinese to be more innovative to stay ahead. This also explains why Chinese firms have continued to thrive during the NEP and NDP decades (Gomez 1999; Benton and Gomez 2001).

The Bumiputeras

From the outset of his premiership, Mahathir voiced his intention to create an ensemble of dynamic, entrepreneurial Malay capitalists. Mahathir's reasoning for the need to hasten the development of Malay capital was that, in 1981, 10 years after the implementation of the NEP, although the government had managed to increase the amount of corporate holdings held in the name of Bumiputeras from 2.4 percent in 1970 to 12.5 percent in 1980 (see Table 5.1 above), little progress had been made in developing Malay businessmen in the control of large corporations. In fact, among the top 100 Malaysian corporations during the mid-1970s, not one single firm was then owned by either the Malaysian government or Bumiputera individuals (Lim 1981). It was precisely this situation that Mahathir sought to rectify.

By the mid-1990s, a number of huge publicly listed conglomerates, controlled primarily by well connected Malays, had emerged in the corporate sector. Given the high degree of autonomy that the office of the prime minister enjoyed from other arms of the Malaysian government, Mahathir was able to distribute government-created economic concessions to a highly selective group of businessmen to help them swiftly develop their corporate interests.[8] Mahathir justified this form of patronage, via policies such as the NEP—and since the mid-1980s, privatization[9]—by arguing that the best way to create Malay capitalists was to distribute concessions to those most capable of generating wealth.

The government's attempt to cultivate Malay industrialists led to the rapid rise of a number of well connected businessmen, including Halim Saad, Tajudin Ramli, Wan Azmi Wan Hamzah, Samsudin Abu Hassan, Rashid Hussain, Hassan Abas, Ahmad Sebi Abu Bakar, Ishak Ismail, Mohamad Sarit Yusoh, Kamaruddin Jaafar, Kamaruddin Mohd Nor, Amin Shah Omar Shah, Mirzan and Mokhzani Mahathir, and the late Yahya Ahmad.[10] As in the case of Chinese capitalists, there was little or no cooperation among these well connected Bumiputera businessmen. The absence of intra-ethnic business cooperation was most evident in the lack of interlocking stock ownership or interlocking directorships among Malaysia's leading Malay capitalists (Gomez and Jomo 1999; Gomez 2002). The relationship between this new breed of Malay businessmen was characterized by competition.[11] In the telecommunications sector, for example, Halim's Timedotcom Bhd and Tajudin's Celcom Bhd were in keen competition with each other. During the bank consolidation exercise promoted in 1998, Azman Hashim and Rashid Hussain made no attempt to merge their financial enterprises.[12]

These arguments indicate that very little cooperation exists among Malaysia's businessmen—from both an intra-ethnic and inter-ethnic perspective. Despite various efforts made by the government during the NEP and NDP decades, the form of development of enterprises owned by the Malay and Chinese business elites reveals rather their desire to lead companies on their own.

Post-NEP/NDP: partnerships and inter-ethnic relations

While there is no evidence of sustained intra-ethnic or inter-ethnic business partnerships among Malaysia's largest enterprises, during the 1990s, among smaller firms, including those quoted on the KLSE, there was growing proof of new inter-ethnic business ties. A review of the 28 companies listed on the KLSE in 1998 (*Malaysian Business*, March 1, 1999) indicated that:

a eight (or 29 percent) of them could be classified as Chinese-Bumiputera partnerships;
b only two were intra-ethnic Chinese partnerships;
c there was no evidence of Bumiputeras only in partnership;
d only one was wholly Bumiputera-owned, the family firm Habib Corp.;
e 12 firms (or 43 percent) were owned by Chinese families and individuals; and
f the remaining firms were owned by government corporations.

The fact that nearly 30 percent of the companies quoted on the local bourse in 1998 were owned by business people of different ethnic groups cooperating in a commercial venture suggests important changes are transpiring in the pattern of ownership and control of corporate enterprises. Moreover, in terms of intra-ethnic business linkages, only two firms were partnerships among members from the Chinese community, while none of them was owned by Bumiputeras working together in business. That there was little evidence of growing intra-ethnic business, specifically among the Bumiputeras, but also among the Chinese, further alluded to conspicuous changes in inter-ethnic corporate ties. Partners in these business enterprises appeared to be equally competent, implying a decline in the "Ali-Baba" alliances. Nearly 46 percent of the firms listed on the KLSE in 1998 were family-owned corporations or under the control of an individual business person, though only one of these 13 firms was owned by a Bumiputera family. This large percentage of firms owned by individuals or families is a further indication that partners in an enterprise eventually prefer to go it alone once accustomed to running an enterprise. It is noteworthy that while there is still evidence of intra-ethnic business partnerships among the Chinese, there is no indication of similar relationships among the Bumiputeras. Since there was also only one family-owned Bumiputera enterprise in this list of firms quoted on the KLSE in 1998, the jewelers, Habib Corp., which had commenced operations during the colonial period, this offered a further manifestation of the government's failure to develop independent Malay capitalists despite sustained efforts through the NEP and NDP.

To determine if the features of the firms listed on the KLSE in 1998 were replicated among companies quoted on the local bourse, a study was undertaken of enterprises that could be classified as inter-ethnic partnerships. A review of ownership patterns of all 757 firms trading equity on the KLSE in the year 2000 revealed that only about 18 (or a mere 2.4 percent) were partnerships (see Appendix 5.2).[13] This rather low figure draws further attention to the issue of the sustainability of partnerships.

These 18 companies, however, share some interesting features. All of them were quoted on the stock exchange in the 1990s. Nearly half of them were incorporated or began operating as inter-ethnically-owned firms during the 1980s and 1990s. A substantial proportion (12 out 18 or 67 percent) are involved in manufacturing, indicating a productive economic dimension to their business activities and the possible emergence of a new breed of entrepreneurs of the Schumpeterian type (Schumpeter 1943).[14] Five (or 18 percent) of these companies are involved in the construction sector, which suggests that some elements of an "Ali-Baba" relationship may still prevail among these newly listed enterprises.[15]

This growing evidence of inter-ethnic business ties indicates a transition in Malaysian society which suggests two things about the NEP and NDP. First, the implementation of these policies has led to the creation of an independent, dynamic Bumiputera middle class, an argument proffered in some

important new studies (Embong 2001). The emergence of the new Bumiputera middle class is also contributing to changes in social relations among
Malaysians, specifically in improved inter-ethnic ties. Second, important changes are transpiring in the way businessmen develop their firms, probably due
to the impact of generational change. Changes in business strategies, organizational structure, and management style within these firms suggest that new
generations of ethnic Chinese and Malays, unlike their forbearers, appear
more inclined to forge inter-ethnic business ties. These new developments
also imply that among this new generation of Malaysians, there is a greater
openness to inter-ethnic business cooperation for mutual benefit. These
business ties also allude to the possibility that non-Bumiputeras born and
bred in Malaysia bear a strong national identity and are comfortable in
inter-ethnic relationships. Among middle-class Bumiputeras, it reflected a
feeling of confidence and ability to hold their own in business, given the
skills they have acquired through state support under the NEP and NDP.

Wazir noted a similar trend of inter-ethnic business linkages among
companies being quoted on the KLSE, attributing it to "significant structural shifts in partnerships or changes from traditional Chinese family-
based organizations to Sino-Bumiputera alliances" (2002:260–61). Wazir
goes on to add:

> There was a time when many of these alliances were linked to Ali Baba
> enterprises, or sleeping partnerships, but it appears that the combina-
> tion of sociopolitical patronage, business acumen and access to finance
> capital is not necessarily dichotomized in terms of what "Malays are
> best at" or "what the Chinese can do better". A subtle combination of
> factors, like access to foreign capital, negotiation for contracts or ten-
> ders, knowledge on strategic personal contacts and smart partnerships
> transcend ethnicity. Malay entrepreneurs have proven their prowess at
> this game just as purely Chinese business acumen in family-based
> companies appear limiting in the wake of global competitiveness.
>
> (Wazir 2002:260–61)

These new developments in the corporate sector bring into question hitherto
rather essentialized understandings of the pattern of development of enterprises owned by ethnic communities in Malaysia. Essentialism has been
defined by Howard Winant as "a belief in unchanging human characteristics,
impervious to social and historical contexts" (quoted in Wong 1999:5). As
noted above, essentializing arguments about Chinese capital exaggerate the
importance of culture in enterprise development and the extent of ethnic
cohesiveness and collective action among members of this community both
within separate nations and across the diaspora.[16] Similarly, among Bumiputeras, in spite of considerable state support to promote Malay capital, and
even though leading corporate figures from this community shared a common
political patron, there was no evidence of any of them cooperating in business.

The growing number of firms that were owned on an inter-ethnic basis by the end of the 1990s is a positive development. From the 1970s until the late 1980s, such cooperative inter-ethnic relationships, where company ownership was on a rather equal basis, were seen to prevail primarily among an elite group. This new development, an outcome of NEP implementation, appears, however, to be primarily a middle-class and urban phenomenon.

Ethnic co-existence and government-forged partnerships

There are two points here that need further elaboration. First, are these partnerships sustainable? History suggests that most of these new partnerships forged in the 1990s will probably not be sustained in the long run. As the studies by Chandler (1962; 1977) and Penrose (1980) have indicated, partnerships are seldom sustainable, though this has not impaired enterprise development. When partners split, new enterprises are formed, precipitating more competition, which in the long run creates a more dynamic environment, and helps promote innovation and productivity. What is important in the context of Malaysia is that although inter-ethnic business relationships may not be sustainable, this is *not* a reflection of unstable ethnic relations.

Second, should the government help forge inter-ethnic business partnerships, especially since there is evidence that they are probably not sustainable? The government has tried to help forge business partnerships in the past, primarily as a means to encourage entrepreneurship and the growth of dynamic domestic enterprises and partly to promote national unity. While these goals are undoubtedly noble, business partnerships cannot be state-driven. At best, joint ventures should only be promoted for a particular project. Instead, the focus should be on creating institutions and providing incentives that help promote entrepreneurship and the implementation of potentially viable business ideas. However, as the experience of NEP and NDP implementation has unequivocally indicated, this type of support should be provided on a one-off or short-term basis, or else it may create a dependency syndrome.

Furthermore, businesses should be allowed to fail, for genuine entrepreneurship thrives on the element of risk and the ability to adapt. Another important lesson from the implementation of the NEP and NDP is that businesses that have managed to develop productively should not be spoiled with too much support, for this will only curtail but not cultivate competitiveness. Voluminous empirical and theoretical research has indicated that the companies that have managed to survive and grow are those that are most exposed to competition (Williamson 1975; Chandler 1977; Scott 1997).

The pattern of evolution of companies in Malaysia since the early 1970s indicates that during policy planning, there should be no mixing of goals. For example, the attempts to develop domestic enterprise and inter-ethnic corporate ties in order to achieve economic development and as a means to unify the nation simultaneously is doomed to fail. This has been a problem with some government policies, evident during the NEP period when public enterprises were established to pursue economic and social goals (Bowie 1991).

Businessmen know who best to work with to develop an enterprise. Decision-making in business is based primarily on how to maximize profits or develop companies of value. When making business decisions, the idea of supporting "national interest" goals of fostering inter-ethnic ties to promote nation building hardly figures; nor should the government expect this of businessmen.

Conclusion

This study of patterns of formation and development of Malaysian firms provides much evidence that business partnerships are not sustainable. The pattern of growth of large-sized firms suggests that these companies have evolved in a manner akin to similarly sized enterprises in the developed economies of the West, as recorded by Chandler (1962; 1977), Penrose (1980), and Williamson (1975). The fact that partnerships are not sustainable brings into question the government's endeavors to use such mechanisms to promote national unity and more equitable distribution of corporate equity among ethic communities. Moreover, inter-ethnic ties that had been forged in the 1970s were hardly ones that reflected an equal relationship between the partners, except possibly in the case of linkages forged between prominent business and political elites.

Inter-ethnic business ties that emerged during the 1980s and 1990s, as UMNO's hegemony over the state increased appreciably, were primarily between Chinese businessmen and well connected Bumiputeras or influential Malay politicians. The extent to which these ties will remain intact depends primarily on whether the political patrons of these well connected businessmen continue to stay in a position of influence indefinitely. This is a highly unlikely scenario. In fact, when Daim resigned from office, his allies in business lost control of major business assets. Similarly, when Deputy Prime Minister Anwar Ibrahim was forced out of UMNO and government in 1998, businessmen linked to him lost control of their assets as well. Even prominent Chinese businessmen, like T. K. Lim of the Multi-Purpose Holdings Group, who was closely aligned with the former deputy prime minister, lost control of his main quoted assets following Anwar's dismissal.[17]

Since the pattern of evolution of large-sized firms in Malaysia is similar to the form of enterprise evolution among companies in industrialized countries, this brings into question the use of terms like "ethnic entrepreneurs" and "ethnic enterprise," concepts that have remained popular in much of the literature on companies owned by ethnic minorities (for example, Light 1972; Light and Bonacich 1988; Waldinger et al. 1990; Light and Bhachu 1993; Waldinger 1996; Light and Gold 2000). These concepts have also influenced how some academics and journalists view the pattern of enterprise development by ethnic Chinese in Malaysia (for example, Seagrave 1995; East Asian Analytical Unit 1995; and Backman 1999). The present study of enterprise development in Malaysia counters essentializing arguments about "ethnic enterprise" or the form of development of ethnically owned enterprises, specifically Chinese firms. Moreover, most enterprises forge business ties that are mutually beneficial to the parties involved.

To substantiate these points, this chapter has provided some evidence of changing trends in inter-ethnic ownership ties that have emerged during the 1990s among smaller sized firms. Contrary to expectation, these business ties are not cultivated on the basis of common ethnic and cultural identity, as was the case during the colonial period among ethnic Chinese migrants. During the NEP and NDP decades, inter-ethnic business ties were nurtured primarily to secure access to state resources as a result of the government's long-running promotion of affirmative action. However, in the present period, the pattern of business formation among more recently incorporated companies suggests that business ties are becoming increasingly inter-ethnic, established on the basis of equal competency among the partners, with both contributing to the productive development of the firm. The ownership of firms by members of different ethnic communities, in a relationship where both partners appear to have equal influence and competency, suggests that important identity transformations have emerged mainly because the class divide between Bumiputeras and non-Bumiputeras has narrowed recently.

The growing evidence of inter-ethnic business ties among KLSE firms, without state intervention, raises important questions about identity transformation, among Bumiputeras as well as non-Bumiputeras. These inter-ethnic investment patterns suggest that among ethnic minorities, the notion of national identity is important, reinforcing the point about their sense of belonging or loyalty to the nation. The attempt by the state to promote inter-ethnic business ties may, however, inadvertently reinforce the idea of ethnic difference among Malaysians, thus undermining the government's policies to create a more unified nation.

Appendix 5.1

Ownership of the top 20 KLSE firms

	Company	Activity	Main shareholder
1	Telekom	Telecommunications	Government
2	Malayan Banking	Finance	Government
3	Tenaga Nasional	Power producer & Distributor	Government
4	Petronas Gas	Gas production	Government
5	Resorts World	Gaming	Lim Goh Tong
6	Malaysia Int. Shipping Corp. (MISC)	Shipping	Government
7	Sime Darby	Plantations/diversified	Government

continued on next page

(*continued*)

	Company	Activity	Main shareholder
8	Commerce Asset-Holding	Finance	Government
9	Genting	Gaming	Lim Goh Tong
10	YTL Corp.	Construction	Yeoh Tiong Lay
11	Public Bank	Finance	Teh Hong Piow
12	Rothmans of Pall Mall	Cigarette manufacturer	Foreign
13	YTL Power International	Power production	Yeoh Tiong Lay
14	RHB Capital	Finance	Rashid Hussain
15	United Engineers (UEM)	Construction/diversified	Halim Saad
16	Renong	Construction/diversified	Halim Saad
17	Berjaya Sports Toto	Gaming	Vincent Tan
18	Magnum Corp.	Gaming	(Unclear)
19	Perusahaan Otomobil Nasional (Proton)	Car manufacturer	Government
20	Kuala Lumpur Kepong (KLK)	Plantations	Lee Loy Seng family

Appendix 5.2

Inter-ethnic partnerships among KLSE firms

1 Company name: Lingkaran Trans Kota Holdings Bhd

Activities	investment holding and provision of management services, primarily engaged in the operation of a roll highway which has yet to commence operation.
Date of incorporation	9.3.1995
Date of listing	19.12.1996
Issued capital	RM300,000,000
Shareholdings	Bumiputera 42.93; Other Malaysians 47.21; Foreigners 9.86
Main shareholders	Irama Duta Sdn Bhd; Gamuda Bhd; Malaysia Nominees (Tempatan) Sdn Bhd; Employees Provident Fund Board; Cartaban Nominees (Asing) Sdn Bhd
Directors	Wan Abdul Rahman bin Wan Yaacob; Yusoff bin Daud; Lin Yun Ling; Nasruddin bin Bahari; Chew Swee Hock; Ng Kee Leen; Saw Wah Theng

2 Company name: Kilang Papan Seribu Daya Bhd

Activities	integrated timber activities consisting of the manufacturing and marketing of timber and timber related products.
Date of incorporation	19.8.1988
Date of listing	17.11.1994
Issued capital	RM19,999,000
Shareholdings	Bumiputera 38.08; Other Malaysians 56.02; Foreigners 5.90

Main shareholders	Hwong You Chuang; Abdullah bin Sepien; Hwong You Soon; SMB Nominees (Tempatan) Sdn Bhd; Syarikat Nominee Bumiputra (Tempatan) Sdn Bhd
Directors	Abdullah bin Sepien; Hwong You Chuang; Henry Chin Poy Wu; Hwong You Soon; Tokuo Wasa

3 Company name: Grand Hoover Bhd

Activities	investment and property holding, construction, manufacturing, trading and distribution of building materials, investment and property holding and provision of management consultancy services.
Date of incorporation	12.3.1071
Date of listing	22.8.1997
Issued capital	RM30,000,000
Shareholdings	Bumiputera 50.35; Other Malaysians 48.98; Foreigners 0.68
Main shareholders	Hoover Corporation Sdn Bhd; Hajjah Rus bte Hj Kachar; Arab-Malaysian Nominees (Tempatan) Sdn Bhd; Mayban Nominees (Tempatan) Sdn Bhd; Yu Kuan Chon
Directors	Hajjah Rus bte Hj Kachar; Hew Kon Ngow; Tan Ah Heng; Tai Ah Kew @ Tai Kim Yok; Thean Lan Chan @ Then Swee Chen; Basar bin Juraimi; IR Hj Md Mazlan bin Hj Md Ismail Merican; Tang Yau @ Tang Lin Yau; Ng Leong Piew

4 Company name: Mercury Industries Bhd

Activities	investment holding; property investment and development, manufacture and sale of under seal and lacquer and paints for automotive and housing industry.
Date of incorporation	20.8.1983
Date of listing	20.6.1991
Issued capital	RM36,182,000
Shareholdings	Bumiputera 44.36; Other Malaysians 44.01; Foreigners 11.63
Main shareholders	BBMB Securities Nominees (Tempatan) Sdn Bhd; Universal Trustee (Malaysia) Bhd; UOLC Nominees (Tempatan) Sdn Bhd; Multi-Purpose Bank Nominees (Asing) Sdn Bhd; Malaysia Nominees (Tempatan) Sdn Bhd
Directors	Peh Teck Quee; Syed Ibrahim bin Syed Mohamed; Ismail bin Yusof; Vijay Kumar Natarajan; Liow Sze Yin

5 Company name: Perfect Food Industries Bhd

Activities	investment holding, manufacture and marketing of biscuits.
Date of incorporation	2.8.1978
Date of listing	15.9.1993
Issued capital	RM19,900,000
Share holdings	Bumiputera 52.87; Other Malaysians 44.94; Foreigners 2.19
Main shareholders	Perfect Pleasure Sdn Bhd; Mayban Finance Bhd; Seagroatt & Campbell Nominees (Tempatan) Sdn Bhd – substantial shareholders; Rothputra Nominee (Tempatan) Sdn Bhd
Directors	Sai Ah Sai; Sai Chin Hock; Abdul Ajib bin Ahmad; Abdul Rahman bin Saad; Augustine Ang Mui Kwong; Su Lee Soon Nee Yeo; Yap Koon Roy

continued on next page

6 Company name: Gamuda Bhd

Activities	investment holding; civil engineering construction.
Date of incorporation	6.10.1976
Date of listing	10.8.1992
Issued capital	RM289,696,409
Shareholdings	Bumiputera 32.94; Other Malaysians 32.82; Foreigners 34.24
Main shareholders	Citicorp Nominees (Asing) Sdn Bhd; Lin Yun Ling; Generasi Setia (M) Sdn Bhd; EB Nominees (Tempatan) Sdn Bhd; Cartaban Nominees (Asing) Sdn Bhd
Directors	Talha bin Mohd Hashim; Lin Yun Ling; Raja Seri Eleena Azlan Shah; Chan Kuan Nam @ Chan Yong Foo; Heng Teng Kuang; Kamarul Zaman bin Mohd Ali; Goon Heng Wah; Ng Kee Leen; Ha Tiing Tai; Wong Chin Yen; Saw Wah Theng

7 Company name: TAP Resources Bhd

Activities	investment holding; infrastructure earthworks; structural and architectural works; manufacturing of non-baked bricks and construction materials.
Date of incorporation	1.11.1994
Date of listing	12.12.1997
Issued capital	RM39,999,999
Shareholdings	Bumiputera 32.886; Other Malaysians 66.827; Foreigners 0.287
Main shareholders	Poh Ah Bah; Cho See Yoo; Rameli bin Musa; Arab-Malaysian Nominees (Tempatan) Sdn Bhd; Merchant Nominees (Tempatan) Sdn Bhd
Directors	Rameli bin Musa; Poh Ah Bah; Cho See Too; Ungku Farid bin Ungku Abd Rahman; Zulhkiple A Baker; Goh Ban Lee; Helinna Hanum Dadameah

8 Company name: Road Builder (M) Holdings Bhd

Activities	investment holding; building and civil construction property development; quarry operations; manufacture of concrete products.
Date of incorporation	27.3.1992
Date of listing	18.2.1993
Issued capital	RM129,980,207
Share holdings	Bumiputera 43.331; Other Malaysians 24.935; Foreigners 31.734
Main shareholders	Chua Hock Chin; Chase Malaysia Nominees (Asing) Sdn Bhd; Tengku Uzir bin Tengku Ubaidillah; Citicorp Nominees (Asing) Sdn Bhd; Tengku Ahmad Rithauddeen bin Tengku Ismail
Directors	Tengku Ahmad Rithauddeen bin Tengku Ismail; Chua Hock Chin; Ong Lee Veng @ Ong Chuan Heng; Tengku Uzir bin Tenku Ubaidillah; Nasruddin bin Bahari; Shamsudin bin Md Dubi; Abd Gani bin Yusof; Huang Chew Siong; Lee Teck Yuen; Mohamed bin Yusoh @ Mohamed bin Yusof; Raja Mufik Affandi bin Raja Khalid; Low Keng Kok

9 Company name: BTM Resources Bhd

Activities	investment holding; logging, sawmilling and trading of sawn timber and logs.
Date of incorporation	10.6.1994
Date of listing	27.3.1996
Issued capital	RM19,999,000
Share holdings	Bumiputera 31.29; Other Malaysians 65.47; Foreigners 3.24
Main shareholders	Yong Tu Sang; Yusof bin Biji Sura @ Mohamad; Permodalan Nasional Bhd (PNB); BBMB Trustee Bhd; Mayban Securities Nominees (Tempatan) Sdn Bhd
Directors	Yusof bin Biji Sura @ Mohamad; Yong Tu Sang; Mohd Zamry bin Yusof; Anpalagan Ramiah; Lau Chen Nai; Tik bin Mustaffa; Yong Yoke Cheng; Yong Emmy

10 Company name: MESB Bhd

Activities	investment holding; supply of engineering equipment, spare parts, and tools.
Date of incorporation	28.3.1995
Date of listing	8.5.1996
Issued capital	RM19,999,000
Share holdings	Bumiputera 50.89; Other Malaysians 44.90; Foreigners 4.21
Main shareholders	Thuraya bte Kassim; DB (Malaysia) Nominee (Asing) Sdn Bhd (DBSPN for; Wan Hussien bin Wan Hamsah); Khoo Loon See; Chea Kok Jiunn @ Sieh Kok Jiun; Sieh Kok Swee
Directors	Abdul Halim bin Ismail; Sieh Kok Swee; Wan Hussien bin Wan Hamzah; Mohamed Nordin bin Sabran; Sivasubramaniam Sivayogarajasingam

11 Company name: Nationwide Express Courier Services Bhd

Activities	provides express courier services
Date of incorporation	9.1.1985
Date of listing	25.5.1995
Issued capital	RM19,082,000
Shareholdings	Bumiputera 49.36; Other Malaysians 48.69; Foreigners 1.95
Main shareholders	Utas Sdn Bhd; Scotia Nominees (Tempatan) Sdn Bhd; Eddy Chieng Ing Huong; Malaysia Nopminees (Tempatan) Sdn Bhd; Malaysia Nominees (Tempatan) Sdn Bhd
Directors	Hj Mohd Noor bin Ismail; Arshad bin Ayub; Ahmad Riza bin Basir; Eddy Chieng Ing Huong; Bazlan bin Osman; Abdullah Sanusi bin Ahmad; Mohd Hassan bin Mohd Hashim

12 Company name: Rohas-Euco Industries Bhd

Activities	manufacture of pressed steel sectional water tank panels design and fabrication of steel structures for high-tension transmission towers.
Date of incorporation	13.3.1961
Date of listing	16.3.1995

continued on next page

Issued capital   RM17,000,000
Share holdings   Bumiputera 49.47; Other Malaysians 47.47; Foreigners 3.06
Main shareholders   UB Nominees (Tempatan) Sdn Bhd – for Wan Azmi;
                          Wan Hamzah; Chan Liew Hoon; BHLB Nominees
                          (Tempatan) Sdn Bhd – for Wan Azmi; Wan Hamzah;
                          Euco International Sdn Bhd; OUB Nominees (Tempatan)
                          Sdn Bhd – for Wan Azmi; Wan Hamzah
Directors   Wan Azmi Wan Hamzah; George Sia Bun Chun; Laurence
                          Yee Lye Eu; Chan Hua Eng; Mustafa bin Mohamed
                          Najimudin; W Mohamed @ Nik Azam bin Wan Hamzah;
                          Peter Sia; Tengku Yunus Kamaruddin; Marizan Nor bin
                          Basirun

---

13 Company name: SP Setia Bhd

Activities   building contractors and investment holding.
Date of incorporation   8.8.1974
Date of listing   2nd board on 12.4.1993; transferred to main board on
                          4.6.1996
Issued capital   RM140,728,715
Shareholdings   Bumiputera 44.42; Other Malaysians 42.84; Foreigners 12.74
Main shareholders   Abdul Rashid bin Abdul Manaff; Multi-Purpose Bank
                          Nominees (Tempatan) Sdn Bhd; Employees Provident Fund
                          Board; Kestral Securities Nominees (Asing) Sdn Bhd;
                          Perconic Resources Sdn Bhd
Directors   Abdul Rashid bin Abdul Manaff; Liew Kee Sin; Voon Tin
                          Yow; Zaki bin Tun Azmi; Mohamad Razali bin Mohd
                          Rahim; Hari Narayanan a/l Govindasamy; George
                          Anthony Dass David; Mohd Radzi bin Sheikh Ahmad;
                          Razali bin Ibrahim

---

14 Company name: Kuala Lumpur City Corporation Bhd

Activities   investment holding; manufacture, assembly, supply and
                          installation of automotive air-conditioning systems,
                          components and related products.
Date of incorporation   10.1.1985
Date of listing   2nd board on 21.8.1998; transferred to main board on
                          18.8.1999
Issued capital   RM84,321,057
Shareholdings   Bumiputera 52.16; Other Malaysians 43.31; Foreigners 4.53
Main shareholders   Kuala Lumpur City Nominees (Tempatan) Sdn Bhd –
                          Kemudi Ria Sdn Bhd; Kuala Lumpur City Nominees
                          (Tempatan) Sdn Bhd – Khadijah Abdul Khalid; Lutfiah
                          binti Ismail; Mohd Nasir bin Ali; Public Nominees
                          (Tempatan) Sdn Bhd – Waterfront; Capital Markets Sdn
                          Bhd
Directors   Hj Anuar bin Hj Zainal Abidin; Lutfiah binti Ismail;
                          Josephine Premla Sivaretnam; Mohd Nasir bin Ali; Loh
                          Yeow Boo @ Lok Bah Bah

---

15 Company name: Rumpun Hijau Capital Bhd

Activities   investment holding; manufacturer and dealer of footwear
                          products.

Date of incorporation 21.8.1978
Date of listing   10.4.1992
Issued capital   RM62,389,334
Shareholdings   Bumiputera 49.89; Other Malaysians 46.71; Foreigners 3.40
Main shareholders   Rumpun Hijau Corporation Sdn Bhd; Ng Tiong Seng
    Corporation Sdn Bhd; Zalaras Sdn Bhd; Panduan Kemas
    Sdn Bhd; Southern Nominees (Tempatan) Sdn Bhd pledged;
    securities a/c for Tandaraya Sdn Bhd
Directors   Mohd Nadzmi bin Mohd Salleh; Arshad bin Ayub; Hj
    Ahmad bin Saad; Hj Mohamad bin Jaafar; Hj Mohd Noor
    bin Hassan; Yahaya bin Yaacob; Abdul Rashid bin Mohd
    Yusoff; Ng Tiong Seng; Ng Chin Heng; Azmin bin Arshad

16 Company name: Syarikat Binaan Budi Sawmill Bhd

Activities   trading, manufacture and sale of molded and sawn timber
    and other wood-based products.
Date of incorporation 6.6.1978
Date of listing   7.7.1997
Issued capital   RM30,000,000
Shareholdings   Bumiputera 49.41; Other Malaysians 49.46; Foreigners 1.13
Main shareholders   Malaysian Trustee Bhd – Qualifier Ceduna Enterprise Sdn;
    Bhd; Amble Impact Sdn Bhd; Malaysian Trustee
    Bhd-Qualifier Sinarplus Sdn Bhd; Malaysian Trustee
    Bhd-Qualifier Kain Ann @ Chua Kien; Lam; Jade Castle
    Sdn Bhd
Directors   Abdul Rashid bin Abdul Manaff; Kain Ann @ Chua Kien
    Lam; Chua Mui Hoon; Zaid @ Rasmi bin Ishak; Jamal
    Mohamed bin Hj AM Sickander; Loo Sin Soo; Tengku
    Anisah binti Tengku Abdul Hamid

17 Company name: United Chemical Industries Bhd

Activities   manufacture and sale of polypropylene and polyethylene
    woven bags and allied products.
Date of incorporation 31.5.1965
Date of listing   20.12.1990
Issued capital   RM18,500,000
Shareholdings   Bumiputera 44.71; Other Malaysians 49.29; Foreigners 6.00
Main shareholders   Merchant Nominees (Tempatan) Sdn Bhd pledged;
    securities a/c for Trafalgar Links (M) Sdn Bhd;
    Arab-Malaysian Nominees (Tempatan) Sdn Bhd;
    Arab-Malaysian Finance Bhd for MBF Leasing Sdn Bhd;
    Tan Ching Ching; Chan Wan Moi; Ke-Zan Nominees
    (Tempatan) Sdn Bhd – Eng Poh Hong; @ Wong Choon
    Ming
Directors   Abg Ahmad Urai bin Abg Hj Mohideen; Abdul Aziz bin
    Abdul Rahman; Ismail @ Mustapha bin Ibrahim; Wong
    Lee Peng; Wong Eng Thiam; Wong Set Moi

18 Company name: Rumpun Hijau Capital Bhd

Activities   investment holding; manufacturer and dealer of footwear
    products.

continued on next page

Date of incorporation	21.8.1978
Date of listing	10.4.1992
Issued capital	RM62,389,334
Shareholdings	Bumiputera 49.89; Other Malaysians 46.71; Foreigners 3.40
Main shareholders;	Rumpun Hijau Corporation Sdn Bhd; Ng Tiong Seng Corporation Sdn Bhd; Zalaras Sdn Bhd; Panduan Kemas Sdn Bhd; Southern Nominees (Tempatan) Sdn Bhd pledged; securities a/c for Tandaraya Sdn Bhd
Directors	Mohd Nadzmi bin Mohd Salleh; Arshad bin Ayub; Ahmad bin Saad; Mohamad bin Jaafar; Mohd Noor bin Hassan; Yahaya bin Yaacob; Abdul Rashid bin Mohd Yusoff; Ng Tiong Seng; Ng Chin Heng; Azmin bin Arshad

Notes

1 For a historical case study of YTL Corp, see Gomez (1999:163–70). See Yeung (2002:200–2) for a discussion on the Hong Leong group.
2 See Gomez (1999:ch. 3) for a historical examination of enterprise development by ethnic Chinese during the NEP decades.
3 In mid-2001, following a feud between Daim and the prime minister, Mahathir Mohamad, leading to the former's resignation as finance minister, Halim Saad would lose control of Renong and UEM. For a detailed discussion on the dispute between Mahathir and Daim that led to ownership changes in firms controlled by Daim's protégé, Halim Saad, see the work of Gomez (2001).
4 The other 16 businessmen listed as among the wealthiest in the country were Robert Kuok, Lim Goh Tong, Quek Leng Chan, Yeoh Tiong Lay, Tiong Hiew King, Teh Hong Piow, Loh Cheng, Yean, Lee Oi Hian, Lee Shin Cheng, Tan Kim Hor, Khoo Kay Peng, Low Yow Chuan, Yaw Teck Seng, Lau Hui Kang, Tan Chin Nam, and Tan Teong Hean (*Malaysian Business* February 1, 2001).
5 In his study of the largest Chinese firms in Malaysia, their growth contextualized within the economic development of the country, Gomez (1999) revealed that their owners had adopted heterogeneous business styles when developing their enterprises. The rise of these firms was due to a variety of factors, including the resources available to these businessmen, the entrepreneurial endowment of individual businessmen, and their access to state patronage through links with influential politicians. Other factors included a productive use of experience gained in an industry before venturing into business, entrepreneurial deployment of resources generated from an initial investment in a company, and a rather focused approach to one trade rather than diversifying into any area of business that appeared potentially profitable. In some cases, entrepreneurial traits, such as the ability to correctly predict market trends and take risks by investing in a potentially lucrative opportunity, have proved crucial.
6 In many cases, however, public enterprises merely acquired between 20 and 50 percent of equity in companies for investment purposes.
7 In the construction and property development sectors, for example, the government's Urban Development Authority (UDA), established in 1971, rapidly secured a prominent presence. In the banking sector, by 1976, two Chinese-controlled banks, Malayan Banking Bhd and the United Malayan Banking Corporation Bhd (UMBC), had fallen under state control following runs on the banks. Subsequently, other Chinese-owned banks like the D&C Bank Bhd, Kwong Yik Bank Bhd, and Bank of Commerce Bhd, as well as the Indian-controlled United Asian Bank Bhd (UAB), would fall under state or Bumiputera control. See Gomez and Jomo (1999:60–66) for details.

8 Apart from Mahathir's desire to rapidly modernize the Malaysian economy, his tenure has also been characterized by growing authoritarianism, involving significant concentration of power in the executive arm of government (see Khoo 1992; Crouch 1996; Munro-Kua 1996; Hilley 2001). This concentration of power has protected the prime minister from being accountable for the pattern of patronage that he has practiced, involving the award of numerous concessions, usually in a non-transparent manner, to select businessmen. For an in-depth study of this political business nexus during the Mahathir era, see Gomez (1994; 2002).

9 For a comprehensive discussion on the implementation of privatization by the Mahathir government, see Jomo (1995).

10 The companies owned by a number of these well connected businessmen were badly affected by the 1997 currency crisis. In some cases, they received either a government bailout or takeover by another state-owned enterprise. In other cases, since many of them were closely associated with leading UMNO figures, internal disputes among powerful politicians led to some losing control of their enterprises. Contrary to the original intention of government policy, this nexus of politics and business based on patronage and political loyalty has undermined the development of Bumiputera entrepreneurship. See Gomez (2002) for an in-depth discussion of the rapid collapse of many corporate groups controlled by these well connected Malay businessmen.

11 Sloane's (1999) study of smaller sized Malay-owned firms also indicates that well connected business people from this community work independently of each other. These business people usually compete with each other to secure as many concessions as possible from the government, a trait that is common among Malay owners of large-scale enterprises as well.

12 There was, similarly, no attempt by Chinese bankers to voluntarily merge their financial enterprises during this consolidation exercise.

13 This figure includes enterprises quoted on the KLSE in 1998.

14 Schumpeter (1943). This is not to negate the point that Schumpeter noted as well that entrepreneurs have also secured economic concessions from the state. Among the directors of firms listed in Appendix 5.2 include Wan Azmi Wan Hamzah, Josephine Premla Sivaretnam, and Mohamad Razali Mohd Rahim, who are closely associated with former finance minister Daim, Raja Seri Eleena Azlan Shah, a member of the Perak royal house, and former cabinet member Tengku Ahmad Rithauddeen, also once an UMNO vice-president.

15 See (Chin 2001) for an in-depth discussion on Ali-Baba-type firms.

16 See Gomez and Benton (2004) for an in-depth critique of essentializing arguments in the literature on Chinese enterprise.

17 For an in-depth review of how business people linked to key politicians have lost control of their corporate assets following the fall of their patrons from positions of power, see Gomez (2003).

References

Books

Backman, M. (1999) *Asian Eclipse: Exposing the Dark Side of Business in Asia*, Singapore: John Wiley.

Benton, G. and Gomez, E. T. (2001) *Chinatown and Transnationalism: Ethnic Chinese in Europe and Southeast Asia*, Canberra: Centre for the Study of the Chinese Southern Diaspora, Australian National University.

Bowie, A. (1991) *Crossing the Industrial Divide: State, Society and the Politics of Economic Transformation in Malaysia*, New York: Columbia University Press.

Brown, R. A. (1994) *Capital and Entrepreneurship in South-East Asia*, New York: St. Martin's Press.

Chan, K. B. (ed.) (2000) *Chinese Business Networks: State, Economy and Culture*, Singapore: Prentice Hall.

Chandler, A. D. Jr. (1962) *Strategy and Structure: Chapters in the History of the American Industrial Enterprise*, Cambridge, MA: MIT Press.

——(1977) *The Visible Hand: The Managerial Revolution in American Business*, Cambridge, MA: Harvard University Press.

Chin. Y. W. (2001) "Usahawan Cina Di Malaysia: Interaksi Budaya dan Transformasi Keusahawanan" (Chinese Enterprise in Malaysia: Cultural Interaction and Entrepreneurial Transformation), unpublished Ph.D. thesis, Universiti Kebangsaan Malaysia, Bangi.

Crouch, H. (1996) *Government and Society in Malaysia*, St. Leonards, NSW: Allen & Unwin.

East Asia Analytical Unit (1995) *Overseas Chinese Business Networks in Asia*, Parkes, ACT: Department of Foreign Affairs and Trade, Commonwealth of Australia.

Embong, A. R. (2001) *State-led Modernization and the New Middle Class in Malaysia*, Basingstoke, U.K.: Palgrave.

Fukuyama, F. (1995) *Trust: The Social Virtues and the Creation of Prosperity*, New York: Free Press.

Gale, B. (1985) *Politics and Business: A Study of Multi-Purpose Holdings Berhad*, Petaling Jaya: Eastern Universities Press.

Gill, R. (1985) *The Making of Malaysia Inc.: A Twenty-five Year Review of the Securities Industry of Malaysia and Singapore*, Singapore: Pelanduk Publications.

Gomez, E. T. (1994) *Political Business: Corporate Involvement of Malaysian Political Parties*, Cairns, QD: James Cook University of North Queensland.

——(1999) *Chinese Business in Malaysia: Accumulation, Ascendance, Accommodation*, Honolulu, HI: University of Hawaii Press.

——(2001) "Why Mahathir Axed Daim," *Far Eastern Economic Review* 5 July.

——(2002) "Political Business in Malaysia: Party Factionalism, Corporate Development, and Economic Crisis," in E. T. Gomez (ed.) *Political Business in East Asia*, London: Routledge.

——(2003) "Capital Development in Malaysia," in J. Yahya, T. N.Peng and Y. K. Kheng (eds.) *Sustaining Growth, Enhancing Distribution: The NEP and NDP Revisited*, Kuala Lumpur: Centre for Economic Development and Ethnic Relations (CEDER), University of Malaya.

Gomez, E. T. and Benton, G. (2004) "De-essentializing Capitalism: Chinese Enterprise, Transnationalism, and Identity," in E. T. Gomez and H. H. M. Hsiao (eds.) *Chinese Enterprise, Transnationalism, and Identity*, London: RoutledgeCurzon.

Gomez, E. T. and Hsiao, H. H. M. (eds.) (2001) *Chinese Business in Southeast Asia: Contesting Cultural Explanations, Researching Entrepreneurship*, Richmond, Surrey, U.K.: Curzon.

Gomez, E. T. and Jomo, K. S. (1999) *Malaysia's Political Economy: Politics, Patronage and Profits*, Cambridge: Cambridge University Press.

Hamilton, G. G. (ed.) (1996) *Asian Business Networks*, Berlin: Walter de Gruyter.

Hara, F. (ed.) (1993) *Formation and Restructuring of Business Groups in Malaysia*, Tokyo: Institute of Developing Economies.

Hilley, J. (2001) *Malaysia: Mahathirism, Hegemony and the New Opposition*, London: Zed.

Jesudason, J. V. (1989) *Ethnicity and the Economy: The State, Chinese Business and Multinationals in Malaysia*, Singapore: Oxford University Press.

Jomo, K. S. (ed.) (1995) *Privatising Malaysis: Rents, Rhetoric, and Realities*, Boulder, CO: Westview Press.

Kao, J. (1993) "The Worldwide Web of Chinese Business," *Harvard Business Review*, March-April.

Khoo, K. J. (1992) "The Grand Vision: Mahathir and Modernisation," in J. S. Kahn and F. K. W. Loh (eds.) *Fragmented Visions: Culture and Politics in Contemporary Malaysia*, Sydney, NSW: Allen & Unwin for Asian Studies Association of Australia.

Kotkin, J. (1993) *Tribes: How Race, Religion and Identity Determine Success in the New Global Economy*, New York: Random House.

Kuala Lumpur Stock Exchange (2000) *Annual Companies Handbook*, Kuala Lumpur: Kuala Lumpur Stock Exchange.

Lee, K. H. and Chow, C. S. (1997) *Biographical Dictionary of the Chinese in Malaysia*, Kuala Lumpur: Institute of Advanced Studies, University of Malaya and Pelanduk Publications.

Lever-Tracy, C., Ip, D., and Tracy, N. (1996) *The Chinese Diaspora and Mainland China: An Emerging Economic Synergy*, New York: St. Martin's Press.

Light, I. (1972) *Ethnic Enterprise in America*, Berkeley, CA: University of California Press.

Light, I. and Bhachu, P. (eds.) (1993) *Immigration and Entrepreneurship: Culture, Capital and Ethnic Networks*, New Brunswick, NJ: Transaction Publishers.

Light, I. and Bonacich, E. (1988) *Immigrant Entrepreneurs: Koreans in Los Angeles, 1965–1982*, Berkeley, CA: University of California Press.

Light, I. and Gold, S. (2000) *Ethnic Economies*, San Diego, CA: Academic Press.

Lim, M. H. (1981) *Ownership and Control of the One Hundred Largest Corporations in Malaysia*, Kuala Lumpur: Oxford University Press.

Liu, H. (1998) "Old Linkages, New Networks: The Globalization of Overseas Chinese Voluntary Associations and its Implications," *China Quarterly* 155 (September).

Malaysia (1996) *Seventh Malaysia Plan, 1996–2000*, Kuala Lumpur: Government Printers.

——(2001) *Eighth Malaysia Plan, 2001–2005*, Kuala Lumpur: Government Printers.

Menkhoff, T. and Gerke, S. (eds.) (2002) *Chinese Entrepreneurship and Asian Business Networks*, London: RoutledgeCurzon.

Munro-Kua, A. (1996) *Authoritarian Populism in Malaysia*, London: Macmillan.

Penrose, E. T. (1980) *The Theory of the Growth of the Firm*, Oxford: Basil Blackwell.

Puthucheary, J. J. (1960) *Ownership and Control in the Malayan Economy*, Singapore: Eastern Universities Press.

Redding, S. G. (1990) *The Spirit of Chinese Capitalism*, Berlin: de Gruyter.

Schumpeter, J. A. (1943) *Capitalism, Socialism and Democracy*, London: Allen & Unwin.

Scott, J. (1997) *Corporate Business and Capitalist Classes*, Oxford: Oxford University Press.

Seagrave, S. (1995) *Lords of the Rim*, London: Bantam.

Searle, P. (1999) *The Riddle of Malaysian Capitalism: Rent-Seekers or Real Capitalists?* St. Leonards, NSW/Honolulu, HI: Allen & Unwin/University of Hawaii Press.

Sieh-Lee, M. L. (1982) *Ownership and Control of Malaysian Manufacturing Corporations*, Kuala Lumpur: UMCB Publications.

Sloane, P. (1999) *Islam, Modernity and Entrepreneurship among the Malays*, Basingstoke, U.K.: Macmillan.

Tan, T. W. (1982) *Income Distribution and Determination in West Malaysia*, Kuala Lumpur: Oxford University Press.

Waldinger, R. (1996) *Still the Promised City? African-Americans and New Immigrants in Post Industrial New York*, Cambridge: Harvard University Press.

Waldinger, R., Ward, R., McEvoy, D., and Aldrich, H. (1990) *Ethnic Entrepreneurs: Immigrant Business in Industrial Societies*, London: Sage.

Wazir, J. K. (2002) "The Globalization of Southeast Asia and Rooted Capitalism: Sino-Nusantara Symbiosis," in T. Menkhoff and S. Gerke (eds.) *Chinese Entrepreneurship and Asian Business Networks*, London: RoutledgeCurzon.

Weidenbaum, M. and Hughes, S. (1996) *The Bamboo Network*, New York: The Free Press.

Whitley, R. (1992) *Business Systems in East Asia: Firms, Markets and Societies*, London: Sage.

Williamson, O. E. (1975) *Markets and Hierarchies: Analysis and Anti-Trust Implications*, New York: Free Press.

Wong, P. (1999) "Introduction," in P. Wong (ed.) *Race, Ethnicity, and Nationality in the United States*, Boulder, CO: Westview Press.

Yeoh, K. K. (1987) "A Study of the Malaysian Chinese Economic Self-Strengthening (Corporatisation) Movement. With Special Reference to MPHB, Other Communal Investment Companies and Cooperatives," unpublished M.Ec. thesis, University of Malaya.

Yeung, H. W. C. and Olds, K. (eds.) (2000) *Globalization of Chinese Business Firms*, Basingstoke, U.K.: Macmillan.

Yeung, H. W. C. (2002) "Transnational Entrepreneurship and Chinese Business Networks: The Regionalization of Chinese Business Firms from Singapore," in T. Menkhoff and S. Gerke (eds.) *Chinese Entrepreneurship and Asian Business Networks*. London: RoutledgeCurzon.

Yoshihara, K. (1988) *The Rise of Ersatz Capitalism in Southeast Asia*, Singapore: Oxford University Press.

Magazines

Asiaweek
Malaysian Business

6 Immigrant transnational entrepreneurship and its linkages with the state/network

Sino-Singaporean experience in a comparative perspective[1]

Hong Liu

Introduction

As one of the most enterprising minorities in Southeast Asia, the nature and characteristics of Chinese entrepreneurship has been a subject of extensive investigations (see, for example, Mackie 1992; Yeung and Olds 2000; Chan 2000; Gomez and Hsiao 2001; Menkhoff and Gerke 2002; Fong and Luk 2007). This line of research has laid a solid ground for an understanding of Asian economic development. However, most of the empirical examples in this literature are drawn either from the first generation of Chinese entrepreneurs who emigrated to Southeast Asia prior to World War II and made their fortune either during the transition from colonialism to independence and/or during the early phase of postcolonial regimes; or from second or third generations of Chinese entrepreneurs who have already been assimilated into the host societies. Such an emphasis reflects dominant academic interests in the study of immigration in economics and sociology; the latter has two central concerns: the determinants of migration and the adaptation of immigrants to the receiving societies (Portes et al. 2002). Unfortunately, the resultant dominant nation-state framework underlying this strand of stylized research has prevented a closer examination of the emerging transnational entrepreneurship and its linkages with the state and business networks under globalization (Liu 2006).

This chapter examines the making and characteristics of "a new breed of Chinese entrepreneurs" in Singapore, by focusing on the new Chinese migrants (*xin yimin*) that have rapidly emerged over the past two decades. While many of them are professionals and labor migrants, a significant segment has followed the footsteps of their entrepreneurial predecessors by venturing into various types of business activities. These entrepreneurs are new in the following two senses: they are new entrants to the diasporic Chinese world and their entrepreneurial experiences have been significantly shaped by new forces engineered by globalization, technological innovation, and new patterns of transnational networks. So far, there has been little attention directed to the characteristics of this new generation of immigrant entrepreneurs, particularly their comparative (dis)advantages with regard to their predecessors and local counterparts. By using several illustrative examples of Sino-Singaporean entrepreneurs, this chapter analyzes the changing roles of transnational entrepreneurship and its linkages with the state. Specific attention will also be drawn to the relevance of those factors that have been considered essential to the conventional pattern of Chinese entrepreneurship such as business familism and social/business networks.

The chapter is divided into three sections. The first part briefly discusses the key attributes of entrepreneurship and the emerging conceptualization of transnational entrepreneurship. The second section analyzes in details the profiles of the new migrant entrepreneurs in Singapore, alternatively called "Sino-Singaporeans" in this chapter to highlight their hybridity, and identifies two major types of entrepreneurial experiences among them: technopreneurs and brokerage entrepreneurs. While there are some significant differences in their emergence, business structure, market focus, and management strategies, they do share a fundamental commonality in the creative use of transnational mobility, which constitutes the core of their entrepreneurial spirit. The last section considers the changing role of the state, network, and familism. Finally, the chapter concludes that transnationality, a close integration between the state and network, and technological innovation are key elements in explaining the dynamic emergence of new Chinese entrepreneurs and shaping their characteristics.

Entrepreneurship in the transnational context

Two perspectives on entrepreneurship

The study of entrepreneurship and its role in modern society has been fundamentally shaped by Joseph Schumpeter (1883–1950), who is considered as "*the* main figure in the literature on entrepreneurship" (Swedberg 2000:12; emphasis original). Schumpeter defines the entrepreneur as someone who carries out new combinations in five different arenas: (1) the introduction of a new good—that is, one with which consumers are not yet familiar—or a new quality of a good; (2) the introduction of a new method of production; (3) the opening of a new market; (4) the conquest of a new source of supply of raw materials or semi-manufactured goods; and (5) the creation of a new organization of any industry, like the creation or the breaking up of a monopoly position. The individuals whose function is to create these new combinations are called "entrepreneurs" (Schumpeter 1961:74). Douglas North (1990:83), on the other hand, sees the individual entrepreneur as "the agent of change" who responds to incentives embodied in the institutional framework. Peter Drucker argues that "entrepreneurs see change as the norm and as healthy. Usually, they do not bring about change themselves. But—and this defines entrepreneur and entrepreneurship—*the entrepreneur*

always searches for change, responds to it, and exploits it as an opportunity …
The entrepreneur, by definition, shifts resources from areas of low productivity and yields to areas of high productivity" (Drucker 1999:23,
emphasis original).

Since its inception as a field of scholarly enquiry, the literature on entrepreneurship can be classified into two schools: the supply-side perspective
and the demand-side perspective (Thornton 1999). In particular, the supply-
side school emphasizes "the availability of suitable individuals to occupy
entrepreneurial roles" and examines entrepreneurship by focusing on the
individual characteristics of entrepreneurs, specifying potential mechanisms
for agency and change. While the majority of entrepreneurship research has
been conducted from this perspective, it has been rightly criticized by others
who claim that that the supply-side arguments are "too simple, making
economic activity too much a function of individuals and underplaying the
role of external structural influences" (Thornton 1999:23). With respect to
ethnic entrepreneurship, scholars often considered the role of *group characteristics* by centering on the intriguing co-relationship between ethnicity
and entrepreneurship; they include "predisposing factors such as selective
migration, culture, and aspiration levels" (Aldrich and Waldinger 1990).
Brigitte Berge (1991) further argues that the cultural embeddedness of
modern entrepreneurship is instrumental in the creation of modern society,
and that "values and economic practices now present in parts of the urban
third world may serve as a preamble to industrialization."

In contrast to the supply-side emphasis on stasis and individuals, the
demand-side perspective examines what entrepreneurs actually do—the decisions they make within social settings that are changing over time, the concern
with the "push and pull of context" such as the activity of the professions,
the policies of nation-states, the development of markets, and the advent of
technological change (Thornton 1999). Scholars of ethnic enterprises also
pay great attention to the *opportunity structures* (market conditions which
may favor products or services oriented to co-ethnics, and situations in
which a wider, non-ethnic market is served) as well as *ethnic strategies*
(emerging from the interaction of opportunities and group characteristics,
as ethnic groups adapt to their environments) (Aldrich and Waldinger
1990). In the work associated with the Research Center for Entrepreneurial
History at Harvard University and through its journal, *Explorations in Entrepreneurial History*, a central theme has been advanced that "entrepreneurship should not be studied by focusing on the individual entrepreneur but
rather by looking at the enterprise, especially the social relations within the
enterprise and the relations between the enterprise and its surroundings"
(Swedberg 2000:35).

It is evident from the above discussion that the standard conceptualization
of entrepreneurship focuses on both the internal dimension and the external
environment of the making of an entrepreneur. Also, as a by-product of the
nation-state era, the research concerns of most studies are predominantly

focused on entrepreneurship within a specific geographical space, should they be the origins of migration or the receiving societies. It is only recently that transnational entrepreneurship has been accorded a greater degree of scholarly attention.

Immigrant transnational entrepreneurship

One of the fundamental issues confronting recent studies of (Chinese) entrepreneurship is the role of globalism and transnationalism; here different conceptualizations and contending views have emerged. According to Portes et al. (2002), transnational entrepreneurs are "self-employed immigrants whose business require frequent travel abroad and who depend for the success of their firms on their contacts and associates in another country, primarily their country of origin." Immigrant transnationalism represents a distinctive form of economic adaptation, and transnational entrepreneurs are different from both the mass of immigrants engaged in wage labor and the more traditional ethnic entrepreneurs whose activities are limited to local markets of the host societies.

Other conceptualizations of transnational entrepreneurship focus on its institutional dimension instead. Yeung (2004:118–19), for example, sees transnational entrepreneurship as

> a learning process because transnational entrepreneurship evolves from experience and learning gained through progressive involvement in foreign operations. Through these cross-border operations, transnational entrepreneurs not only learn how to deal with unexpected contingencies in the host countries, but also develop a deeper understanding of their realities ... Another attribute defining transnational entrepreneurship is foresight in foreign ventures, which is important at least from the perspective of strategic management.

He further suggests that there are three key attributes in facilitating the transnational operation of Chinese firms: "their greater opportunities for internalizing overseas markets, their trust and goodwill in host countries and their enrollment in transnational social and business networks." In the meantime, transnational entrepreneur is defined as "a social actor capable of bearing risks and taking strategic initiatives to establish, integrate, and sustain foreign operations" and by "three inter-related attributes that must be simultaneously present in the entrepreneurial process: (1) control of resources in different countries; (2) capabilities in strategic management in different countries; and (3) abilities to create and exploit opportunities in different countries" (Yeung 2002:37).

However, the concept of transnational entrepreneurship and its application to Chinese businesses in the multi-ethnic Southeast Asia has also been criticized as being "dangerously close to essentializing ethnicity." The idea is on shaky ground because it is based on "a sense of cohesiveness among individuals of a particular ethnic group acting in concert, usually for the economic progress of the community as well as of the "homeland," that is not the country of their birth, but the country of origin of their ancestors" (Gomez 2004:111).

With the recognition that entrepreneurship is part and parcel of changing times and spaces, this chapter draws upon its theoretical framework from the emerging field of transnational studies by focusing on the regularity and multiple impact of transnationalism. The latter can be formally defined as "the processes by which immigrants form and sustain multi-stranded social relations that link together their societies of origin and settlement. I call these processes transnationalism to emphasize that many immigrants today build social fields that cross geographic, cultural, and political borders ... An essential element [of transnationalism] is *the multiplicity of involvements that transmigrants sustain in both home and host societies*" (Basch et al. 1994:6; emphasis mine). Therefore, transnationalists represent "a growing number of persons who live dual lives: speaking two languages, having homes in two countries, and making a living through *continuous regular contact across national borders*" (Portes et al. 1999:217; emphasis mine).

While earlier conceptualization of transnationalism provides little room for the role of the state and power relations, recent (re)formulation offers some remedies by pointing out that the connections between "here" and "there" are contingent outcomes subject to multiple political constraints, and that states and state politics shape the options for migrant and ethnic trans-state social action. The state, therefore, should be brought back into the emerging field of transnationalism, with an emphasis upon "the *interactions* of migrants with states and civil society actors in both sending and receiving countries" (Waldinger and Fitzgerald 2004:1179; emphasis original).

This chapter considers transnationality as a defining characteristic of Sino-Singaporean entrepreneurship. In particular, I argue that since its early inception, new migrant entrepreneurs have always been a *transnational construct*. This is true in terms of their transnational education and experiences, transnational knowledge of business and culture, sources of capital, the composition of top management and their orientation, corporate strategies and transnational division of labor within the firm, and, to be sure, the heavily reliance on a transnational market. Meanwhile, transnational familism and social network constitute an important support system for the creation and growth of transnational entrepreneurship. Finally, the benefits of the state–network interactions are largely materialized through transnational mechanisms. As will be demonstrated shortly, the development of transnational Sino-Singaporean entrepreneurship is largely an indigenous activity, relatively free from any direct involvement of foreign corporations and international operations.

Two patterns of Sino-Singaporean transnational entrepreneurship

After a brief overview of Chinese new migrants in Singapore over the last two decades, this section looks at two patterns of Sino-Singaporean entrepreneurship: technopreneurs and brokerage entrepreneurs. I will first examine their characteristics from the supply-side perspective, or those attributes that are internal to the entrepreneurs concerned. Later I will then go beyond this paradigm and consider the question from the demand-side perspective by focusing on the role of the state, transnational familism and networks, and transnational management.

New Chinese migrants in Singapore

New Chinese migrants, or the so-called *xin yimin*, refer to those who have emigrated since the late 1970s and have lived outside of mainland China, either (semi-)permanently or as sojourners. In my other works elsewhere (Liu 2002; 2005a), I categorize the new migrants into four major types: students-turned-immigrants (those studying abroad initially but staying more permanently outside China after their graduation), chain migrants (those joining their families and relatives who are foreign citizens or permanent residents), emigrating professionals (those emigrating to the West because of their educational credentials and professional experience), and illegal immigrants (those going overseas illegally or over-staying their temporary visas after legal entrance as tourists or visitors). Based upon various sources, I estimated that by the end of 2003 the number of emigrants originating from the PRC (excluding Hong Kong, Taiwan and Macao) over the last two decades amounted to more than 3 million.

These Chinese new migrants can be further divided into two major categories: those with "portable skills" such as students and professionals, and those who posses only menial labor skills such as the majority of chain migrants and almost all illegal immigrants. In terms of the time frame, the past 20 years of China's international migration can also be divided into two periods. During the first decade (that is, the 1980s), the major source of growing emigration came from chain immigrants. On the other hand, during the second period (the 1990s), many new migrants were former students who had finished their overseas education and the emigrating professionals. It should be noted that illegal immigration remained an acute problem throughout both periods. Three major reasons explain the rapid rise of new migrants from China: the trend of globalization of migration; changing political and economic environments in China and the destination nations, respectively (see next section); and the growing role of intermediary agencies in facilitating the new wave of emigration, both legally and illegally (Liu 2005a). The emergence of new migrants could also be understood within a historical perspective that examines their origins and their internal structure (Wang 2004).

As a newly industrialized nation with a predominant Chinese population, Singapore is a major and an ideal destination for new migrants. By the end of 2000, there were approximately 290,000 permanent residents in the country. Together with foreigners who stay on with visas of one year or longer, they represent the fastest growing segment against the backdrop of decreasing percentage of citizens (from 86 percent in 1990 to 74 percent in 2000) (*Lianhe Zaobao*, September 1, 2000). A significant portion of the new permanent residents came from the mainland and belonged to the first or second categories of new migrants, namely students-turned-immigrants and professionals. The outcome largely reflects the fairly stringent criteria set by the Singaporean government when granting permanent residency, particularly in terms of the level of educational attainment and salary of the applicant.[2] As there are no official statistics available, the number of new Chinese migrants has been estimated at approximately 300,000 (*Yazhou Zhoukan*, cover story "Chinese New Migrants Have Transformed Singapore," April 25, 2004). This probably constitutes the largest concentration of new Chinese migrants in Asia, excepting Hong Kong.

The new migrants in Singapore share some common demographic characteristics as their counterparts elsewhere. For one thing, the new wave of emigration has gradually redrawn the map of the Chinese diaspora in terms of their native-place origins, characterized by the diversity of their geographical origins. While many recent immigrants still originate from the *qiaoxiang* in South China, the percentage from non-*qiaoxiang* regions of China has increased remarkably. In comparison with other categories of new migrants and the Chinese society at large, those new migrants with portable skills are generally much better educated, even prior to their exit (Liu 2005a).

The changing characteristics of new migrants have important implications for our understanding of Sino-Singaporean entrepreneurship. First, the identity of new migrants is multifaceted, hybridized, and fluid. This is in sharp contrast with the past, where the pattern of overseas Chinese identity was quite clear-cut: one either would return to China eventually to fulfill the dreams of *luoye guigen* (as most did or hoped for before 1945) or settle down to become *luodi shenggen*, which was the predominant pattern after 1945 for the offspring of the Chinese overseas.[3] The new migrants, as I have demonstrated elsewhere (Liu 2002; 2005b), have been vacillating between these two identities and constitute what I called the "transnational Chinese." At least in the foreseeable future, their identities would be characterized as neither *luoye guigen* nor *luodi shenggen*. Many of them are in the process of developing a new, mobile identity. For some, Singapore is not the first or the only site of their migratory journey; many actually came to the "Lion City" by way of a third country, and this transnational mobility is embedded into their ways of life and mentality.

Second, they were all born and received their early socialization in China, and still have close family and personal connections there. Even though they have become citizens or permanent residents of Singapore, China remains as an important source of ethnic strength and a cultural reservoir. The rapid growth of the Chinese economy and its integration with the global market (contrasting to the limited market of Singapore) makes this transnational connection both indispensable and highly feasible. Finally, many of the new migrants, particularly those with portable skills, have had educational and professional experiences in more than one location (China, the West, and/or Singapore); such transnational knowledge of cultures and technology, as well as transnational experiences, thus play a significant role in shaping their entrepreneurial behavior.

Technopreneur as innovative wealth creator

"Technopreneurs" refers to those entrepreneurs who use technological innovations and translate such technology into successful products or services (Milton-Smith et al. 1999). While they share similar attributes with traditional entrepreneurs in their risk-taking and profit-driven propensities, technopreneurs rely heavily on the application of (new and/or advanced) technology to their products and services, from the stage of starting-up the company through its growth and to its (for some) initial public offering (IPO). The defining characteristic of a technopreneur is their ability to convert technological inventions into innovative use for production and services. To be sure, this is in tandem with the core spirit of entrepreneurship conceptualized by Schumpeter and others. As Peter Drucker states clearly, entrepreneurs must innovate. "Innovation is the specific instrument of entrepreneurship [and it] endows resources with a new capacity to create wealth" (1999:27). To a great extent, technopreneurship is analogous to what he calls "knowledge-based innovation," which is "the 'super-star' of entrepreneurship. It gets the publicity [and] the money" (Drucker 1999:98). In his pioneering work on innovation and entrepreneurship, Drucker further specifies three main requirements for knowledge-based innovation: (1) careful analysis of all the necessary factors, whether knowledge itself, or social, economic, or perceptual factors; the analysis must identify what factors are not yet available so that the entrepreneur can decide whether these missing factors can be produced; (2) a clear focus on the strategic position (such as developing a complete system that would then dominate the field and create a market focus for its products); and (3) the need to learn and practice entrepreneurial management (Drucker 1999:105–9).

As mentioned earlier, a significant portion of Chinese new migrants in Singapore are well educated and tech-savvy. A small segment of them are even able to transfer their technological know-how to innovative use for a broader market, thus converting from scientists/professionals into technopreneurs. The following section begins with the profiling of four entrepreneurs who have recently emerged on the Sino-Singaporean business scene by successfully combining technological edge with business acumen;[4] it is followed by an examination of their common entrepreneurial attributes, especially from the supply-side perspective.

Lan Weiguang

Born in 1964 in a village of Wuping county, a rural region of western Fujian province, Lan is the eldest son of five children whose father was a cashier in a local state-owned factory, earning approximately 32 yuan (US$4) a month. Taking a typical route of upward social mobility available to people like him, Lan Weiguang passed the national college entrance examination in 1981 and was admitted into the department of chemistry of Xiamen University, one of the key national universities. After graduation in 1985 he worked as a lecturer in the department of food engineering at Jimei University and married Chen Ni, a school teacher from his neighboring village. Encouraged by a professor from the National University of Singapore (NUS) whom he met at an international conference in Beijing, Lan applied for and won a scholarship, and went to Singapore to pursue Ph.D. training in 1992. Upon graduation in 1995, he joined Hyflux, the largest water-treatment company in Singapore, as its technical and sales director in China, while his family stayed behind in Singapore. He became a permanent resident of Singapore in 1995 and a naturalized citizen two years later.

While on the job in Shanghai, Lan increasingly recognized the business potentials of using membranes for filtration and purification to improve the quality of pharmaceutical products.[5] After one and a half years with Hyflux, he left the company and set up Suntar Xiamen in 1996. Along with other companies he established later, Suntar is now part of the Singapore-incorporated Sinomem Technology group controlled by Lan. From the onset, Lan faced the challenge of formulating a clear market focus—one of the three major requirements in a knowledge-based economy as specified by Peter Drucker. The profit margin for water-treatment products is much lower than those in the pharmaceutical industries. Furthermore, membrane products for water-treatment need to be replaced once every three to five years whereas the replacement frequency for pharmaceutical products is once a year. Hence, Sinomem has expanded into the manufacturing and installation of membrane systems. The firm owns and controls numerous different proprietary advanced membrane processes that can be applied in the pharmaceutical industries, such as in the production of antibiotics, vitamins, and amino acids. The pharmaceutical industry currently accounts for about 90 percent of the company's total revenues.

The company's headquarters are located in Singapore's science park, while its production facilities are in Xiamen. The company's sales grew by a stunning 547 percent between 2000 and 2002. Its business volume, which is almost entirely derived from operations in China, grew to S$31.3 million and the net profit was S$10.6 million in 2002. The sale of Lan's membrane products and technology accounted for nearly 10 percent of the 2 billion yuan market in China. Sinomem has completed more than 50 projects in China and was listed at 28 in the 2003 Deloitte Touche Tohmatsu Asia Pacific Technology Fast 500[6] (*Straits Times*, December 23, 2003; *The Edge Singapore*, May 26, 2003; *Xiamen Wanbao*, November 22, 2003).

Meanwhile, the size of Lan's company increased from an initial staff of three to more than 170, 65 percent of whom had at least university education. In June 2003, Sinomem successfully launched its initial public offer (IPO) at the Singapore Stock Exchange (SGX). The market capitalization of the company was over S$150 million. According to the Forbes' China's Richest 100 in 2003, Lan's family, who controlled about 75 percent of Sinomem valued at US$137 million, was ranked as the 75th richest person in China. He was the only entrepreneur on the list whose wealth was not based upon IT or high tech (*Dongnan Zaobao*, November 12, 2003). He was also named "Young Chinese Entrepreneur 2003" in Singapore, an award organized by *Yazhou Zhoukan*, an influential Chinese-language news magazine published in Hong Kong. In 2004 Sinomem purchased Shandong-based Reyphon Agriceutical, a Chinese company that produces chemicals that increase crop yields. Sinomem, through its wholly owned unit Suntar Investment, owns 68 per cent of Reyphon, which made its debut on the Singapore Exchange in August 2007 (*Straits Times*, August 2, 2007).

Lin Yucheng

Born in 1963 in Quanzhou, southern Fujian, Lin studied physics at Nanjing University from 1981. Upon graduation in 1985, he won a government scholarship to pursue a doctoral degree in applied environmental geochemistry at the Imperial College of Science and Technology in London. After completing his Ph.D. in 1991, the Economic Development Board (EDB) in Singapore arranged an interview with him and Lin eventually received two job offers in Singapore: one from the Nanyang Technological University (NTU) and the other from the then Singapore Institute of Standards and Industrial Research. He chose the latter and became a senior research fellow. He subsequently served as head of the Environmental Technology Centre of the then Productivity and Standards Board (PSB). In 1993 Lin became Singapore citizen.

Lin moved into entrepreneurship in 1996 when he and PSB set up a joint venture, NOVO Environmental Technology Services Pty. Ltd. (NOVO ETS), with him taking 30 percent stakes of the company whose main business was in environmental, health and safety standards consultancy and environmental engineering. He immediately spearheaded NOVO ETS's initiative into the PRC market and established NOVO Safety and Environmental Technology (Guangzhou) in April 2001. In July 2003, he sold his stakes back to PSB. Together with Goh Ching Wah, an entrepreneur with directorships in and co-founder of 44 publicly listed companies in Singapore, they acquired several businesses and expanded the existing businesses of the group and started United Envirotech (UE), with Lin serving as chairman and CEO. UE's two principal activities are environmental engineering solutions and environmental consultancy solutions. The former includes the design and implementation of integrated systems for engineering solutions, based mainly on its membrane technology, to address the specific needs of its customers. The latter includes the provision of consultancy services and training in the management of environmental health and safety (*Dow Jones Newswires*, March 19, 2004; www.unitedenvirotech.com/aboutus.html).

United Envirotech's revenue grew from S$1.9 million in 2001 to S$14.6 million in 2003, and pretax profit grew from S$177,000 to an estimated S$8.8 million over the same period. Similar to Sinomem, China represents the key market focus of UE. For instance, the giant Chinese petrochemical group, Sinopec, accounted for 49 percent of its total revenue. Following the successful footsteps of Sinomem, the company became the eighth water-treatment player listed on the Singapore exchange in April 2004, selling 63.8 million IPO shares at 47 cents apiece. Lin instantly became another multi-millionaire: he received S$5.2 million from the direct sale of shares and his remaining 29 percent stake was valued at S$34 million (*Straits Times*, April 19, 2004; *The Edge Singapore*, April 19, 2004).

Shi Xu and Zhang Lu

Born in 1964 in Shanghai, Shi Xu received his Bachelor of Science degree in physics from Tongji University in 1987 and doctoral degree in thin film technology from the University of Reading. After his graduation in 1991, he became the youngest lecturer at the time at the Nanyang Technological University (NTU) and was later promoted to Associate Professor. In 1999 he quit his academic job and became the chief executive officer of Nanofilm Technologies International, where he applied his patented techniques to produce ultra-hard, ultra-thin diamond films. In the same year, Japanese multinational Shimazu Corporation signed a multi-million-dollar exclusive agreement with Nanofilm to supply the company with the key component to produce the coating for disk-drive readers or slider heads. According to Shi, the company has been profitable from the start and has plans to go public in the near future.

Among his significant achievements, Shi received two major awards: the National Technology Award in 2000, conferred by the National Science and Technology Board of Singapore (now known as A*STAR), and the Inno-vation Award in 2001, conferred by the Singapore government in recognition of the company's outstanding technological contributions. His company has also been ranked as one of the "Asia-Pacific Technology Fast 500" compa-nies, as compiled by Deloitte Touche Tohmatsu (DTT) in 2003.[7]

Zhang Lu, another China-born Singapore citizen in her early 40s, studied electrical engineering at the Beijing Broadcasting College. After obtaining a MBA degree from the University of Melbourne, she was recruited by Philips

Electronics Singapore as a quality-assurance engineer and soon became a senior engineer. Taking advantage of her working experience, she and four friends established Treasureway Limited Singapore in 1993, specializing in systems management and office automation. In the following year, she formed three other companies in Shanghai, Guangzhou, and Xuzhou in Jiangsu province, bringing back the technological know-how and the experience acquired overseas to China. In 2001 alone the total value of the contracts that her companies won amounted to 100 million yuan, an increase of 60 percent over the previous year (*Lianhe Zaobao*, December 23, 2001). In recognition of her contribution to China's development, she was granted permanent residency by the Shanghai municipal government in 2002, a privilege that is available only for a handful of former PRC nationals (*Ziben Zazhi* [*The Fund*] vol. 1, no. 1, October 2004, p. 53).

Attributes behind business success: the supply-side perspective

As argued earlier, the supply-side explanation of (ethnic) entrepreneurship tends to focus on the psychological, social, cultural, and personal characteristics of individual entrepreneurs and examines their need for achievement, locus of control, risk-taking propensity, problem-solving style and innovativeness, leadership style, values, and socialization in explaining entrepreneurial success. Before turning to the demand-side perspective, I will first discuss some common characteristics of technopreneurship from the supply-side perspective, as exemplified by these Chinese new migrants

First, they all have a high risk-taking propensity and a hard-working attitude. As discussed above, risk-taking is one of the main components of entrepreneurship. For our Sino-Singaporean technopreneurs, they all had well paid and stable careers prior to starting their own businesses. But they were willing to take significant risks in exchange for the potential rewards that appear to be much more attractive, both financially and sentimentally. For example, Lan Weiguang's wife remembered that when her husband decided to quit the Hyflux job to become an entrepreneur, "I supported him but at first, I was anxious" (*Straits Times*, May 23, 2003). Similarly, Lin Yucheng knew that giving up job security was indeed risky but it could be more rewarding. "I wanted to do big things," he says (*Straits Times*, April 19, 2004). As for Shi Xu, "sometimes the pressure is tremendous, so you need to believe in yourself and have a strong mind." "Being an innovator is like riding a roller-coaster—it's not for the faint-hearted," according to him. "Before you become successful, there's no reward and no recognition. Apart from the difficulties you face from the work itself, you also encounter cynicism and people who don't believe you. You need a strong mind to keep going." He also recognized that the better-educated are sometimes less likely to innovate: "The better educated you are, the more comfortable you get because you lose the drive and guts to take a risk" (*Straits Times*, November 13, 2001). In one sense, our technopreneurs are extraordinary in taking risks and breaking with the traditional route of (Chinese) social hierarchy which places "scholar-gentry" at the top of the society.

To partially offset the risks derived from the loss of job security, our technopreneurs worked extremely hard. Just like Lan, whose initial staff numbered just three when he set up his Sinomem, NOVO ETS had only three consultants. "I worked hard, sleeping only three to four hours a night," said Lin Yucheng. During the first year of Shi Xu's company, he had to leave his two-day-old baby and his wife in hospital to rush to Japan to see one of his first clients, a multinational company which had bought a coating system from Nanofilm. He really had little choice, as this was a big client and would have represented a vital business breakthrough if he won them over. As he recalled: "They told me that their company was not an experimental ground, and I had better make sure that everything was working well."

Second, and perhaps more importantly, the ability to translate technological know-how and advantages into production and marketing is the key attribute that explains their success. This ability, to be sure, is embedded with the conception and practice of technopreneurship. It constitutes the main divide that sets people like Lan, Lin, and Shi apart from other prominent inventors with advanced scientific knowledge. Describing himself as "an entrepreneurial scientist instead of a scientifically-minded entrepreneur," Lan sensed the huge business potential of the membrane market in China, especially in the filtration and purification processes to improve the quality of pharmaceutical products. At this strategic juncture, his knowledge of the transnational market and the status of technological development gave him further confidence in making the transition from professional manager to entrepreneur: "In addition to my familiarities with situations in both China and overseas, I also know well the technological status of industries in China" (*Guanming Ribao*, February 20, 2003). "Our philosophy is simple: innovation and market leadership will drive growth and enhance shareholder value," Lan states. "By making breakthroughs in membrane applications across industries and entrenching our leadership positions in markets, we are well positioned to serve our customers better, attract strategic partners and R&D talents and embark on a growth path that will inevitably benefit our shareholders" (*Straits Times*, May 17, 2003). In a speech delivered in February 2004 at the Singapore Chinese Chamber of Commerce, Lan shared his views on the requirements for entrepreneurial management as: (1) a keen foresight for potential business opportunities; (2) regarding the client's problem as a subject of scientific research and translating advanced technology into productivity; (3) never giving up in face of difficulties; (4) an effective combination of technology and marketing; (5) a strong interest in the business; and (6) seizing opportunities that could quickly slip away.

The third attribute is the strategic focus of their businesses. As pointed out by some scholars, "an entrepreneur is someone who specializes in taking *judgmental decisions* about the coordination of scarce resources" (Casson 2003:19–20; emphasis mine). In fact, the question of how to maintain strategic focus becomes a key challenge for technopreneurs when they make the transition from scientist to entrepreneur. Our cases indicate that they took Drucker's advice (one of the main requirements of knowledge-based entrepreneurship is "a clear focus on the strategic position") wholeheartedly, even though they may not have read his work.

For instance, the market for filtration membranes was still in its nascent stage. According to Hyflux CEO Olivia Lum (Lan's former boss), "Membrane technology has started only recently in Asia. And increasingly, with all the pollution in the rivers and nature reserves, it is already becoming a must to use the membrane technology. We are talking about either upgrading or building new membrane plants." She further added that, "Singapore is one of the pioneers in membrane technology in this region" (Pek 2003). Lan Weiguang's training and work experience in Singapore and China led him to believe that membrane technology would be a fertile field of business opportunities and strategic focus. Lan emphasized that Sinomem's expertise lies in membrane processing technology rather than membrane production. "Membranes can be procured by anybody from a number of suppliers," he said. "We are different in that we assemble and integrate the different kinds of membranes as part of a process which meets the needs of our customer." He claimed that Sinomem is also the pioneer of the membrane software business in China. After the successful listing of his company on the main board of the Singapore Stock Exchange, he told *Yazhou Zhoukan* that "even though I already have had plenty of capital and opportunities, I will never give up the field of my specialization. After all, along with opportunities, there are traps everywhere" (*Yazhou Zhoukan*, January 2, 2004). Similarly, Lin Yucheng was firmly aware of his technological advantage and the core strategy. "Pharmaceuticals and petrochemicals [are] our focus currently," Lin said. "The reason is very simple. Firstly, the entry barrier is quite high; they really need good technology. Secondly, the profit margin is much higher than the traditional process, for example in sewage water treatment. [This has been our focus because competition] is not as strong in the other industry sectors" (*Channel News Asia*, April 12, 2004).

In brief, the supply-side argument considers the combination of risk-taking, technological know-how, hard work, business acumen, and strategic focus to account for the rise of technopreneurs like Lan and Lin. These attributes alone, however, cannot fully explain their success. In the following section, I will examine the role of the state, transnationalism, familism, and network in the making of Sino-Singaporean entrepreneurship.

Entrepreneurs as brokers

Unlike technopreneurs, who are well educated and tech-savvy, contemporary brokerage entrepreneurs resemble more closely their predecessors who set foot in Southeast Asia more than 150 years ago. They usually started small, normally working for others as manual laborers. After accumulating sufficient capital and experience, they then set up their own companies in the service or manufacturing sectors that are mostly labor-intensive. The major source of business profits derives from their brokerage activities: between their clients (contractors) and their customers (laborers) in the local settings, and more importantly, as an intermediary between China and Singapore in the transnational setting, by bringing "scarce commodities" (which could be knowledge of investment opportunities, laborers, students, or prospective immigrants) from one side to the other. It is the latter characteristic that brokerage entrepreneurs share with the technopreneurs discussed earlier.

Wang Quancheng

Born in 1965 in Anxi county in southern Fujian, Wang received only high school education. At the age of 21 he went to Singapore as a construction worker with only 20 yuan (S$4) in his pocket, laboring for more than a dozen hours and earning a mere S$15 a day. Realizing that he did not have any special skills that would help him to move up the financial and social ladder, he started paying attention to all kinds of details at the construction sites, from how to lay bricks to how to read construction blueprints. This effort in upgrading himself soon paid off handsomely; six months later, he was promoted to become a foreman in the construction company. Three years later, using personal savings and loans from friends and other lenders, he set up his own construction company, Lianquan Construction Company. Like his predecessors, he too had to work hard. In the early phase of his company, he worked together with more than 100 laborers in construction sites, sleeping only three hours a day (*Lianhe Wanbao*, November 12, 2001).

The construction boom in the early 1990s and the ability to bring in cheap labor from China helped his business tremendously. His firm soon reached a reported annual business volume of S$50 million, and Wang himself became a Singapore citizen and a director or board member of more than 30 different local companies. Wang also invested nearly 100 million yuan to build a four-star hotel in his hometown Anxi (*Wenhui Bao* [Hong Kong], October 8, 2003). Keenly aware of the importance of social networking among newcomers, he founded the Huayuan Association in June 2001, which had a membership of nearly 2,000 and is the largest local association oriented toward new migrants. Its membership was composed of new migrants who were either citizens or permanent residents. The majority of these were professionals with at least a bachelor's degree, and more than 100 of them had doctoral degrees (see below). He also participated actively in various local social activities, serving, for example, as vice chairman of the Singapore Basketball Association.

Du Zhiqiang

Born in Sichuan (perhaps in the early 1960s), Du was a cadre in the local government of Chengdu. He migrated to Singapore in 1992 and became naturalized two years later. His first job in Singapore was as a factory director of a chicken slaughterhouse, where he worked more than ten hours a day and performed all kinds of chores. He recalled that this experience gave him "an understanding of the local situation, an opportunity to know more people, and the awareness of the need to work extremely hard in the new environment." He set up his own companies in Singapore and China in 1993, named Asia-Link Technology. Unlike technopreneurship, there is not much technology involved in these businesses. Instead, the focus was on brokerage activities between China and Singapore. In China, a large number of individuals wanted to go to Singapore, either as students or laborers, while many government officials and business people were eager to take part personally in the development of the city-state. In Singapore, on the other hand, there was a consensus in the business sector that investments in China (especially in inland provinces such as Sichuan) could be more effectively executed with the help of those who understand China and have valuable local connections. Du's company served mainly as an agent in six types of business service: an agency for international students to study in Singapore; labor employment; international migration; international investment; international trade; and international business tourism. The company has brought in several thousand professionals and laborers to work and settle in Singapore, and has helped Singaporean firms to invest in Sichuan and Guangdong (*Sichuan Qiaobao*, January 15, 2003; www.asialink.com.sg).

There are two commonalities among brokerage entrepreneurs. First, unlike technopreneurs who have an edge in technological knowledge, they rely heavily on personal connections, hard work, social capital, and family networks. In fact, they share similar attributes of the pre-1965 generations of Chinese entrepreneurs in Southeast Asia (see for example, Chan and Chiang 1994; Liu and Wong 2004). Therefore, it is by no means accidental that brokerage entrepreneurs are keen on networking through Chinese associations. Second, unlike their predecessors, they live in an age of globalization and information, whereby they can take advantage of an expanding mainland Chinese market and the growing expectations of mainland Chinese for studying and working overseas. It is by serving this transnational clientele that they have accumulated their capital and profits. Viewed in this light, transnationality itself, too, becomes a defining characteristic of brokerage entrepreneurship.

Interactions with the state and network

So far, the above discussion has focused on the individual characteristics of Sino-Singaporean entrepreneurship. However, it is necessary to go beyond the supply-side argument by considering Chinese new migrant entrepreneurs in the transnational framework, within which the role of the state and network can be better understood. This section investigates the role of the Chinese and Singaporean states, familism, and social network in the making of Sino-Singaporean transnational entrepreneurship.

The state goes transnational

As mentioned earlier, the linkages between "here" and "there" are contingent upon state politics. The state—in both China and Singapore—has played a key role in the making of Sino-Singaporean entrepreneurship. Without their interventions at various critical conjunctions, this new breed of transnational entrepreneurship could not have emerged in the first place. Furthermore, the continuing growth of the latter depends significantly upon the participation of the state on both sides of the South China Sea.

China as the reformist state

Since its opening-up in 1978, China has been profoundly influenced by the process of globalization. In fact, "the Chinese state *per se* has been a part of globalization, and a major driving force behind the process" (Zheng 2004:22). One important consequence of the rising influence of this process has been the role of transnational migrants from China, perhaps an (un)-intentional by-product of the state policy.

Since the institution of market reform policies, regulatory control over emigration has been significantly reduced. The first stage of China's evolving policies on emigration began in the early 1980s when controls on overseas travel for private reasons were significantly relaxed. The response from the public was more than enthusiastic: during the first six years (1979–85) of the open-door policy, an estimated 350,000 Chinese citizens went overseas (Liu 2005a). The policy, "Regulation Concerning Chinese Citizens Going Abroad and Returning," promulgated in November 1985, made overseas travel a basic right, and the red tape was subsequently reduced, which further facilitated the "leave-the-country-fever" (*chuguo re*). From February 2002, Chinese citizens going abroad have no longer been obliged to submit a foreign invitation together with their application, nor do they need to obtain prior approval (*chu jing ka*) from the local Public Security Bureau.

More specifically, one of the new state policies is the encouragement of "overseas Chinese talent" (mainly students-turned-immigrants) to serve the country. In his address to the Sixth World Chinese Entrepreneurs Convention held in Nanjing in 2001, the then prime minister Zhu Rongji appealed specifically to those overseas Chinese with professional credentials and experiences: "We have Chinese friends everywhere in the world," said Zhu:

Among them, there are specialized professionals in all areas, who know very well both the international market practices and Chinese cultural traditions. They have unique advantages in developing their business in China. They will find a lot of good opportunities for big development in China no matter whether they have already made investment here or are still looking for business opportunities.

(cited in Liu 2005b)

More importantly, by the mid-1990s, realizing that many Chinese students were becoming new immigrants and were likely to settle overseas in a more permanent manner, the government formulated the policy of "supporting overseas studies, encouraging the return of Chinese students, and upholding the freedom of their movement" (*zhichi liuxue, guli huiguo, laiqu ziyou*). The official slogan of "returning to serve the country" (*huiguo fuwu*) was replaced by "serving the country" (*weiguo fuwu*) in 1993 (Liu 2005b; see also Thuno 2001), thus making new migrants' physical return to the homeland not a prerequisite of demonstrating their patriotism. Zhang Xuezhong, minister of personnel, reportedly said that "China ought to seize the opportunity to encourage more overseas Chinese with genuine ability and learning to come back and run high-tech enterprises." To achieve this goal, various incentive regulations are being formulated. It is in this context that an increasingly large number of new migrants are returning to China, where they constitute an important segment of the urban elite. There are now 56 industrial zones in China, specifically designed to attract returned Chinese students/scientists, and 4,100 have responded by working there so far. More than 2,600 new migrants (nearly half with doctoral degrees) took part in the Fourth Technological Exchange Fair for Chinese Scholars/Professionals Abroad, held in Guangzhou in late 2001. Among them, 28.8 percent planned to return to set up enterprises, and 34 percent intended to seek domestic partnership (*Yazhou Zhoukan*, January 20, 2002). A recent survey of 3,000 returnees shows that some 60 percent are satisfied with the government's preferential policies (*People's Daily* [overseas edition], September 13, 2007).

Like their counterparts in North America, Sino-Singaporean technopreneurs benefited significantly from the new policies of the state. Indeed, people like Lan Weiguang, Lin Yucheng, and Shi Xu are the products of the open-door policy that encouraged them to study overseas, and they made good use of the facilities provided by various levels of the Chinese government designed specifically for the purpose of attracting new migrants with technological know-how and international experience. Lan's Sinomem, for instance, was the first factory in Xiamen's Torch Industrial Park, which is targeted specifically at returned students and professionals from overseas. Encouraged by He Kaijun, director of the industrial park, who had good knowledge of membrane technology and its potential, Lan decided to settle down in Xiamen (*Xiamen Wanbao*, November 22, 2003). Subsequently,

Hong Yongshi, then mayor of Xiamen, enthusiastically endorsed Lan's plan to develop the city as major center for research and application of membrane technology in China. Lan acknowledged publicly that his company's success during the early stage "depends significantly upon the support of the [Chinese] government" (*Dongnan Zaobao*, November 22, 2003). In a TV interview in Singapore (Channel 8, June 16, 2003), he expressed his "gratitude to Deng Xiaoping and the government of Singapore. Because of Deng, I had the opportunity to study in college; thanks to the government of Singapore, I have had my subsequent opportunity of development."

The state not only provides an environment that is conducive to the growth of technopreneurship, but it also directly participates in the process. For instance, when Lan established the Xiamen University Suntar Membrane Scitechonlogy (Xiamen) Company Limited in 1996, it was a joint venture between multiple parties. Lan's investment was 7.2 million yuan; an equal amount was put in by the Xiamen Resources Group Company, a company wholly owned by the Xiamen municipal government; and the remaining 9 million yuan was from three other companies including Xiamen University. In March 2003, Suntar Xiamen entered into an agreement with Xiamen Resources Group Company to establish another joint venture company, named Suntar Desalination, to develop a seawater desalination plant in Xiamen by 2004 to produce and sell drinking water. Today, the desalination plant produces about 5,000 tons of drinking water daily. Lin's success was further significantly facilitated by his close, both personal and professional, relations with China's gigantic state-owned enterprise, the Sinopec Group (as well as its subsidiaries throughout China). In fact, the latter accounted for almost half of UE's sales in 2003 (*Lianhe Zaobao*, April 13, 2004).

Singapore's search for global talent

Unlike China, which has a large pool of human talent and enormous markets, Singapore's economic growth has been significantly constrained by its limited domestic market and human resources. The state's main strategy has been to encourage local companies to go regional and attract "foreign talents" to expand the local economy. On the domestic front, the government policy aimed to develop a knowledge-based economy by providing various types of direct financial assistance and preferential treatment. It is this environment that provides the background for the emergence of new Chinese immigrants in general and Sino-Singaporean entrepreneurship in particular.

Demographically, there has been a trend of steady decline in fertility for the last two decades in Singapore. With a total fertility rate of 1.26 in 2003, far below the replacement rate of 2.1, the country's population would decline in the long run and may create structural problems for the local economy (*Straits Times*, August 30, 2004). Therefore, the government implemented the foreign talents policy aimed at attracting professionals and entrepreneurs, many of them are ethnic Chinese from Greater China or the diasporic Chinese communities elsewhere. One of the earliest manifestations of this newly formulated policy was a speech by Lee Hsien Loong, then minister for trade and industry and second minister for defense, in August 1989, just two months after the Tiananmen Incident that alienated a significant number of Hong Kong professionals. "Let us welcome fresh immigrants, so long as they bring with them the same grit, enterprise, and ability as our forefathers did" (Lee 1989). "Our rapid economic growth has created a severe shortage of talent and labor, at all levels. We need more skilled workers, technicians, professionals, entrepreneurs, and administrators. Our growth is constrained by our [limited] supply of talent. If we had more good people, we could grow even faster." After the establishment of formal diplomatic ties between China and Singapore in 1990, an increasingly large number of Chinese went to Singapore, where the government was particularly interested in attracting individuals with technological know-how and entrepreneurial drive. Speaking at the National Day rally in 1999, then prime minister Goh Chok Tong announced that "without talent, we cannot become a first-world economy and a world-class home. We must import talent from overseas to supplement the local talent" (*Lianhe Zaobao*, August 23, 1999). Senior minister Lee Kuan Yew stated candidly that "we will be overtaken if we do not recruit foreign talent." He also disclosed that in order to better understand the Chinese [from the mainland], it was important to recruit intelligent Chinese to work and study in Singapore so that they too could understand Singaporeans better and eventually become members of the Singapore community (*Lianhe Zaobao*, August 15, 1999; October 24, 2001). Starting in 1992, the government offered full scholarships to Chinese students to study in local junior colleges and universities. One of the major requirements was that they had to work in Singapore for at least six years upon graduation. A survey indicated that the policy had great success: among those 1,195 students who came to Singapore under this scheme, 74 percent eventually became permanent residents (*Lianhe Zaobao*, November 7, 2002).

The Singapore government is also keen on encouraging business alliances and networks among companies in the Asian region, a continuation of the long historical pattern of regional networking (Liu and Wong 2004). As Lee Kuan Yew declared at the Second World Chinese Entrepreneurs Convention held in Hong Kong in 1993, "We would be foolish not to use the ethnic Chinese network to increase our reach and our grasp of these opportunities" (cited in Liu 1998). In his speech at the Global Entrepolis @ Singapore in October 2003,[8] Goh Chok Tong also highlighted key strategic thrusts that would enable Singapore to meet the challenges of the new economy—through networking and alliances, its unique connections and connectivity, and the availability of global talent (*PR Newswire*, October 30, 2003). Similarly, the trade and industry minister George Yeo remarked in March 2004 that "Singapore's most profound links to China, India, and Southeast Asia are not just economic, but also cultural. If Singapore was able to nourish its cultural core, its economic trunk would be strong and its branches would spread wide" (*Straits Times*, March 26, 2004).

When Drucker (1999:237–41) speaks of the incompatibility between government and innovation, he argues that the former focuses on "planning" and produces policies that would be "obsolete fairly fast." Innovation, on the other hand, has to be "decentralized, ad hoc, autonomous, specific, and micro-economic." The Singaporean experience seems to provide a contrasting example. Just like the East Asian developmental state's role in "picking up the winners" from the 1970s to the early 1990s (Hawes and Liu 1993), the Singapore government has been deliberately promoting specific economic sectors, of which knowledge-based entrepreneurship has received special attention. Since 1999, Singapore has strived to create conditions that would stimulate and support high-tech enterprise, or technopreneurship. In fact, the development of high-tech businesses constitutes a key component of the country's economic strategy in the twenty-first century. The chief goal is to develop new economic activities and new markets to supplement its manufacturing sector and as a services hub for the region. Under this general policy guideline, a wide range of programs has been instituted. For example, a scheme called DATE, or Directors and Advisors for Technopreneurial Enterprises, introduces highly experienced business people who need expert guidance for start-ups, particularly in key areas such as finance and marketing. By the end of 1999, about 20 programs were available to new technopreneurs to assist them in the areas of finance, IT application, technology application, business development, human resources, and business innovation (Milton-Smith et al. 1999:52–67).

This series of policy initiatives was warmly received by the new Chinese migrants as well as entrepreneurs from the PRC. According to the 2003 Economic Development Board (EDB) statistics, among 180 Chinese companies in the manufacturing and service sectors, 60 of them were in the high-tech sector (though still significantly lower than those from India, which numbered 385), some of whom received EDB's Start-up Enterprise Development Scheme (SEEDS); the total amount of funding exceeded S$13.1 million. According to Shi Xu, "If Chinese high tech companies intend to raise capital and acquire new technology, or to look for a platform for going to the global market, Singapore is a natural choice."[9] On the other hand, the new Chinese entrepreneurs also believed that the Singapore market was too small, and it was imperative to go global (including to China) after transforming their inventions into innovations for market purposes. This dual strategy—raising funds and developing productivity-oriented technology in Singapore and tapping the emerging China market—has reinforced the transnational characteristics of Sino-Singaporean entrepreneurship.

The Singapore state also joined hands with the new migrant entrepreneurs in direct collaboration. Lin Yucheng's NOVO EST, for example, was a joint venture with a government agency, the Productivity and Standards Board (PSB). The government also purposefully involved new migrant entrepreneurs in numerous government-sponsored business dealings with China. For instance, four members of the official delegation to China in 2002 led by George Yeo were new migrant entrepreneurs who were thought to be able to play a useful role in bridging the two countries. Lan Weiguang has accompanied a number of Singapore government teams in the latter's business trips to the provinces of Fujian and Zhejiang.

In short, the state has not been marginalized by globalization. Instead, through systematic policy preferential treatments and direct collaboration, both the Chinese and Singapore states have played a significant role in the emergence and growth of Sino-Singaporean entrepreneurship. Unlike the older generation of political entrepreneurs who relied on state and elite patronage in accumulating social and economic capital (cf. Liu 2001), the state–business relationship governing the growth of Sino-Singaporean entrepreneurship is more transparent, and the policy-oriented preferential treatments for specific sectors of the economy have benefited Chinese new migrants who possess portable skills and business acumen. This collaboration has resulted in a win-win situation for the parties involved.

Familism, network, and transnational management

What is the role of familism and network in the making of Sino-Singaporean transnational entrepreneurship? Have they, as some commentators claimed, become insignificant in Chinese entrepreneurship, especially in technopreneurship? Our empirical cases demonstrate that they remain an important component of transnational entrepreneurship, though the degree of their significance depends on specific business sectors and the background of the entrepreneurs.

Familism

In his seminal essay, Wong Siu-lun (1985) declares that "[t]he core of Chinese economic organization is familism." Here, we argue that business familism and its underpinning element—Chinese culture—do not disappear with the emergence of the knowledge-based economy and still provide a useful support system in the transnational arena. To be sure, the families of Chinese new migrants have been socially constructed and strengthened by "transnationalism, which reproduced the 'reality' of family solidarity through mundane everyday life activities acted out across borders" (Chan and Seet 2003).

In his speech at the Singapore Management University in October 2003, Lan Weiguang remarked that in order to venture into the China market, one needed to have a deep understanding of Chinese culture: "This is important mainly because Confucian ideas still have a great impact upon Chinese ways of thinking." As a matter of fact, his initial impulse to venture into some form of private business prior to coming to Singapore was out of family obligation—being the eldest son of five siblings, he had to take good care of them when their father passed away. "A few hours before he died, he spoke to me about many things. He told me [that] he didn't like this world as life was hard," Lan once recalled tearfully about the final hours of his father. "But he didn't want to die yet because my siblings were still young. He had not fulfilled his fatherly responsibilities ... I promised him that I'd look after the family." After his father passed away, Lan gathered all his savings of around 3,000 yuan to give to his family and found a part-time job to earn more money (*Straits Times,* June 8, 2003; *Xiamen Wanbao*, November 22, 2003).

Familism is manifested not only in the sentiment, but more importantly, in the structure of his firm, which is family-controlled. Sinomem's top management team consists of five persons, reflecting a mixture of familism, social networking, and transnationalism. As the founder and managing director of the Group, Lan controls 67.5 percent of its stock, and is "responsible for setting strategic directions for the Group and oversees the overall management and operations; he also spearheads and supervises all R&D activities." His wife, Chen Ni, who holds a diploma in Biology from Ningde Teachers' College as well as an MBA from Shanghai Jiao Tong University, controls 7.5 percent of the stock. She is the "co-founder and Executive Director, responsible for the overall administration and day-to-day management functions of the Group." Together with her husband, she is also on the five-person board of directors. Her role as women in business, indeed, represents a major departure from the traditional pattern of Chinese business familism, whereby as a rule female members of the family do not directly control the business. As part of the restructuring effort in 2000, Lan Weiguang hired a non-family member for the CEO position. This person left the firm after just six months, apparently an outcome of internal disagreements. Now the general manager is Lan's younger brother, Lan Xinguang, who has an accounting diploma from the Fujian Fisheries Administrative School. He is responsible for "the management and day-to-day operations of the group activities in China." In an interview on Chinese national television, while regretting not having a CEO from outside the family, Lan Weiguang made it clear that the CEO he was looking for should have three characteristics: professional integrity; managerial capacities; and identifying with his company's existing corporate culture and enhancing it further.[10]

Networks

Various forms of network—personal, institutional, and social—remain an important source of Sino-Singaporean entrepreneurship. This is a continuation of the importance of networking in Chinese business (e.g. Hamilton 1996), though the current practice is characterized by a significantly greater degree of transnationality. Take the example of Lin Yucheng: his relationship with Sinopec began in the late 1990s when he was still a managing director of NOVO EST. Lin volunteered to be a tour guide for a group of high-level managers from Sinopec who were visiting Singapore in 1997. They left with good impressions of his personality and technological capacity and subsequently initiated a series of cooperative projects. "It is more important to know how to behave with propriety (*zuo ren*) than how to do business," recalled Lin:

> I had no intention of doing business with them when we first met, nor did I imagine that I would have an inseparable relationship with Sinopec later. I just thought that they were guests from afar and I should be doing my best as host. It was by chance that I came to know that they were looking for the applied technology in petrochemical products and environmental solutions; this happened to have been a subject of my research and practice for over 20 years.

One can safely assume that without this initial harmonious personal connection, subsequent collaborations could not have been materialized. Unlike traditional personal networking, the continuation of sustainable business networks today has to be built upon core competence, especially for a technology-driven firm like Lin's UE. He frankly acknowledges that "in order to establish long-term relationships, it is not enough to rely merely on *renqing* [personal feelings], we must be at the technological cutting-edge and have a core group of top-notch scientists" (*Lianhe Zaobao*, March 13, 2004).

In addition to using the family network as the core of his business organization, Lan Weguang relies on a modern form of networking that is based upon alumni connections. Apart from his spouse and his brothers in the top management team, the only non-family member is Cao Min Jie, a senior manager, who is responsible for research and development activities, process development and application studies. Cao was a colleague of Lan at Jimei University. He also received a transnational education: a bachelor's degree in food engineering from Shanghai Fisheries University, a master's in food science and a Ph.D. in biotechnology from Nagasaki University, and post-doctorial training at the National University of Singapore. One of the five directors, Robin Lin Lu Ping, is also Lan's college classmate who also holds a B.Sc. in Chemistry from Xiamen University. Lin is currently the finance and tax manager at the John Deere (China) company, and has extensive transnational working experience in various key finance positions such as the Banca Commerciale Italiana, the Royal Bank of Canada, the Dell Computer Corporation in China, and the Xiamen Paktank Co. Finally Lin has an MBA from Queens University and an M.A. in economics from the University of Western Ontario.

As to the patterns of institutionalized social networking that involve various types of Chinese associations such as locality- and occupation-based associations (cf. Liu 1998; 2001), these do not appear to be significant for technopreneurs, but they are essential for brokerage entrepreneurs. Lan Weiguang, for instance, is a member of the Singapore Chinese Chamber of Commerce, arguably the single most important business organization in the country. As a member of the Xiamen University Alumni Association in Singapore, he has replaced the entrepreneurs of the older generation as the main patron. There is no evidence of his participation in any locality or dialect associations. Both Lin Yucheng and Shi Xu, on the other hand, are vice presidents of Huayuan Association, which serves as one of the platforms from which business information is disseminated, especially in the early stage.

For brokerage entrepreneurs, however, social networking through various organized forms is essential. For one thing, their brokerage activities need to be built upon all kinds of connections in both Singapore and China. Wang Quancheng, for instance, is the founder of the Huayuan Association, which has sponsored a series of activities such as investment talks, business trips, and hosting Chinese entrepreneurs. Through these activities Wang could accumulate social capital which may not be easily obtained by an entrepreneur with limited financial capital in the traditional line of business (construction): he got to meet personally with influential people like Lee Hsien Loong, Zhang Jiuhuan, Chinese ambassador to Singapore, and local leaders in Fujian province. These connections and their associated prestige could be valuable asset for his investment in his hometown of Anxi.

In a similar vein, Du Zhiqiang, whose agency is mainly in the line of recruiting students, laborers, prospective immigrants, and investors from China, the building of a social network has become an indispensable asset. To overcome his minority status within the Chinese community in Singapore (the ancestors of the majority of the Chinese were from Fujian and Guangdong, while Du is from Sichuan, a traditionally under-represented province but increasingly becoming a more popular source of emigration), Du founded the Tianfu Hometown Association (Tianfu is an alias of Sichuan Province) in 1999. Just like the Huayuan Association, the Tianfu Hometown Association has gone beyond the age-old principles of social classifications in Chinese associations: they are not mainly based upon locality, dialect, or kinship ties, but more inclusively on ethnicity and collegiality in general. While the Huanyuan Association is open to all new Chinese migrants who have become permanent residents or citizens of Singapore, the Tianfu Hometown Association's membership (of nearly 1,000) is composed of those who were born in Sichuan and/or used to study and work there. The latter also enlists members of the Singapore parliament and the vice governor of the Sichuan province as advisers. In 2006, the organization was renamed the Tianfu Association, thus downplaying its locality linkage. A chamber of commerce was established in October 2006 within the association, aiming to attract businesspeople in Singapore as well as those originating from other regions of China. The Tianfu Association signed an agreement in July 2007 with two other established locality associations in

Singapore to promote cooperation in the areas of trade, education, and culture, especially among different generations of Chinese in Singapore (*Lianhe Zaobao*, December 26, 2006; July 13, 2007).

Transnational management

One of the major characteristics of Sino-Singaporean transnational entrepreneurs is the transnational composition of their top management teams, whose members include those who were born either in Singapore or China, well educated in multicultural environments, and with substantial working experience in transnational corporations. These characteristics significantly bolster their transnational outlook.

Take the example of Sinomem. One of the five members of its top management team is Choo Beng Lor, the financial controller, who oversees the finance department and manages all financial functions within the group. He holds a bachelor of accountancy degree from Nanyang Technological University and has worked for six years as an auditor with Deloitte and Touche Singapore, a multinational corporation. The other two directors are Teng Cheong Kwee amd Hee Theng Fong. Teng was a graduate of the University of Newcastle in Australia and an Executive Director of Pheim Asset Management, a fund management company in Singapore. He was previously an executive vice president at the Singapore Exchange, where he was in charge of the review of listings, member broker supervision and investigation, and market surveillance. On the other hand, Hee, who obtained a LLB from the University of Singapore in 1979, is concurrently the managing partner of law firm Hee Theng Fong & Co., legal advisor to several organizations, and director of several listed companies.

The composition of top management at Lin Yucheng's UE is also transnational. It was jointly founded with Goh Ching Wah, a Singaporean who is president and executive director of the Internet Technology Group (ITG), listed in SXG, as well as deputy chairman of Ossia International Limited and international chairman of the Rebel Sport Limited, a listed company in Australia. He and his brothers (Messrs. Goh Ching Lai and Goh Ching Huat) co-founded World of Sports and Ossia International Limited ("Ossia"). According to UE's IPO prospectus, ITG controls UE's 300,000 shares and Goh Ching Wah is an executive director. His brothers and sister, Goh Ching Huat, Goh Ching Lai, and Goh Lee Choo, each control 500,000 shares and are non-executive directors of UE (*Lianhe Zaobao*, April 21, 2004).

The top management of Shi Xu's Nanofilm Technologies is also composed of people with transnational backgrounds. Cheah Li Kang, its CTO, holds a B.Sc. in engineering and a Ph.D. from NTU, where Shi had taught for seven years before founding Nanofilm. Cheah was previously the centre manager of advanced substrate and bombardment technologies at the Gintic Institute of Manufacturing Technology. Eugene Chiang, the vice president in Sales and Coating Services, is "a promising entrepreneur who started his business abroad more than 10 years ago in Thailand at the early age of 25." Wei Hao, general manager in Design and Engineering, received his Ph.D. in technology from Massey University in New Zealand and has held senior positions at Westinghouse, International Power Technologies, the Beijing Institute of Communications, and Signal Design. Finally, Shen Chunhui, general manager in Production and Logistics, was previously a lecturer in Jiao Tong University in Shanghai and worked previously at Seagate and Conner Peripherals.

As illustrated elsewhere (Dosi et al. 1998), knowledge is influenced by processed information, but it also involves insight and creativity. Vision is the dominant set of beliefs a firm has about its internal circumstances and external environment. In the meantime, interlocking directorates play an important role in corporate knowledge transfer, and the transnational composition of these new enterprises is beneficial to their rapid growth and expansion into the transnational market (O'Hagan and Green 2004). It is the combination of vision, transnational knowledge, and technological advantage that give an edge to the Sino-Singaporean entrepreneurs, who are also encouraged by an environment that is conducive to state–network interactions. Therefore, the integration of transnational knowledge, technology, and networks in the transnational arena is an emerging area that calls for greater attention to our empirical understanding of Chinese entrepreneurship, as well as its reconceptualization.

Concluding remarks

What was happening in the United States in the 1980s, wrote Peter Drucker, was "a profound shift from a 'managerial' to an 'entrepreneurial' economy." He contends that what made possible the emergence of the entrepreneurial economy in America were the new applications of management, especially systematic innovation in the "search for and the exploitation of new opportunities for satisfying human wants and human needs" (Drucker 1999:13). The long march toward the same entrepreneurial economy has been under way in Singapore (and to some extent, in China as well), and the cases illustrated above are just some illuminating examples of how a specific segment of Chinese entrepreneurs has systematically and innovatively introduced "new combinations" for new products, new methods of production, and new markets. In the following discussion, I will provide a few preliminary observations about the Sino-Singaporean entrepreneurs.

First, being bi-cultural, bilingual, and making a living through *continuous regular contact across national borders*, these entrepreneurs are transnationalists in the truest sense of transnationalism. After completing their education in a transnational and multicultural setting, our entrepreneurs further expanded their horizons through working in a transnational environment, either in TNCs or through cross-border activities. Their economic activities constantly traverse between multiple locations. Lan, for example, spends one third of his time in Xiamen, Singapore, and elsewhere. He once remarked in 2003 that the reason why he set up businesses in China was because of his intention to "do something for my country [China] with my capacities" (*Guangming Ribao*, February 6, 2003), even though he had become a Singapore citizen a few years earlier. Ke Hongjing, another China-born entrepreneur involved in importing and exporting in Singapore, remarks that whenever he goes to China on a business trip, he is always eager to return "home"—Singapore (*Lianhe Zaobao*, December 17, 2003). These people are the prototypes of what I called "transnational Chinese" (Liu 2002), and their transnational experiences and knowledge—and the mentality of being "both here and there at the same time"—have significantly shaped their business strategies and patterns of alliance in the commercial world.

Second, it is precisely this transnationality that has become a defining characteristic of Sino-Singaporean entrepreneurs. Unlike other types of transnational entrepreneur who first began their businesses in a specific nation before venturing overseas, our entrepreneurs have been transnational from the inception of their business. This transnationality is also embedded in the internal structure of their companies. Many of them started their business with the aid of transnational knowledge and experiences which gave them confidence and necessary connections. Their companies are run by people with global outlooks/experiences and aim at reaching a transnational market. The spatial and strategic division of labor in Singapore and China has been undertaken within this framework, whereby Singapore serves as the source of finance and technological innovation and China constitutes the key manufacturing base and market outlet. The windfalls generated through this transnational arrangement of business activities have been significant. Indeed, in comparison with locally born technopreneurs in the same business who, however, lack substantial transnational experience and knowledge (see Milton-Smith et al. 1999 for illustrative examples), Sino-Singaporean technopreneurs have consistently out-performed their local counterparts and become successful within a considerably shorter period of time. As a testament to the Weberian conception of entrepreneur as agent of change, Sino-Singaporean entrepreneurs generate change by involving a collection of transnational actors and transforming the local environment in the two geographical domains. They are indeed a new breed of entrepreneur in an increasingly globalizing Asia-Pacific region.

Finally, the characteristics of immigrant transnational entrepreneurship have to be understood in their changing interactions with the state and network. The state has actively participated in the process of transnational entrepreneurial economy by formulating accommodating and conducive policies and being directly involved in the business transactions. As a vertically constructed hierarchy and multilayered entity, the state interacts closely with the horizontally structured transnational networks. Therefore, the possibilities of new hybridizations—between culture and institution, between national and transnational, between the state and network, and between familism and modern management—need to be given sharper focuses in our search for a new breed of Chinese entrepreneur in a rapidly changing Asia-Pacific setting. All these interactions, in the final analysis, take place amidst the increasing pace of transnational flows of knowledge and population, where technological advancement becomes another key dynamic in the transformation of Chinese business and entrepreneurship in contemporary Asia and beyond.

Notes

1 Research for this paper was partly funded by the Toyota Foundation, for the project on "Modern Asian Knowledge Networks," which is gratefully acknowledged.
2 Take the example of the National University of Singapore: Among its 1,671 full-time teaching faculty members in 2001, 887 (53 percent) were Singapore citizens and the remaining 784 (47 percent) were foreigners, of whom 110 (14 percent) were PRC citizens (the majority of whom were permanent residents of Singapore). Among the university's 842 full-time researchers, only 221 (26 percent) were Singapore citizens, and 621 (73.7 percent) were foreigners, with those from the PRC numbering 329 (53 percent). See *National University of Singapore Annual Report 2001* for details (www.nus.edu.sg/annualreport/2001/appendix.pdf).
3 *Luoye guigen*, "fallen leaves return to their roots," refers to those Chinese who remain loyal to their native places and wish (usually in vain) to return to the homeland; and *luodi shenggen*, "falling to the ground and striking root," refers to an assimilation project, which includes permanent settlement abroad and the renunciation of Chinese citizenship.
4 Unless otherwise specified, the material concerning the life and business of Sino-Singaporean entrepreneurs has been drawn from various primary sources, including Chinese and/or English interviews and company reports that are either published or broadcast in China and Singapore.
5 A membrane is a barrier that permits the separation of the different components of a pressurized fluid stream. By forcing a fluid through a membrane, it is possible to separate, concentrate, and purify the fluid.
6 The program provides a ranking of leading technology companies that have achieved an average revenue growth rate of 385 percent over three years across the Asia-Pacific region.
7 The author's personal interview with Shi Xu (Singapore, 2005). Detailed rankings can be found at www.nanofilm.com.sg/.
8 Organized by the Economic Development Board, the Global Entrepolis @ Singapore is

> a world premier event for enterprise, innovation, and technology. More than just an event, it is a unique marketplace where deals are made, funds are raised, creative ideas are exchanged, new innovative enterprises and partnerships are forged. A key highlight is the Enterprise Exchange exposition where the latest technology and innovations are displayed and traded. The event is also specially designed to facilitate enterprises, both big and small, to network, interact, and create business opportunities with some of the world's most successful and innovative companies and individuals.
> (*Lianhe Zaobao*, September 3, 2003)

More than 1,000 entrepreneurs from China participated in this event which attracted over 10,000 entrepreneurs from the world.

9 See www.cvcht.com/wenzhang/list.asp?id=696 for details.
10 See www.cctv.com/lm/123/19/59608.html for details.

References

Aldrich, H. and Waldinger, R. (1990) "Ethnicity and Entrepreneurship," *Annual Review of Sociology* 16:111–35.

Basch, L. G., Schillier, N. G., and Blanc-Szanton, C. (1994) *Nations Unbound: Transnational Projects, Post-colonial Predicaments, and De-terrirorialized Nation-States*, Langhorne, PA: Gordon and Breach.

Berge, B. (1991) "The Culture of Modern Entrepreneurship," in B. Berge (ed.) *The Culture of Entrepreneurship*, San Francisco, CA: Institute for Contemporary Studies.

Casson, M. (2003) *The Entrepreneur: An Economic Theory*, 2nd edition, Cheltenham, U.K.: Edward Elgar.

Chan, K. B. (ed.) (2000) *Chinese Business Networks: State, Economy and Culture*, Singapore: Prentice Hall.

Chan, K. B. and Chiang, C. N. (1994) *Stepping Out: The Making of Chinese Entrepreneurs*, Singapore: Prentice Hall.

Chan, K. B. and Seet, S. C. (2003) "Migrant Family Drama Revisited: Mainland Chinese Immigrants in Singapore," *Sojourn* 18:171–200.

Dosi, G., Teece, D. J., and Chytry, J. (eds.) (1998) *Technology, Organization, and Competitiveness: Perspectives on Industrial and Corporate Change*, New York: Oxford University Press.

Drucker, P. (1999) *Innovation and Entrepreneurship: Practice and Principles*, 2nd edition, Oxford: Butterworth Heinemann.

Fong, E. and Luk, C. (eds.) (2007) *Chinese Ethnic Business: Global and Local Perspectives*, London: Routledge.

Gomez, E. T. (2004) "Intra-Ethnic Cooperation in Transnational Perspective: Malaysian Chinese Investments in the United Kingdoms," in E. T. Gomez and H. H. M. Hsiao (eds.) *Chinese Enterprise, Transnationalism, and Identity*, London: RoutledgeCurzon.

Gomez, E. T. and Hsiao, H. H. M. (eds.) (2001) *Chinese Business in South-East Asia: Contesting Cultural Explanations, Researching Entrepreneurship*, Richmond, Surrey, U.K.: Curzon Press.

——(2004) *Chinese Enterprise, Transnationalism, and Identity*, London: Routledge-Curzon.

Hamilton, G. (ed.) (1996) *Asian Business Networks*, Berlin: de Gruyter.

Hawes, G. and Liu, H. (1993) "Explaining the Dynamics of the Southeast Asian Political Economy: State, Society and the Search for Economic Growth," *World Politics* 45:629–60.

Lee, H. L. (1989) "Let Us Welcome Immigrants," *A Bimonthly Selection of Ministerial Speeches*, vol. 13, no. 4 (Information Division, Ministry of Communications and Information, Singapore), July-August, pp. 76–78.

Leong, C. T. (2003) "From a Few Dollars to the Ring of $100m," *Straits Times*, June 8.

Liu, H. (1998) "Old Linkages, New Networks: The Globalization of Overseas Chinese Voluntary Associations and Its Implications," *The China Quarterly* 155: 582–609.

——(2001) "Social Capital and Business Networking: A Case Study of Modern Chinese Transnationalism," *Southeast Asian Studies (Tonan Ajia Kenkyu)* 39:357–81.

——(2002) "Transnational Chinese: Empirical Analyses and Theoretical Reformulations" (in Chinese), *21st Century*, June, pp. 108–21.

——(2005a) "Explaining the Dynamics of Chinese Migration since 1980: A Historical and Demographical Perspective," *Journal of Oriental Studies* 39:92–110.

——(2005b) "New Migrants and the Revival of Overseas Chinese Nationalism," *Journal of Contemporary China* 14:291–316.

——(2006) "Introduction: Toward a Multi-dimensional Exploration of the Chinese Overseas," in H. Liu (ed.) *The Chinese Overseas, vol. 1: Conceptualizing and Historicizing Chinese International Migration*, London and New York: Routledge.

Liu, H. and Wong, S. K. (2004) *Singapore Chinese Society in Transition: Business, Politics and Socio-economic Change, 1945–1965*, New York: Peter Lang Publishing.

Mackie, J. (1992) "Overseas Chinese Entrepreneurship," *Asian-Pacific Economic Literature* 6:41–64.

Menkhoff, T. and Gerke, S. (eds.) (2002) *Chinese Entrepreneurship and Asian Business Networks*, London: RoutledgeCurzon.

Milton-Smith, J., Lee, R., Chan, Y. L., and Tang, K. F. (1999) *The Making of a Technopreneur*, Singapore: ITE Alumni Association.

North, D. (1990) *Institutions, Institutional Change and Economic Performance*, Cambridge: Cambridge University Press.

O'Hagan, S. B. and Green, M. B. (2004) "Corporate Knowledge Transfer via Interlocking Directorates: A Network Analysis Approach," *Geoforum* 35:127–39.

Pek, T. G. (2003) "Cover Story: Taking Competition in Its Stride," *The Edge Singapore*, 26 May.

Portes, A., Guarnizo, L. E., and Landolt, P. (1999) "The Study of Transnationalism: Pitfalls and Promise of an Emergent Research Field," *Ethnic and Racial Studies* 22:217–37.

Portes, A., Haller, W., and Guarnizo, L. E. (2002) "Transnational Entrepreneurs: An Alternative Form of Immigrant Economic Adaptation," *American Sociological Review* 67:278–98.

Schumpeter, J. A. (1961) *The Theory of Economic Development: An Inquiry into Profits, Capital, Credit, Interest, and the Business Cycle*, Cambridge, MA: Harvard University Press.

Swedberg, R. (2000) "The Social Science View of Entrepreneurship: Introduction and Practical Applications," in R. Swedberg (ed.) *Entrepreneurship: The Social Science View*, Oxford: Oxford University Press.

Thornton, P. H. (1999) "The Sociology of Entrepreneurship," *Annual Review of Sociology* 25:19–46.

Thuno, M. (2001) "Reaching Out and Incorporating Chinese Overseas: The Transterritorial Scope of the PRC by the End of the 20th Century," *The China Quarterly* 168:910–29.

Waldinger, R. and Fitzgerald, D. (2004) "Transnationalism in Question," *American Journal of Sociology* 109:1177–95.

Wang, G. W. (2004) "New Migrants: How New? Why New?" in G. Benton and H. Liu (eds.) *Diasporic Chinese Ventures: The Life and Work of Wang Gungwu*, London: RoutledgeCurzon.

Wong, S. L. (1985) "The Chinese Family Firm: a Model," *British Journal of Sociology* 36:58–72.

Yeung, H. W. C. (2002) "Entrepreneurship in International Business: An Institutional Perspective," *Asia Pacific Journal of Management* 19:29–61.

——(2004) *Chinese Capitalism in a Global Era: Towards Hybrid Capitalism,* London and New York: Routledge.

Yeung, H. W. C. and Olds, C. (eds.) (2000) *Globalisation of Chinese Firms*, London: Macmillan.

Zheng, Y. N. (2004) *Globalization and State Transformation in China*, Cambridge: Cambridge University Press.

7 Transforming *guanxi* networks

Taiwanese enterprises' production networks in Thailand and Vietnam

Dung-Sheng Chen, Sue-Ching Jou, and Hsin-Huang Michael Hsiao

Introduction

Research on Chinese capital in foreign investment and overseas economic organizations can be roughly divided into two paradigms. The first one is an economic and Western-centric approach that emphasizes the importance of incentive mechanisms in determining how and why enterprises divest investments from their own developing countries into other developing countries. The second one is the social embeddedness approach. The latter stresses that the decision-making and organizational structures of Chinese companies engaging in foreign investment are influenced by their local cultural, social, and political contexts (Biggart and Hamilton 1997; Redding 1990; Yeung 1997; 1998). Economic profits are only contingent, but not determining, factors for Chinese enterprises to practice foreign investment and organize their production structures. Some even push their arguments further and suggest that network relations based on personal relationships are causal mechanisms of transnational economic operations for Chinese enterprises (Yeung 1997:4–5).

The economic approach treats the behavior of economic organizations operating in different countries as essentially the same. It fails to consider how particular cultural traditions and social institutions can influence companies' decision-making and organizational structures. On the other hand, although the social embeddedness approach is able to pinpoint unnecessary and unrealistic constraints of the economic paradigm, it over-emphasizes the impact of local particularities and downplays the structural embeddedness of these companies in the global economic and institutional contexts. We are inclined to take a middle-of-the-road approach and are interested in investigating why some global conditions *do* activate local mechanisms such as personal relationships, while others are able to operate closer to the principles of economic efficiency. We also believe that the globalization process has strongly infiltrated numerous institutional arrangements, including the diffusion of management education and the competitive structures between transnational companies. Consequently, such deep interpenetration should result in organizational and network isomorphism, that is, a tendency toward homogenization rather than differentiation, even though the actual extent of such development may vary across countries. At the same time, we are keenly aware that the presence of organizational and network isomorphism does not and cannot completely eliminate local particularities.

Based on the above arguments, this chapter seeks to highlight how and why the mechanisms of transnational operation for Chinese companies over time are more prone to develop hybrid or even formal mechanisms rather than a continuation of the initial person-oriented or network-oriented mechanisms. To paraphrase our central argument, we believe that personal relationships among overseas Chinese indeed provide important assets for Taiwanese companies in Southeast Asia, as one form of Chinese business arrangement, to exercise their cross-border investments and establish their production organizations at the initial stage. However, as time unfolds, many of these Taiwanese companies that are built with specific ethnic connections should gradually utilize, either voluntarily or involuntarily, other mechanisms to coordinate their collaborative production networks as they face rapid changes in the global economic and institutional environments.

In short, we believe that it is only through the adoption of a historical and dynamic approach that we can specify how local and global factors affect the operation of overseas Chinese businesses during different periods of organizational development. Furthermore, no singular causal mechanism among Chinese companies, such as personal relationships, should dominate transnational economic activities either universally or trans-historically.

Literature review

The most popular understanding of Chinese production networks is their overt reliance on personal relationships in general or overseas Chinese ethnic connections in particular. According to this perspective, owing to the prevalence of person-oriented norms in Chinese society, huge potential benefits exist for business leaders if and only if they know how to utilize family ties, friendships, or common local origins effectively to establish business relationships. Although this cultural explanation highlights the particularity of Chinese capitalism, it has been subjected to challenges from at least three different theoretical approaches.

The first one is the thesis of organizational imperatives. The thesis argues that the most important objective for an organization or a production network is survival. Organizational leaders will use all means, including personal relationships, to fulfill this objective. Therefore, the personal relationship is just one major instrument for maintaining business operations, a practice that is not unique to any (Chinese included) business community. If we want to explain why Chinese enterprises are more dependent on personal relationships, we should investigate the specific benefits these relationships can bring to them. Viewed under this light, the thesis construes that it is organizational imperatives that shape the practices and behaviors of Chinese business owners, rather than unique Chinese cultural norms and values (Chang and Tam 2004). Furthermore, when new contingent factors emerge in the market, personal relationships tend to be replaced or incorporated by other coordination mechanisms, resulting in network dynamics. For instance, economic globalization has enabled instant exchanges of information, market fluctuations, and transactions among various business partners in the global commodity chain. As economic organizations envisage frequent and new challenges and demands from their customers, it becomes necessary for the production networks to adjust their organizational strategies and structures accordingly. Consequently, competition acts as a strong selective force to settle on the most fitted or adapted organizational form to accommodate the turbulent external environment, as would have been predicted by the population ecology model as well (Hannen and Freeman 1977).

The second perspective focuses specifically on the homogenizing influences of globalization. Economic globalization tends to decrease differences among various economic entities formed by different business cultural systems, market barriers, and policy systems. Its influences can be witnessed in several important areas. First, the establishment of global economic organizations, such as the World Trade Organization, has contributed to the formation of comparable institutional environments and structures for enterprises to facilitate global cooperation and competition. Second, the increase of international division of labor has forced many business organizations to broaden their scope from local to global markets. To enhance global competitiveness, they have to follow standard procedures specified by independent standards organizations, such as the International Organization for Standardization (ISO), to fulfill basic demands from multinational buyers. These similarities in economic institutions tend to stimulate further isomorphism of business organizations, as proposed by neo-institutional theorists (DiMaggio and Powell 1983; Meyer and Rowan 1977). In his empirical study on Hong Kong business enterprises, Wong (2004:65) argued that having been operated in global institutional environments, Hong Kong enterprises either copy or learn the organizational arrangements of successful companies locally and elsewhere in order to gain organizational legitimacy. The thesis of institutional isomorphism has correctly pointed out that the increasing similarity of the global institutional environment gradually produces many common characteristics in business organizations and networks for companies in different countries.

Supporters of the social embeddedness approach, however, criticize these strong globalization theories for their failure to acknowledge the effects of local cultural and social characteristics on business networks (Crawford 2000:69–86; Yeung 1997). They instead emphasize how the cultural tradition of Chinese societies facilitates the formation of trust among business partners and the development of organizational networks. Chinese culture is one of the major factors that facilitate the success of many Chinese enterprises under the world economy. This argument, while appealing, can be problematic for the following two reasons. First, supporters of the social embeddedness approach overlook that most Chinese firms are embedded in the global economic milieu as well, which would subject them to experience the organizational shift from a personal, relational, or informal base to a more formal one. Under this transformative process, Chinese enterprises would share similar characteristics with their non-Chinese counterparts over time, although the former may still be able to uphold certain particularities or idiosyncrasies. Second, while the social embeddedness approach may correctly highlight the contributions of local cultural or social characteristics to ensure the survival of economic organizations, it nonetheless fails to identify changes in the efficiency boundaries of the same local factors in the emergence of new economic structures, institutional environments, and organizational characteristics. It is only through the adoption of an historical comparative perspective that one can envision clearly how and why Chinese enterprises and their economic networks have to combine personal relationships and other governance mechanisms in order to survive economically.

In an increasingly homogeneous and constraining institutional and competitive environment, we believe that businessmen are certainly able to exercise freedom and select strategies, within specific boundary conditions of course, in order to better prepare themselves for new opportunities and economic survival. The spectrum of strategic choices available for these leaders is undoubtedly affected by the immediate environmental conditions, as well as the learning and educational processes of the owners themselves. With regard to the latter, the better educated the owners are (especially from Western-style institutions), the more likely they will be able to adopt management strategies other than those of traditional or family businesses. In addition, increasing interaction between Chinese and Western entrepreneurs has facilitated the diffusion and learning of Western business strategies. As a result, we postulate that the growing exposure of Chinese entrepreneurs to non-family business styles and practices would contribute to the transformation of personal networking into other patterns of networking in Chinese collaborative production structures.

Although they differ in direction and emphasis, the above theses reveal why conventional cultural explanations of Chinese capitalism and Chinese production networks fail to incorporate significant impacts of macroeconomic and institutional conditions on the development of Chinese economic organizations. For the purpose of economic survival, Chinese business organizations must adjust themselves to external requirements in order to gain competitive advantage and legitimacy in the global economy. It is therefore arguable that under globalization, even though the traditional Chinese cultural system may still be important in some areas, its influence on business activities should be weaker than before. We would argue further that these global structuring processes of Chinese business organizations and networks may even be the deliberate outcomes or intentional plans of (new) business leaders, particularly among those second- and third-generation entrepreneurs who received non-traditional but formal/Western educational and business training experience.

Using Taiwanese production networks in Thailand and Vietnam as illustrative case studies, this chapter seeks to demonstrate how those pre-existing networking mechanisms of Chinese production networks formed during the early stage of transnational investment have subsequently undergone rapid transformation in the global economic system. Contrary to predictions derived from the cultural perspective, we argue that the competitive global market forced Taiwanese businessmen to implement quasi-hierarchical mechanisms rather than ethnic or personal connections to improve the efficiency and productivity of their production systems. As a result, the networking principles have now shifted from personal relationships into various hybrid patterns.

Data and research method

The case studies are drawn from our multi-year research project on transnational production networks and the co-ethnic business relationships of Taiwanese enterprises in Southeast Asia and China since 1998. Our data collection concentrates mainly on in-depth personal interviews, with occasional supplementary information from various secondary sources. Our targeted interviewees are mostly high-ranking managers of Taiwanese enterprises with investments in Southeast Asia and China. Before conducting the in-depth interviews, we systematically analyzed the background of the companies involved, including their organizational structures, production methods, and foreign investment strategies. The project involves an historical study of the foreign investment patterns of each company as well. We obtained such information from company annual reports as well as various secondary sources such as magazines, newspapers, and scholarly publications. In order to solicit detailed information about the transnational activities of these companies, we deliberately sampled interviewees who were senior administrative/managerial staff in charge of the planning of foreign investments or operating overseas subsidiaries. For companies that are headquartered in Taiwan, we conducted interviews both in Taiwan and the host countries to cross-validate information from different sources. Information on transnational strategies and intra-firm coordination arrangements was usually obtained from interviews conducted at their headquarters. On the other hand, specific information on how these companies developed factories and enterprises abroad was obtained from executives based in Thailand and Vietnam.

A fundamental requirement of network research is to collect information on *all* participants within the network. This criterion, however, is very difficult to fulfill empirically. In this study, we first selected different types of Taiwanese firms and then collected data on both the focal companies in the network and their collaborative suppliers. Because of personnel and resource constraints, we were unable to interview all executives and owners of companies involved in the production network. We also encountered reluctance in some focal companies to provide a complete list of their suppliers, for business and confidential reasons. To partially overcome this limitation, we systematically collected secondary data, as detailed as possible, to supplement the missing links.

Findings

Network transformation

Based on the evidence compiled from our fieldwork on Taiwan enterprise networks in Southeast Asia, we can indeed conclude that the production networks have been transformed from those based on personal ties to more formalized mechanisms in the midst of cut-throat competition in the global market. In the following section, we select a few cases of Taiwanese production networks in Thailand and Vietnam and analyze their trajectories of network transformation as evidence to support our key argument.

Our first example is the production network led by Kinpo Inc., a major Taiwanese electronic manufacturing company in Thailand.[1] Similar to the steps taken by other electronic original equipment manufacturers (OEMs) in Taiwan, Kinpo implemented foreign direct investment (FDI) in Thailand in the early 1990s when the company was seeking ways to improve its profit margins amid tremendous pressure from global competitors and, perhaps more importantly, with the consent of their business partners, namely international trading companies and multinational firms in the West. Indeed, the final choice of FDI locations was not an independent one. Rather, it was dictated and directed by their Western counterparts. Their position as subcontractors and OEMs has rendered their role in FDI rather passive. This eventually led to the "wholesale" relocation of their production networks elsewhere (Chen 1998:40–41).

Given that the pressure to provide low-price and high-quality products is enormous, almost immediately after the completion of FDI and when production began, the safest and risk-averse strategy for Kinpo is to bring along their most trusted overseas partners. At the initial stage of its foreign direct investment in Thailand, Cal-Comp Electronics, as the leader of the production network, invited its long-term partners to establish overseas plants jointly to assure an efficient supply of high-quality parts. Seven important suppliers came along with Cal-Comp to Thailand in the early 1990s. It is evident here that trust and free communication generated by strong ethnic ties helped the successful extension of the production network to overseas manufacturing sites. The strategy also alleviated many difficulties commonly encountered during the start-up stage.

Currently, Cal-Comp Electronics has six manufacturing plants in Thailand. When the company began its expansion to build its fourth and fifth factories, it reserved several production sites within the factory premises for its collaborative partners. In other words, these collaborative suppliers were asked to implement in-house manufacturing for the dominant leader of the production network. As tenants, they also had to pay rent to the core company for using manufacturing space and utilities (Cal-Comp:5; Jet-Thai:11–12; Jet:6; Yuan-Deng:2).[2] We call this new collaborative model an "in-house production network." Its sole purpose is to minimize costs and achieve efficiency in the production process by eliminating all unnecessary intermediaries and logistic arrangements.

Under this arrangement, the focal company of the network saves both time and money in the transportation of parts because the suppliers provide the materials in-house and there is no physical distance separating different stages of the production process. Since the parts are stocked at the suppliers' production site, the storage cost is paid entirely by the suppliers rather than by the focal company. Moreover, the focal company is able to change its procurement orders when necessary. This guarantees that orders will always be fulfilled on time (Yuan-Deng:5). This in-house model is a realization of the just-in-time (JIT) collaborative system to achieve maximum production capacity. The development of such a physical production arrangement ensures that the dominant actor in the network can respond to price fluctuations and competition more efficiently and flexibly in the electronic devices market. The production processes and quantity of parts produced by the suppliers can be monitored by the focal company more transparently under this in-house model. The suppliers not only have to manage the delivery of parts on time with no excuses, but they also have to adjust production whenever there are changes in quantity or cancellation of orders, without complaint.

When we examine the pattern of personal relationships within the in-house model, we find that the governance structure of the collaborative relationships, in the case of Cal-Comp, has changed to exhibit the following characteristics. First, the focal company exercises management authority over the suppliers even though the former does not hold any ownership of the latter. Through their participation, the suppliers essentially lose or give up their limited negotiation capability to the focal company and merely act as "divisions" within the factory system of the focal company. The change in the physical arrangements of the collaborative production system has not only increased their geographical proximity, but it has also legitimized an authoritative pattern of coordination. In short, the new arrangement further enhances existing asymmetrical collaborative relationships of the production network.

Second, when the suppliers move their production lines to within the focal company's factory, they risk forgoing opportunities to gain parts orders from other leading manufacturing companies. and even jeopardizing any pre-existing collaborative relationships with other suppliers. For these in-house suppliers, their first priority now is to fulfill various requests from the core actor of the production network. Therefore, they should have little capacity left to match the demand from other customers. In the case of core companies from different production systems, their major concern would be the unnecessary disclosure of significant product information and trade secrets to their competitors and the possible slow response in production from these in-house suppliers. Therefore, they would be very reluctant to offer orders to these "exclusive" suppliers.

Of course, the creation and the maintenance of the in-house pattern to maximize efficiency in the production network are viable only when the focal company experiences continuous growth (Yuan-Deng:6). This, in turn, is contingent upon the growth prospects of the global electronic market. In other words, it is only under the condition of growing demand that the core actor of the production network can provide sufficient business to their in-house suppliers without making any guarantee of parts orders to them. Because of constant fluctuations in the market, the in-house production network can respond quickly as well as reduce its losses by intensively exchanging information about market forecasting and making appropriate monthly or even weekly production plans. It is possibly true that this pattern is sustained because of the stiff competition among numerous suppliers. By dedicating themselves solely as in-house suppliers, these companies can acquire the status of "priority" suppliers in the collaborative relationship. Relatively speaking, this privileged status grants these suppliers a better position from which to retain a significant degree of sales and financial stability. This is quite significant for the Taiwanese business communities, as their business models are still predominantly based on social networks.

Last but not least, the close and continuous interaction among various in-house partners contributes significantly to proficient production modifications, product design, and management innovation for the suppliers (Jet:18; Yuan-Deng:8). In fact, one can even argue that the constant improvement in their production efficiency and coordination capability by means of reciprocal learning is the key for the whole network to survive successfully in the rapidly changing environment.

Although another major production network of electronic devices in Thailand, led by Delta (Thailand), has not established a similar in-house model to that of Cal-Comp, it nonetheless has created in-house parts warehouses for its suppliers. These warehouses do not implement parts production by the suppliers and function merely as on-time delivery stations for the core company. According to one interviewee, the company learned about the idea of the in-house warehouse from its major buyer, Dell Inc. (Delta:27). The logic of coordination in Delta's model is similar to that of Cal-Comp.

In sum, the governance structure of these two Taiwanese production networks in Thailand has been changed, to a certain degree, from a personal-based to a formal-based model. With severe competition pressures from the global market, both the core companies and the suppliers in the production networks established by Taiwanese companies at the foreign site have to continuously adjust their coordination mechanisms in order to lower production costs as well as maintain high-quality products. Whenever personal or ethnic ties reached their limits for generating profits under network coordination, the core actors do not hesitate to initiate new models of production collaboration. Under the newly formulated arrangements, a transparent exchange of production information, in-house parts delivery stations, and an internal price bidding system are set up to improve the efficiency of network operations. Indeed, the imperative for network partners to survive in the global market forces them to move beyond personal or ethnic networks (Chang and Tam 2004).

From the example of these two major cases of Taiwanese investment in Thailand, it is evident that most Taiwan focal companies in the production networks have strong links with Western multinational firms or large trading companies. The latter continuously exert price pressure on their Taiwanese subcontractors to maximize profits as well as provide new ideas to transform their production networks accordingly. To satisfy their demands, the Taiwanese firms must be sensitive to changes and demands in the global market, particularly by constantly looking for ways to reduce prices and improve management practices. Operating under volatile and uncertain environments, they must choose appropriate mechanisms of network operation at various stages of network transformation in order to survive. While these mechanisms certainly continue to include personal or local ethnic ties, they are now increasingly combined and fused with other (formal) mechanisms in order to accommodate the market challenges successfully for their own survival as well as that of the entire production network.

Network reconstruction

In the early 1990s, many local motorcycle companies in Taiwan faced flattened sales and an increasingly saturated market amid intense competition from giant Japanese corporations such as Honda, Suzuki, and Yamaha. Many investors considered Vietnam as a location with great opportunity for market expansion, particularly for mid-range motorcycles. Unlike the experience of their counterparts in the case of the export-oriented sector for electronic devices, the major motivation of the motorcycle companies in their foreign direct investment (FDI) in the destination countries is to pursue local, not global, market opportunities instead (Jou and Chen 2001).

In 1992, the Sanyang Industry Co., a major motorcycle company in Taiwan, established its subsidiary, the Vietnam Manufacturing and Export Processing Co. Ltd. (VMEP), in Vietnam. In order to ramp up the local production rate, VMEP invited some of its suppliers to join its overseas venture. As a result, 13 collaborative suppliers went along with Sanyang and established their production branches in Vietnam. Table 7.1 provides a summary of the basic details of these companies. Most of them are long-term, first-tier parts suppliers of Sanyang in Taiwan and have already established strong ties with each other within the production network. To minimize unnecessary horizontal competition, each of them specializes in only one major part of motorcycle manufacturing, excepting Haysheng and Yuchi, the two manufacturers of motorcycle seats. The average amount of foreign investment of these suppliers was approximately three and a half million U.S. dollars, slightly lower than the average investment of Taiwanese companies in Vietnam for the past 10 years. Indeed, the investment by VMEP has been showcased as a major foreign investment by the Vietnamese government, although the actual amount of capital investment by its suppliers tended to be small- to medium-sized. It is perhaps interesting to note that the largest investment was by the Kenda Rubber Company, a minor tire supplier of Sanyang in Taiwan. We suspect that the reason is probably due to the fact that its major tire supplier already had significant investments in mainland China and did not consider another large-scale investment in Vietnam economical or profitable (KENDA:6).

All of these companies concentrated their locations in Ton-Nai at the Lu-Hao industrial district near Ho Chi Minh City and are only about fifteen kilometers away from the focal company, VMEP. Based on the responses collected from the interviews, they received direct assistance from VMEP in both the selection of the plant location and the subsequent construction of factories and production lines (SANYANG:6; PRECISION:5). Today, the total number of Taiwanese collaborative suppliers within the production network has expanded from the original 13 to 19, all residing in the same geographical district. Together, these suppliers employ a total of 1,200 employees and produce approximately 35 percent of the motorcycle parts needed by VMEP. On the other hand, the focal company purchased about 10 percent of parts from national enterprises in Vietnam and produced about 15 percent of the parts internally. Finally, VMEP still had to import some motorcycle components from abroad.

To entice its suppliers to participate in the joint venture, VMEP initially invested money and owned a minority stake (about 9.9 percent) in each of

Table 7.1 Basic details of VMEP and its collaborative producers

Company	Total capital ($)	Major products	Company	Total capital ($)	Major products
VMEP	120,000,000	Engine and other motorcycle parts	Yushwen	3,830,000	
Kenda	15,000,000	Tire	Kaifa	3,700,000	Buffer
Hornchi	1,500,000		Broad bright	2,830,000	
Shinlin, Vietnam	2,678,000	precision switch	Vietnam	6,500,000	Metal frame
President	3,230,000	Battery	Yuchin	1,940,000	Seats
Linyuan	1,280,000	Screw	Jaysheng	815,000	Seats
ShuShui	3,500,000	Light	Chifa	–	Plastics

the 13 collaborative suppliers, though it never participated in their daily operation (SHILIN:1). The move was intended to share the risks associated with their foreign direct investment in Vietnam. Even though these companies already had long-term collaborative relationships with Sanyang in Taiwan, a minority equity investment would consolidate their relationships even further. It should be noted that this kind of investment strategy is seldom adopted by other large-sized Taiwanese companies and might prove to be useful if successful. Unfortunately, the equity investment strategy did not last long, as VMEP later had to sell the shares back to its suppliers several years later when the company encountered financial difficulties (PRECISION:5).

At the beginning, the strong ties within the production network benefited the suppliers tremendously. The core company not only provided crucial help in land development and company registration, but it also offered negotiation on their behalf with the Vietnamese government at the central and local levels. On several occasions during 1996 and 1997, VMEP even provided short-term loans to its suppliers (SANYANG:17). The active involvement of VMEP reduced the transaction and operational costs of these suppliers significantly. Under such a production network arrangement, these suppliers are all exclusive collaborators, that is, they may provide parts *only* to VMEP. As one interviewee noted unequivocally, "the original suppliers from Taiwan have an understanding with VMEP that they cannot sell any parts to other companies, especially VMEP's competitors in Vietnam such as Honda, Suzuki, and Yamaha" (SANYANG:6). As benefactors of the production network, it is an obligation that these suppliers must observe and contribute back to the core company. Since the norm of reciprocity had been adequately exercised within the network, it further reinforced trust among its members, even though VMEP never made any guarantee of stable and sufficient orders to its suppliers.

In addition to personal ties, both the suppliers and the core company instituted mechanisms to effectively communicate and coordinate their activities as a collective. For instance, the suppliers of VMEP established an association to hold regular meetings to exchange information about Vietnamese government regulations or the industrial district's committee, important market information about their foreign competitors, production details of the focal company, and so on. The core company, on the other hand, also held irregular meetings with its suppliers to announce important decisions about the adjustment of component orders or price reduction (BROAD BRIGHT:14).

If we just examine the process of the VMEP's transplantation of production networks, we may conclude that it is indeed a well planned and well executed project. VMEP invested in Vietnam about two years ahead of its suppliers, and its business activity was selling assembled final products to the local market. It was only after the sales figures had reached a certain target and the response from the market was satisfactory, that VMEP began to establish its foreign production subsidiary and introduce its key parts suppliers into Vietnam. In addition, the collaborative relationships within the networks have been further strengthened by its minority equity investment in each accompanying supplier.

However, we also need to examine the experience of the production network after the transplantation, particularly the difficulties that the production network might have encountered after the venture and the necessary adjustments taken by its members. One key concern is whether there was anything inherent in the network that made it unable to cope with the new and changing environment. Before we analyze the kinds of difficulties faced by the venture and why these eventually led to a partial breakdown of the VMEP production network, it is necessary to understand the nature of the motorcycle industry in general and its production in Vietnam in particular. First, the Taiwanese motorcycle companies faced a host of related problems including a saturated local market, increasing labor costs, and tough standards of environmental protection (Lu 1999). These major motorcycle companies must carry out foreign direct investment in China, Southeast Asia, and elsewhere to seek and create new business opportunities, just like other traditional industrial enterprises. But unlike these counterparts, their goal is to capture the local market and compete with other foreign, global manufacturers. According to the argument of some literature, Taiwanese enterprises tend to be strong in manufacturing but weak in creating their own brands and establishing sales channels in the local markets. This is exactly the situation faced by VMEP in Vietnam, where the company faced tough competition from foreign companies dominated by the Japanese at the high end of the market and at the low end by local competitors such as IKD.[3]

In 1999, the total number of motorcycles produced by foreign companies in Vietnam was about 300,000 units. Of all the motorcycles manufactured in that year (about 1 million), about 300,000 units were high-end vehicles. The market leaders of these expensive high-quality motorcycles were Honda, followed by VMEP and Suzuki. More specifically, Honda seized about 60 percent of the top-class market while VMEP gained another 25 percent, with the remaining share captured by Suzuki. The opportunity for rapid expansion, however, is limited. In fact, the projected demand is only expected to increase by 100,000 units in 2010 to 1,200,000.[4] As the leading brand in the market, Honda motorcycles can command very expensive prices because of brand reputation and loyalty. Although the motorcycles manufactured by VMEP have comparable quality, they can only sell at two thirds of the latter's asking price. In the low-end market, motorcycles manufactured by IKD are sold at half the price of those of VMEP, thus exerting tremendous price pressure on VMEP. Being squeezed in the middle, VMEP has found it difficult even to maintain its own market share in the domestic market in Vietnam (SANYANG:5).

Facing intense pressure from both ends, VMEP is in a precarious and awkward position in formulating its marketing strategy. On the one hand, because of Honda's marvelous brand reputation and advanced research and development capabilities in design and manufacturing, it is extremely difficult and unlikely for the company to dislodge Honda as the high-end market leader. As a result, VMEP would not be able to increase market share through high-end production or improve profits by raising prices. On the other hand, prices of low-end motorcycles are simply too low to meet the company's bottom line, as VMEP cannot reduce production costs to compromise on the quality of its products and after-sales service. In other words, any expansion into the low-end market is likely to meet with failure. The annual sales of motorcycles were 26,000, 32,000, 40,000, and 60,000 units in 1995, 1996, 1998, and 1999, respectively (SANYANG:5). Although the numbers indicated a significant improvement in sales over time, the growth was far below the potential production capacities of the entire production network and was insufficient to sustain its stable operation in the long run.

After several years without stable and sufficient orders from VMEP, many of the collaborative parts suppliers were unable to wait indefinitely but had to develop alternative organizational strategies to solve their own underproduction problem. They generally adopted two different strategies, which, as a result, eventually eroded and broke both the boundary of the network and the intensity of network connections. The first strategy was to search for new business opportunities in the local market as well as markets in other Southeast Asian countries. In order to survive, they even tried hard to contact their Japanese competitors in order to become their alternative suppliers. The latter efforts, however, were largely unsuccessful. As one interviewee from a tire company pointed out bluntly, "strong nationalism among Japanese companies is the main reason why they tend to use products exclusively from Japanese suppliers" (KENDA:4). Another company was more successful and eventually became the supplier to a specific Japanese production system in Vietnam. However, the success of the latter is not accidental. In fact, its parent company in Taiwan has already been part of this Japanese manufacturer's system. It was through such pre-established links that the company was able to obtain additional orders from the Japanese production system in Vietnam (KAIFA:4). It is evident that because of the rigid network boundary and strict standards of parts quality within the Japanese production system, only those Taiwanese suppliers that have prior relations or have high-quality products could successfully become suppliers to the Japanese production system (PRECISION:7; KAIFA:4; KENDA:4).

The second strategy was to transform its products into parts suitable for other products. Shilin V.E., a major supplier of circuits for VMEP and its parent company in Taiwan, has long-term collaborative relationships with Sanyang, and offers a good illustration. Shilin V.E. in Taiwan supplied about 70 to 80 percent of the total demand for circuits by Sanyang. Such close collaborative relationships imposed a very strong obligation on Shilin V.E. as an exclusive supplier of competitive as well as low-priced parts to VMEP in Vietnam. Without the permission of Sanyang, Shilin V.E. simply may not provide any parts to its competitors. Although VMEP eventually agreed to let Shilin V.E. supply some manufactured parts to other companies, Shilin V.E. committed at least 10 percent of its production capacity to producing electric switches for its focal company (SHILIN:5–11).

Another example of the second strategy is Vietnam Precision, a supplier that specializes in metal pressing and provides the metal frame and metal parts of the motorcycle to VMEP. Today, in addition to motorcycle manufacturing the company also manufactures metal frames for various products ranging from wheelchairs to walking carts. In fact, the amount of sales from the latter rose considerably over time and represented close to 60 percent of the company's sales (PRECISION:3, 8, 10). While the development of new products unrelated to motorcycle manufacturing contributed significantly to the company's financial health, it also reduced its level of dependence on VMEP and, as a result, weakened their close collaborative relationship as well. The success of these two Vietnamese subsidiaries also gradually transformed their mother companies in Taiwan, and they eventually became manufacturing bases for their mother companies to save labor costs. For these companies, the intra-firm production network became more important than their collaborative connections with VMEP. In addition, as their business relationships with the new customers deepened, they may gradually replace or supplant the existing production network.

Conclusion and discussion

Based on these case studies of cross-border investment by Taiwanese companies in Vietnam and Thailand, we can identify different trajectories in the transformation of their production networks. In the case of Thailand, although ethnic relationships and personal ties helped the networks to survive and prosper during the initial stage, the network leaders eventually opted for either formal or hybrid models to later cope with the daily demands. In most instances, the new management models are learned, borrowed, or modified from their multinational customers. In the case of Vietnam, the effectiveness of the production network had been under tremendous stress because of tough competition from both Japanese and local producers, and it has even faced the danger of eventual breakdown. Such a development occurred even though the core firm had a well organized and executed investment plan, solid support from its suppliers, and strong pre-existing personal ties. These strong ethnic connections among network members, although important, failed to guarantee any success in their foreign ventures. Without adequate business orders to sustain their own economic survival in a foreign environment, the subcontractors frequently had to recourse to their old personal ties in Taiwan and elsewhere to obtain new business opportunities. Such activities not only weakened their dependence on the leading firm, but also transformed their business nature and enhanced their flexibility for growth.

On the one hand, the export-oriented manufacturers in Thailand have made successful investments and remarkable transformations in their management structures. Since they are deeply embedded in both the global competitive environment and the local production setting, they are probably more adept (sometimes even forced to do so) at integrating and operating various positive mechanisms into their production networks at different periods when necessary. It appears that the global economic and institutional environments shaped and influenced these Taiwanese manufacturers more significantly and effectively after their foreign investment had become established and rooted locally. We suspect that this pattern is indeed quite common, as a similar trajectory of network transformation can be found in many large Taiwanese electronic enterprises in Penang and Kuala Lumpur (Chen et al. 2004:179–85).

On the other hand, while the local-market oriented Taiwanese manufacturers were initially successful in transplanting their production network, its failure to increase market share in Vietnam subsequently weakened the entire ethnic network. In order to survive financially, the parts suppliers reduced their personal connections with, and dependence on, the core company in Vietnam and instead utilized their old connections at home to solicit new business opportunities. Paradoxically, while the strength of personal ties with the core company has been reduced significantly in Vietnam, personal ties with their home companies were amplified significantly. Again, the situation here is not entirely unique for those companies facing similar problems. In a related work, we found that subcontractors of the Taiwanese motorcycle production networks in Indonesia also sought business orders from other foreign customers in order to survive economically (Chen et al. 2004:186).

The empirical findings provide partial support of our underlying framework that different economic actors are necessarily embedded in global and local environments differently and therefore run the operations of their foreign network accordingly. As a result, it is important to specify the conditions under which these Taiwanese enterprises are embedded, the specific factors operating at different stages of foreign investment, and how the production networks have been transformed as a result of these changing factors. Our findings here suggest clearly that the condition of market competition is a critical factor in shaping the development of production networks. Since export-oriented Taiwanese enterprises consider the host countries merely as production sites, their immediate concerns are subject to the demands of their multinational trading partners, as well as seeking ways to achieve efficiency in production. Any reorganization of the production system that increases efficiency and flexibility to quickly take into account the conditions of the changing global market would not be resisted or rejected. This explains why the governance structure of their production networks has a tendency to become a hybrid model rather than retaining its genuine, original mode with superficial alterations. However, the experience of their overseas counterparts targeting the local markets was dramatically different. Tough conditions and insurmountable challenges in marketing, sales, and production all seriously damaged or eroded the operation of these transplanted production networks, and even weakened their long-term survivability.

The degree of integration of these enterprises in the global production chains is another determining factor in the development of their production networks. The more integrated they are, the greater the tendency and necessity for the development of institutional isomorphism in their governance structures. Many of these management strategies, such as internal bidding practices and just-in-time logistic control, have already been well developed by their multinational customers. It is therefore easier for them to learn and adapt quickly. Although the particularities of some long-standing local governance structures will remain and may even persist for quite some time, more and more formalized rules and procedures are expected to flourish in these export-oriented production networks, both in Taiwan and elsewhere.

Finally, we believe that the size of firms is another important factor in shaping the trajectory of production networks in the host and recipient countries and changes in the governance structures. Obviously, the size of the core firm is highly correlated with the amount of economic resources, power, and information that its production networks can employ. Consequently, larger companies would have greater economic clout to oblige their subcontractors to follow more transparent rules on quality, price, and delivery time. Also, larger firms can devote more resources to innovations in management, process control, and product design, which undoubtedly would tilt the governance structures further away from the reliance on personal relations and toward formal and institutionalized mechanisms.

Appendix 7.1: list of abbreviated company names

CAL-COMP	Cal-Comp Electronics (Thailand) Co. Ltd.
YUAN-DENG	Yuan Deng Industrial Co. Ltd.
DELTA	Delta Electronics (Thailand) Public Co. Ltd.
JET	Jet Industries (Thailand) Co. Ltd
JET-THAI	Jet Thai Plastic Industries Co. Ltd.
SANYANG(VMEP)	Sanyang Industry
SHIHLIN	Shihlin Vietnam Co. Ltd.
PRECISION	Vietnam Precision Industrial Co. Ltd.
BROAD BRIGHT	Vietnam Broad Bright Ind. Co. Ltd
KENDA	KENDA Rubber (Vietnam) Co. Ltd.
KAIFA	Kaifa Vietnam Industrial Co. Ltd.

Notes

1 The company name for Kinpo in Thailand is Cal-Comp Electronics.
2 These abbreviations come from our research field notes for each company under investigation, and the number indicates the page number of each interview transcript.

See Appendix 7 at the end of the chapter for the complete list of the companies cited in this study.

3 IKD motorcycles are those assembled by local companies by using very cheap parts imported from China, which are sold without branding or any guarantee of service.

4 See www.cpbjlf.com/Vmotor/motorcycle.htm.

References

Biggart, N. W. and Hamilton, G. (1997) "On the Limits of a Firm-based Theory to Explain Business Networks," in M. Orru, N. W. Biggart, and G. G. Hamilton (eds.) *The Economic Organization of East Asian Capitalism*, Thousand Oaks, CA: Sage.

Chang, L. Y. and Tam, T. 2004. "The Making of Chinese Business Culture: Culture versus Organizational Imperatives," in E. T. Gomez and H. H. M. Hsiao (eds.) *Chinese Enterprise, Transnationalism, and Identity*, London: RoutledgeCurzon.

Chen, D. S., Jou, S. C., and Hsiao, H. H. M. (2004) "Interfirm Networking by Taiwanese Enterprises in Malaysia and Indonesia," in E. T. Gomez and H. H. M. Hsiao (eds.) *Chinese Enterprise, Transnationalism, and Identity*, London: RoutledgeCurzon.

Chen, T. J. (1998) "FDI by Small- and Medium-Sized Enterprises from Taiwan," in T. J. Chen (ed.) *Taiwanese Firms in Southeast Asia: Networking Across Borders*, Cheltenham, U.K.: Edward Elgar.

Crawford, D. (2000) "Chinese Capitalism: Cultures, the Southeast Asian Region and Economic Globalization," *Third World Quarterly* 21:69–86.

DiMaggio, P. J. and Powell, W. W. (1983) "The Iron Cage Revisited: Institutional Isomorphism and Collective Rationality in Organizational Fields," *American Sociological Review* 48: 147–60.

Hannen, M. T. and Freeman, J. (1977) "The Population Ecology of Populations," *American Journal of Sociology* 82:929–64.

Jou, S. C. and Chen, D. S. (2001) "Latecomer's Globalization: Taiwan's Experiences in FDI and Reproduction of Territorial Production Networks in Southeast Asia," in H. H. M. Hsiao, H. Z. Wang, and I. C. Kung (eds.) *Taiwanese Business in Southeast Asia: Network, Identity, and Globalization* (in Chinese), Taipei: Academia Sinica.

Lu, C. F. (1999) "Current Impacts and Challenges of Taiwan's Motorcycle Industry" (in Chinese), *Newsletter of the Taiwanese Motorcycle Association* 62:7–13.

Meyer, J. W. and Rowan, B. (1977) "Institutional Organizations: Formal Structure as Myth and Ceremony," *American Journal of Sociology* 83:340–63.

Redding, S. G. (1990) *The Spirit of Chinese Capitalism*, Berlin: Walter de Gruyter.

Wong, R. S. K. (2004) "Chinese Business Firms and Entrepreneurs in Hong Kong," in E. T. Gomez and H. H. M. Hsiao (eds.) *Chinese Enterprise, Transnationalism, and Identity*, London: RoutledgeCurzon.

Yeung, H. W. C. (1997) "Business Networks and Transnational Corporations: A Study of Hong Kong Firms in the ASEAN Regions," *Economic Geography* 73:1–25.

——(1998) *Transnational Corporations and Business Networks: Hong Kong Firms in the ASEAN Region*, New York: Routledge.

8 Born out of networks

A sociological analysis of the emergence of the firm[1]

Yanjie Bian

Introduction

China currently has more than 8 million small and medium-sized companies; a majority of them are family businesses and private enterprises
coming to life in the post-1980 reform era. As of 2002, these firms accounted for approximately 60 percent of the country's GDP, 40 percent of the
national revenue, and 75 percent of non-agricultural jobs (Wu 2003:181).
Each year, hundreds of thousands of new firms have emerged. Although a
good number of them have been short-lived, many have survived and grown
rapidly in an increasingly competitive market economy.

How do firms come about? What roles do social networks play in the
start-up of a business? In this chapter, I try to answer these two questions
with the assistance of two kinds of data. The first is based on the in-depth
interviews that I conducted with Chinese entrepreneurs in Hong Kong and
the Pear River Delta region of Guangdong Province. These interviews offer
vivid evidence that, while firms are created in response to a market demand
that is yet to be satisfied, they are born out of entrepreneurs' embedded
social networks in which information, opportunity, and resources are utilized in the starting up of a new business. Based on these self-reported
stories, I then formulate a typology of market and network images of the
emergence of the firm in contemporary China. The second source of data is
based on a survey of 830 firms in the Pearl River Delta region. The latter
provides the basis for testing hypotheses about the specific roles of social
networks in a business' starting up process. Below I will begin with three
stories of how businesses started up.

Three stories about business start-ups

The Mr. L story

Mr. L is a mainland Chinese entrepreneur, currently residing in Hong Kong,
who engages in international trading of copper materials. His economic
success can be reflected by his grandiose residence (350 square meters) in a

gated upper-class neighborhood in the Red Hill Peninsula. Besides a magnificent ocean view, his residence has a completely carpeted living room, a grand piano, a large collection of art, a wide-screen TV in the family studio, and furniture that together signify one of the prototypical "luxurious homes" (or *hao chai*) of Hong Kong. When we discussed how he started his business, Mr. L immediately brought up the point that it was "born out of my networks" that were rich in both information and opportunities in the international trade of copper materials.

During the 1980s and 1990s, prices of copper materials fluctuated tremendously. Trading opportunities for Chinese players, however, were slim since the market was dominated by Western buyers and had high international standards for the quality of copper materials. Among Chinese traders, the market was dominated by the state-dominated copper industry. The latter held to relatively lower standards in quality even though it had the potential to supply and export low-priced copper materials to the international market. Drawn from his work experience as a foreign diplomat in China's Canadian embassy and as a manager in the China Tourist Company in Hong Kong, Mr. L quickly established a close network of business relationships with Western and Chinese entrepreneurs. In fact, Mr. L recalled that it was his Western business friends who offered him both the information and opportunities for a possible international trading business in copper material with China.

Back home, Mr. L grew up in the Jiangsu Province. He received a B.A. degree in English language and literature from Nanjing University, which situated him in advantageous classmate and friendship networks and connected him to leaders and other strategic people in the copper industry. Capitalizing on these domestic and overseas connections, Mr. L started up his international trade business in Hong Kong in the early 1990s. Profits from his business venture were instant and all bank loans for his start-up investment were paid off quickly and handsomely. The volume of copper trading and the earnings of his company grew substantially over time.

The Mr. S story

Mr. S never dreamed of owning any business until the opportunity suddenly came upon him. Growing up as a city kid in Guangzhou, he played Chinese checkers regularly and was a very good player. One of his senior chess playing friends, "lao Cao" (or "old Cao"), in his previous neighborhood happened to be the director of logistics in a state-owned factory. In 1995, with just one more year of study to obtain his undergraduate degree in sociology from Zhongshan University, the top college in the city and the province, Mr. S began thinking of what to do in his future career. Knowing Mr. S well, lao Cao urged him to think about doing something on his own in an increasingly marketized and privatized economy. "Why don't you make money by selling the junks from my factory?"

"The junks?"

"Yes, the used cotton gloves that rise high as a hill in the factory's back-yard. No one from my factory wanted to sell or reuse them because we the employees would not be allowed to do anything with the factory property for money making purposes. But they could sell at a good price."

"But even if I wanted to do it, would your factory allow me?"

"I'm in charge of my factory's logistics and this is under my jurisdiction!"

This is how Mr. S began his first business from of a social tie to a chess playing friend who happened to have a business opportunity to offer.

This business opportunity did not last long, however. For one thing, a single factory's junks were insufficient to satisfy and sustain the operation of a business indefinitely. Mr. S did look to other factories for a similar business opportunity, but as competition increased, the profit margins were getting extremely low, and eventually forced him to give up this particular business altogether. For another thing, the "junk business," in Mr. S's own words, was clearly not "his type." He wanted to use his knowledge of sociology to start a different kind of business development. Nonetheless, the "junk business" helped Mr. S to save a good amount of money that was sufficient to open and operate a marketing survey firm. Today, his company is one of the top 10 national marketing firms.

The Mr. F story

As a self-trained carpenter working as an ordinary peasant in a village in southern China, Mr. F had the dream of making and selling furniture as a *getihu* (self-employed) owner as early as 1982 when the province was given special permission from the central government to authorize self-employment and private enterprise in many industries, including the manufacturing of furniture. During that time, furniture, particularly red-wood furniture, had an increasing demand locally and regionally (and later nationally), making the sale of furniture a rather easy job with an impressive annual profit margin of more than 100 percent! This strong seller's market inspired Mr. F to pursue his goal of becoming an entrepreneur.

Raising the required start-up capital of $5,000 RMB in 1982 was the major obstacle for Mr. F. Of course, this would be a small, negligible amount in 2003, by which time his furniture company had a workforce of 500+ workers and an after-tax profit of $4.7 million RMB. But back then, the amount was insurmountable when Mr. F had an annual income of $500 RMB and personal savings of $250 RMB, or 5 percent of the required capital. He made great efforts to borrow from relatives and friends, increasing his capital to $2,000 RMB. To make up the rest, Mr. F recruited a village cadre, "San Ge" (or third brother), as a partner. The latter used his power and connections to take a loan of $3,000 RMB from a savings and loans office at the commune, the lowest level the state banking system in the countryside, that had jurisdiction over the village. San Ge also helped Mr. F to get registration and all other necessary paperwork done with the government for the jointly owned furniture shop.

A recounting

These stories represent many similar ones that I learned from personal interviews with entrepreneurs in Hong Kong and the Pearl River Delta region. Common to them is that market opportunities for business start-ups are obtained through the entrepreneurs' own network connections. Of course, the ability to capitalize on these opportunities would require a risk-taking attitude (though Mr. F faced a more favorable seller's market situation in his furniture business back in the early 1980s). Although the risk-taking attitude and the desire to become one's own boss are important supply-side determinants, the above examples clearly suggest that learning about these opportunities is equally, if not more, important. The latter appears to be structurally constrained by at least two factors. The first is the opportunity itself, that is, whether the entrepreneur is situated in an environment where there is a pent-up demand for a specific product or service that entails money making opportunities. The second is the structure of opportunity itself, specifically whether the entrepreneur is located in a network that offers information about different market demands and opportunities that would permit him/her to capitalize on the information obtained. How do these two factors influence business start-ups? In the following section, I offer a schematic typology to answer this specific question.

Market and network images about business start-ups

A new business establishment emerges in response to a market demand for a specific product or service that is yet to be provided. This is a well known understanding in neoclassical economics about economic equilibrium (Becker 1976). According to this perspective, equilibrium arises when the match between supply and demand in the market is perfect. Disequilibrium occurs when there are unsatisfied demands that call for the expansion of the economy, creating room for new establishments to supply the demanded products or services (McKenzie and Tullock 1989). A new establishment may be short lived if that demand proves to be instantaneous or weak; but it will survive and grow if demand for the product or service is strong and continuous (provided of course that quality and price both satisfy market demand). In short, the emergence and growth of a business establishment can be explained in terms of market demand, where a new establishment is created precisely to satisfy such a demand.

The establishment of a new business is not the only way to meet unsatisfied market demand. An alternative solution common to any economy is to expand or restructure existing producers and service outlets to achieve greater efficiency (Becker 1976). Such an alternative for China in the 1980s, however, was not viable because all existing economic organizations back then were exclusively state-owned (as broadly defined and including urban collectives under local government) and largely inefficient (Wu 2003). Property rights arrangements in the state sector provided little or no room to satisfy the interests of producers, who instead would prefer business opportunities beyond the confines of the state. In fact, one could argue that the key to China's post-1980 reforms was the strategy of "letting the birds out of the cage" so that new economic activities and organizational forms grew *outside* the state sector (Naughton 1995). It was under such a macro-structural and business environment that individuals like the entrepreneurs that I interviewed were drawn to starting up their own businesses when opportunities knocked.

These stories also lend strong support to the importance of "structural embeddedness" in economic action described by Granovetter (1985)—economic opportunities are rooted in the networks of ongoing social relationships that disseminate business information and build transaction-relevant trust between economic actors. One should, however, note that this experience is not entirely unique to the Chinese context. There is rich empirical evidence in the West on the roles of social networks in the expansion of British textile businesses (Kerridge 1985), the growth of the American glass industry (White 2002), and the operation of loans by a Chicago bank (Uzzi 1997). Under China's transitional economy, social networks have played important roles in diffusing economic information because existing formal institutions are ineffective (Boisot and Child 1996), protecting private businesses from the threats of predatory local governments (Peng 2004), securing and operating business contacts under a weak legal system (Zhou et al. 2003), and functioning as social capital to increase economic performances of the firm (Bian 2002). What are the specific roles that social networks play in the process of a business's starting up? Or, to put it more bluntly, how do people learn and catch money making opportunities?

Based on the personal experiences of Chinese entrepreneurs interviewed, it appears that network-facilitated information and trust are involved and critical in all three initial steps taken to start up a business. The first step involves obtaining valuable information regarding the availability of business opportunities and the possibility that they could establish an entity to exploit such opportunities. This access of information may be unintentional, as in the case of Mr. S who learned about it via a chess playing friend, or intentional, as in the case of Mr. L who actively sought information from a collection of Western and Chinese business friends. The second step involves the mobilization of start-up capital. Like their predecessors in Hong Kong and elsewhere, these Chinese entrepreneurs in the Pearl River Delta all started their businesses without sufficient financial capital. Because of the underdevelopment of the Chinese capital market, very few entrepreneurs obtained their start-up capital from state and local banks when their personal savings fell short of the required working capital. Instead, they borrowed money from their families, kinsmen, friends, and associates through other social relations. The capital raised is either in the form of informal loans or even partnerships (as for Mr. F). The third step involves the securing of a business order through network ties with strategic individuals. The latter may either be the person who provided the information in the first place (like Mr. S's lao Cao) or the prospective partner of the new business (in the case of Mr. F). In sum, in terms of information, start-up capital, and first business order, the ability to access and mobilize these valuable resources and the success in founding a business establishment are heavily embedded in the dense social networks that dominate Chinese society.

Figure 8.1 presents a typology in which the establishment of a new business has to operate under an interaction between two contrasting images of the economy (network and market images). Specifically, the network image depicts an economy as relationally rooted and allows variation between network embeddedness (for past and current information and opportunities) and network cultivation (for future information and opportunities). The market image, on the other hand, depicts an economy from the supply and demand perspective and allows variation between continuous (strong) and instant (weak) demand. Thus, the cross-classification of these two dichotomies creates four types of start-up business.

Network image	Market image	
	Continuous demands	**Instant demands**
Network embeddedness	I New businesses are embedded in networks in which market demands for a specific product or service are strong and continuous. Therefore, businesses are likely to last long and grow over time. At the start-up stage, investment capital and business orders are obtained through network ties that continue to play a long-term role in the growth of the business.	II New businesses are embedded in networks in which there is an instant but discontinuous demand for a specific product or service. Therefore, businesses are likely to be short-lived or quickly change the products or services they provide. At the start-up stage, investment capital and business orders are obtained through network ties that continue to play a role in the transformation and therefore survival of the business.
Network cultivation	III New businesses are a response to strong and continuous market demand. Therefore, businesses are likely to last long, but their growth will depend upon the cultivation of network ties and resources. At the start-up stage, investment capital and business orders are not necessarily obtained through network ties, but the development of the business will rely in substantive ways on the cultivation of network ties and resources.	IV New businesses are a response to an instant but discontinuous market demand for a specific product or service. Therefore, businesses may be short-lived or quickly change the products or services they provide. At the start-up stage, investment capital and business orders are not necessarily obtained through network ties and resources, which, however, must be cultivated successfully for the transformation and therefore survival of the business.

Figure 8.1 Network and market images of a business' starting up: a typology

The type I business is born out of networks in which market demands for a specific product or service are strong and continuous, and the start-up investment capital and business orders are obtained through network ties that will continue to play a long-term role in the growth of the businesses. The type II business is also born out of networks, but it differs from the former type in that there is only an instantaneous and discontinuous market demand for that specific product or service. Therefore, the maintenance of such networks will be crucial and the latter will continue to play an important role in the transformation and hence survival of the business. Similar to the first one, type III businesses also emerge in response to strong and continuous market demand. But during the start-up phase, these businesses do not necessarily rely on network-facilitated information or opportunity since they are readily available in the marketplace anyway. However, increased competition may force these businesses to rely on the cultivation of network ties and resources in order to survive and grow. Finally, type IV businesses, similar to their counterparts of type II, represent responses to an instant but discontinuous market demand for a specific product or service. As a result, they may be short-lived or have to quickly change the products or services they provide. Although their investment capital and business orders are not necessarily obtained through network ties during the start-up, the need to cultivate network ties and resources successfully will play an important role in the transformation and eventual survival of these businesses.

A survey of firms in the Pearl River Delta

Case studies are useful for establishing a broad understanding but weak in testing the empirical implications of a theory. For hypothesis testing, I now turn to a survey of 830 firms in three Pearl River Delta cities (Zhongshan, Fushan, and Jiangmen) in 2003. These three cities were chosen for three reasons. First, they underwent great economic transformation from rural townships into industrial centers from the 1980s. Numerous new firms were founded in southern China during this period and they should provide valuable insights about start-up businesses as well as the basis for a random sampling of firms. From a scientific sampling point of view, it may not be easy to locate new firms in Guangzhou, an old city that still has many well established firms with a long business history. Second, in the newly developed industrial centers in the Pearl River Delta, factories in a particular city are highly concentrated in one or two industries, making it relatively easy to control the effects of industry. In particular, these three cities have a concentration of factories in furniture, garment, textile, china, construction materials, and small-scale manufacturing. Finally, my collaborating institution Zhongshan University has used these cities as sites of continued research, and their extensive prior knowledge about the industrial structure and social situations there was extremely useful for designing and implementing the survey effectively and efficiently.

The survey was conducted in the fall and winter of 2003 by locally trained interviewers. Because it was extremely difficult to conduct interviews in factory settings, we deliberately selected interviewers who had prior connections with strategic players in each sampled factory. Our research design covered all factories within each chosen industry. The overall response rate was 70 percent. Preliminary analyses reveal that the size distribution of factories surveyed is indeed comparable to that of the population. The targeted respondents were initially general managers or their deputies, although in factories with more than 500 employees it was usually the lower-level management personnel who completed the questionnaire.

To our surprise, the most difficult task was to convince respondents that the study was indeed a scholarly investigation with no implication whatsoever for tax assessment or other measures of state monitoring. Indeed, this false assumption on the part of the respondents made them unlikely to answer economic performance questions (revenues, earnings, etc.) or they simply offered unreliable and invalid responses. Because fixed capital and tax contributions are recorded more clearly and consistently from year to year, we were able to track this information from official records. We also found that after controlling for individual industries, there is a high correlation between economic performance and consumed electricity; the latter therefore may be considered as a more reliable substitute or instrumental variable of the former. Finally, we found that respondents were open to answering questions about social networks and their roles in the factory's start-up processes and the operation of business orders.

Table 8.1 describes the characteristics of the 830 firms at the time of survey and at the point of start-up. At the time of survey, 12.5 percent of the firms were in the furniture business, 15.9 percent in garment, 24.3 percent in textile, 14.2 in china, 21.9 percent in manufacturing, and 11.1 percent in the production of construction materials. Most of these firms are private enterprises (82.3 percent), and the remaining ones are legally recognized as either state-owned (0.5 percent, or four firms), collective (2.9 percent), foreign (7.0 percent), or shareholding (7.4 percent). The average size of employment is slightly more than 230 workers, but the variation is tremendous. Small firms with 50 or fewer workers account for 44.2 percent, medium-size firms with 51–500 workers for another 46.6 percent, and large firms with more than 500 workers constitute another 9 percent. As of 2002, these firms have an average fixed asset of $18.3 million RMB, contribute $1.46 million RMB of tax to the state, and spend more than $2.2 million RMB on electricity. The statistics suggest a ratio of approximately 0.67, or $67 RMB tax contribution to $100 RMB consumption of electricity. In terms of the management structure and labor mobility, 45.3 percent of the firms have a board of directors, 8.3 percent (mostly state-owned, collective, and shareholding firms) have the Communist Party organization built into the company structure, and they experienced rather high annual rates of worker inflow (24.2 percent) and outflow (17.6 percent). Most of these firms

Table 8.1 Sample of firms from Zhongshan, Fushan, and Jiangmen, Guangdong Province

At the time of survey		At the point of startup	
Industry (%)		*Year of establishment (%)*	
Furniture	12.5	1990 or before	21.1
Garment	15.9	1991–93	13.3
Textile	24.3	1994–97	22.7
China	14.2	1998–99	18.1
Manufacturing	21.9	2000–2001	14.7
Construction materials	11.1	2002–3	10.1
Economic sector (%)		*Form of organization (%)*	
Private	82.3	Family business	51.3
State	0.5	Partnership	28.2
Collective	2.9	Private enterprise	6.6
Foreign	7.0	Shareholding and foreign	7.6
Shareholding	7.4	Other	6.3
Size of employment (%)		*Investment (in $10,000 RMB)*	609.2
Up to 10 workers	7.7	*Source of investment (%)*	
11–50 workers	36.5	Network	61.8
51–100 workers	20.6	Family/individual	28.9
101–500 workers	26.0	Organization	9.3
More than 500 workers	8.9	*Mobilizing investment via (%)*	
Average	230.1	Family ties	66.1
Economic indicators (in $10,000 RMB)		Kinship ties	36.1
Fixed assets	1829.9	Friendship ties	23.0
Tax contribution	146.0	Other social ties	22.2
Power expenses	222.6	Not though any social tie	2.9
Structure and mobility		No answer	7.2
% firms with a board of directors	45.3	*First business order*	
% firms with CCP organization	8.3	% Founder's prior ties with client	73.5
% workers inflow (n = 749)	24.2	% Written contract	48.7
% workers outflow (n = 748)	17.6	% Business continued	52.5

hire "migrant peasant workers" to handle skilled and unskilled work tasks and these migrant workers are responsible for the high turnover rates.

Not surprisingly, virtually all of these factories were the product of China's economic reforms. About 21.1 percent of them were established in the 1980s, 54.1 percent in the 1990s, and 24.8 percent since 2000. Because private ownership gained legitimate status only after 1993 and especially after the post-1998 property rights reforms, firms established earlier might have been registered under a different legal status currently than when they were new start-ups. Of course, these concerns as of today are, if any, historical. Therefore, rather than soliciting information about the existing form of corporate ownership, we asked respondents to report the form of organization at the point of start-up instead. Slightly more than half of them (51 percent) began as a family business, 28.2 percent as a partnership, 6.6 percent as a private enterprise, 7.6 percent as a shareholding or foreign firm, and 6.3 percent did not mention any specific form but chose "other forms." As of 2003, some of the latter firms were state-owned and collective while the others were shareholding. It is reasonable to assume that firms in the "other" category might have been "township and village enterprises" which were operated like any private enterprise.

On average, the surveyed firms required a start-up investment capital of slightly more than $6 million RMB. This represents a substantial sum of capital for any form of business arrangement even by today's standard. The efforts to mobilize financial resources of such size should be substantial as well.[2] Of the three major reported sources of investment, a combination of both the founder's own money and that of his/her social contacts or affiliated organizations, which we termed "network," represented the dominant mode. About 61.8 percent of the sampled factories claimed to raise capital through this particular channel. On the other hand, about 28.9 percent of the factories raised capital solely from individual founders themselves and/ or their immediate families. Less than one tenth of the factories (9.3 percent) utilized the formal channels, such as a foreign firm, a state-owned work unit, a nonprofit institution, or a state bank.

In terms of a detailed breakdown by the sources of investment capital, one can conclude unequivocally that much of capital raised was network-embedded. Under the heading of "mobilizing investment via," factory founders are likely to mobilize the financial resources from their immediate families (66.1 percent), followed by kinship ties (36.1 percent), friends (23.0 percent), and other social ties (22.2 percent). Together, they constituted about 90 percent of the sampled factories, indicating that the mobilization of start-up investment capital is heavily embedded within the founders' social networks. Only a very small minority, less than 3 percent, admitted that they never utilized any form of social tie to raise start-up capital. Additional analyses reveal that these factories tended to be foreign firms and state-owned firms at the start-up stage. Finally, about 7.2 percent provided no answers since the respondents were not the founders and knew little about the specific arrangements. Further analyses revealed that these factories started up either as a family business or partnership. If we assume that a family business must invest one's own capital and a partnership rely on investment from all partners, one may assume that the major source of investment was the family/individual in the case of the former and the network for the latter. These conversions will be used later to examine the role of social networks in the mobilization of start-up investment capital.

The last set of descriptive results concerns the source of the first business order. Note that the results may be biased upward because the numbers are based on "successful" factories. Three questions are designed specifically to address the nature of the first business order: the form of contract, the existence of prior ties with the business client, and whether the business order with this particular client continued or discontinued after the first order was completed. As shown in Table 8.1, about half of the factories used written contracts for the first business order whereas the other half used oral contracts instead. The former might simply be a fax message, showing only the content and price of the order and the expected date of delivery. Nonetheless, these fax messages are legally binding according to Chinese corporate law. Oral contracts, in contrast, do not have any legal protection and thus require a high degree of trust between the parties involved. Of course, this does not constitute a problem since close to three fourths of the factory founders had a prior social tie with the client. The evidence provides strong support to the importance of embedded networks in developing business opportunities among newly established firms in the Pearl River Delta. Finally, there is some indication that the business opportunity was not just an instant market demand: 52.5 percent of the surveyed factories stated that their business relationships with the first client continued, with some stretching into a year-long or even longer project.

Networks and the start-up investment capital

Table 8.2 presents results concerning the role of social networks in the mobilization of start-up investment capital. Panel A in the upper section displays a cross-tabulation between sources of investment and methods of investment mobilization. The cross-classification indicates clearly that when the source of start-up investment capital comes from social network, social ties, by default, become the exclusive mode for mobilizing financial resources. All of the firms within this category or close to two thirds of all firms (61.8 percent to be exact) reportedly used this particular investment mobilization strategy. Similarly, among those who use family or self in raising capital, an overwhelming majority (97 percent) of the responses or 28.1 percent among all firms had to rely on the founders themselves, their family members, close kin, and/or friends. Capital raised from family members, close kin, and friends is most likely in the shape of informal loans. Only in some rare occasions (0.8 percent) would the capital be raised solely out of the individual social circle.

Among those firms that utilize formal institutions as the source of investment capital, over three quarters, or 7.2 percent among all firms, are based on social ties to a state bank or other formal organization. In sum, the utilization of social ties is the predominant method (97.1 percent) to mobilize start-up investment capital. To further understand what factors are more likely to be associated with specific sources of investment, we estimate a multinomial logistic regression model as the dependent variable has three response categories, namely network, family/self, and organization. The results are presented in the lower panel of Table 8.2 (panel B).

Relative to foreign/shareholding firms, factories that began as family businesses or partnership/private enterprises are more likely to rely on networks and family/self to provide the major source of investment capital, whereas foreign firms, shareholding firms, and firms that are classified as state- or collectively owned have the advantage of obtaining investment

Table 8.2 Source and mobilization of investment capital

A. Percent cross-distribution

Source of investment	Mobilization of investment via		
	Social ties	No tie	Total
Network	61.8	0.0	61.8
Family/self	28.1	0.8	28.9
Organization	7.2	2.1	9.3
Total	97.1	2.9	100.0
N			830

B. Multinomial regression on source of investment

Predictors Form of organization	Network/organization		Family-self/organization	
	β	Exp(β)	β	Exp(β)
Family business	2.302***	9.997	2.250***	9.490
Partnership and private	1.016**	2.763	0.939*	2.558
Other (state and collective)	0.580	1.786	1.097	2.994
Foreign/shareholding (omitted)				
Start up with a million RMB or more	−0.652**	0.521	−0.690***	0.502
Year of establishment				
1994–98	1.097**	2.996	1.197**	3.309
1999–2001	1.355**	3.877	1.672***	5.321
2002–3	2.254***	9.530	2.305***	10.027
1993 or earlier (omitted)				
Industry				
Furniture	1.537	4.650	1.196	3.307
Garment	1.206	3.341	1.006	2.735
Textile	1.563**	4.776	0.884	2.420
China	0.793*	2.210	−0.207	0.813
Manufacturing/construction (omitted)				
Intercept	1.875***		1.428***	

Summary Statistics:

Model χ^2	154.644
df	22
Nagelkerke coefficient (R^2)	0.226

Notes:
*p<0.05, **p<0.01, ***p<0.001

capital from formal institutions. It is important to recognize that the mobilization by the latter via the formal channels entails the assistance of social ties as well. After controlling for industry-specific differences, firms are unlikely to secure the investment from social network or family/individual when the amount of start-up capital involved is large (greater than 1 million RMB). The founders would rather seek assistance through formal channels. Finally, the results suggest that recent establishments are more likely than earlier ones to rely on social networks and family/self for securing invest-ment capital. We caution not to interpret the results as evidence regarding the declining influence of formal organizations as a major source of invest-ment capital. This perhaps instead signals that many entrepreneurs in the Pearl River Delta today might have already accumulated significant finan-cial resources earlier and are therefore increasingly more able to invest their own capital in new business ventures.

Networks and the first business order

One important indication about the significance of the social network is its role in securing the first business order. In fact, the first business order arguably constitutes the lifeblood of any new business. The key question here is where it usually comes from. As indicated earlier, the entrepreneurs in the qualitative interviews all mentioned that not only did they typically begin their busi-nesses accidentally after learning about a particular money making oppor-tunity from business associates/friends, the latter also became their first clients. Table 8.3 displays the survey results to aid further understanding about the nature of the first business order and its associated factors. Among those 751 firms that provided valid answers, it is evident that the existence of prior ties is critical, disregarding whether oral or written contracts are used. Among those who utilized oral contracts, roughly 40 percent of the firms had prior ties with the first business clients (see upper panel A). Among those who utilized written contracts, slightly less than one third actually did so. Although the importance of prior ties is stronger in oral contracts than in written con-tracts, the actual gap is much smaller than our initial expectation.

More importantly, the relationship between prior ties with clients and the use of oral/written contracts is found to be robust even after controlling for other extraneous factors in the multivariate statistical model (see lower panel B). More specifically, firms that had prior ties with clients are more likely to use oral rather than written contracts. Other things being equal, the odds of using oral contracts vis-à-vis written contracts are 50 percent (= 1/0.67) more likely among those who had ties with the first business order clients. We interpret the relative importance of the oral contract as an indication of the importance of trust.

The logistic regression model also reveals some interesting results regarding the use of a specific form of contract in the first business order. Relative to shareholding/foreign firms (the reference category), family busi-nesses, partnerships, and private enterprises all have significantly lower ten-dencies to use written contracts, even after the founder's prior tie to the client is controlled. Furthermore, firms with an initial investment of over 1 million yuan (RMB) are more likely to use written contracts than firms with lower capitalization. Finally, other things being equal, firms established recently (in 2002 and 2003) are more likely to use written contracts in their first business orders. After considering the signs and increasing strength of

Table 8.3 Analysis of first business order

A. *Percent cross-distribution*

Prior tie to client	N = 751 Form of contract		N = 766 Business continuation	
	Written	Oral	Continued	Discontinued
Yes	32.5	38.6	53.9	17.8
No	16.2	12.7	19.2	9.1
Total	48.7	51.3	73.1	26.9

B. *Logistic regressions of contract form and business continuation*

Predictors Networks	Written = 1/Oral = 0		Continued = 1/Discontinued = 0	
	β	Exp(β)	β	Exp(β)
Founder's prior tie to client	−0.398*	0.672	0.361*	1.434
Form of organization				
Family business	−1.607***	0.201	0.879**	2.409
Partnership/private	−0.801*	0.449	0.059	1.061
Other (state and collective)	−0.762	0.467	−0.274	0.760
Shareholding/foreign (omitted)				
A million yuan investment or more	0.301***	1.351	-0.006	0.994
Year of establishment				
1994–98	−0.231	0.794	0.059	1.061
1999–2001	0.463	1.589	0.363	1.438
2002–3	0.691*	1.995	0.934***	2.544
1993 or earlier (omitted)				
Intercept	−0.026	0.974	−2.190	0.112
Summary statistics				
Model χ^2		219.024		35.101
df		8		8
Nagelkerke coefficient (R^2)		0.351		0.071

Notes:
*p<0.05, **p<0.01, ***p<0.001

the coefficients of the dummies for the year of establishment, they appear to signal a growing trend of formalization, that is, the use of written contracts as the business norm, in the Pearl River Delta.

If the existence of prior ties is important for first business orders, the next logical question is whether they continue to play an important role in business continuation. A cross-classification table displaying its relationship with business continuation is shown in the last two columns of panel A. Close to three quarters (73.1 percent) of the firms maintained continuous business with their first business order clients. Among those firms that maintained a continuous relationship, 74 percent had pre-existing ties with clients, as compared to 66 percent with a discontinued relationship. This bivariate relationship is confirmed in the multivariate logistic regression model (last two columns of panel B). The coefficient for the existence of prior ties with company owners is 0.361, suggesting that these kind of companies are 43 percent more likely to maintain continuous business transactions with their first business order clients than those without prior ties. This effect, together with earlier results on the nature of the contract, offers impressive support for the importance of the social network in the start-up of new businesses. Finally, firms established recently, in 2002 and 2003, are more likely to continue their businesses with the first business client, indicating that network embeddedness and network cultivation is still strong and important in the contemporary setting.[3]

Conclusion and implications

This study demonstrates impressive results about how Chinese firms in the Pearl River Delta were born out of the social networks of their founders. For anyone interested in starting up a business venture, information regarding business opportunities, start-up capital, and the first business order are all critical. These three processes are highly embedded and inter-twined within the entrepreneurs' social networks. The in-depth personal interviews reveal that many entrepreneurs learn about valuable money making opportunities via their social contacts, either intentionally or unin-tentionally, which are subsequently carried through by strategic persons in the business community. Pre-existing social ties to these informants/partners prove to be indispensable. An investigation of 830 firms further demon-strates that financial investment at the start-up point is indeed highly embedded in the social networks of the entrepreneurs, not only because these investments mostly originate from family and social ties as a source of capital, but, perhaps more importantly, because the mobilization of these investments is heavily operated through social ties. It is only in some rare occasions (about 3 percent) that a new firm does not have to rely on the founder's social ties to mobilize financial resources. Finally, the survey also illustrates the importance of prior ties in the first business order, and shows that these ties entail trust that helps to forfeit the unnecessary complexity and hidden cost of drawing up written contracts, and that these prior ties increase the likelihood of the continuation of the business partnership rather than its discontinuation after the first order has been completed.

The findings from this study offer several directions for future research. First, the survey results have been produced largely to test the implications of the image of network embeddedness, focusing on how start-up invest-ments and first business orders are rooted in the founder's social network. However, the images of network cultivation and the market have not been explored. These images require longitudinal data to map the trajectories of new businesses in the middle and later stages of development, as well as data on changes of market demand within specific industries. Second, the analyses focus narrowly only on specific firm characteristics and the networks of the firm founders, and have purposely excluded the characteristics of founders themselves. Founders who are older, highly educated, with prior entrepreneurial experience, and/or with prior managerial experience, such as state officials and managers would all have important implications on how they start-up their businesses and how they might utilize their social ties differently at various stages of the start-up process. A former-state-official founder, for instance, is expected to garner greater network resources to mobilize investments from the formal institution channel. Former-entrepreneur founders, on the other hand, are expected to secure business orders, especially large ones, from former clients, and their business relationships with the latter are likely to be sustained as long-term partnership, perhaps not because of their ties per se, but rather because of a proven record that entails a high level of trust. How these various factors play out will enrich our understanding about how a business starts up and how it will grow under the interaction of network and market images.

When a new business starts up, a new entrepreneur comes to life. Researchers have long been reminded of the Schumpeterian notion of entrepreneurship: the entrepreneur as risk-taking innovator. However, based on the findings from the present study, we should add that an entrepreneur ought to be a social innovator in the first place. More specifically, under the transitional economy of contemporary China, not only does economic information remain largely uncoded and not diffused openly (Boisot and Child 1996), but the capital and production markets are also operating in a manner that is unfriendly to brand-new entrepreneurs. Therefore, individuals having risk-taking attitudes and desires to become entrepreneurs must necessarily be socially innovative about the existence, value, and mobilization of information, opportunity, and resources from their social networks. It is the social awareness of this potentiality and the ability to convert the latter into a business operation that constitute the integral components of entrepreneurship in China, and probably elsewhere as well.

Notes

1 An earlier version of this chapter was presented at the conference, "Chinese Entrepreneurship," HKUST, May 20–21, 2004. I acknowledge the financial support of a RGC grant (HKUST6007/00 H), the collaboration of Professor Qiu Haixiong, the assistance of data management and analysis of Zhu Bingyu, and helpful comments from the participants of the conference.

2 The start-up investment capital varies across industries; factories need a relatively larger start-up investment if they produce furniture, construction materials, and china than if they produce garments, textiles, or small manufactured products; and larger investments at start-up are more common in the most recent years.

3 Of course, part of its continued importance reflects the recency effect as well, that is, the importance of prior ties occuring predominantly within the first few years of business operations and their influence declining over time. Given the lack of longitudinal data, we are unable to disentangle the two effects empirically.

References

Becker, G. (1976) "The Economic Approach to Human Behavior," in G. Becker (ed.) *The Economic Approach to Human Behavior*, Chicago, IL: University of Chicago Press.

Bian, Y. J. (2002) "Social Capital of the Firm and Its Impact on Performance: A Social Network Analysis," in A. S. Tsui and C. M. Lau (eds.) *The Management of Enterprises in the People's Republic of China*, New York: Kluwer Academic Publishers.

Boisot, M. and Child, J. (1996) "From Fiefs to Clans and Network Capitalism: Explaining China's Emerging Economic Order," *Administrative Science Quarterly* 41:600–628.

Brown, J. and Bose, M. B. (eds.) (1993) *Entrepreneurship, Networks, and Modern Business*, Manchester, U.K. and New York: Manchester University Press.

Granovetter, M. (1985) "Economic Action and Social Structure: The Problem of Embeddedness," *American Journal of Sociology* 91:481–510.

Kerridge, E. (1985) *Textile Manufactures in Early Modern England*, Manchester, U.K.: Manchester University Press.

McKenzie, R. B. and Tullock, G. (1989) *The Best of the New World of Economics … and then some*, Homewood, IL: Irwin.

Naughton, B. (1995) *Growing Out of the Plan: Chinese Economic Reform, 1978– 1993*, New York: Oxford University Press.

Peng, Y. (2004) "Kinship Networks and Entrepreneurs in China's Transitional Economy," *American Journal of Sociology* 109(5):1045–74.

Uzzi, B. (1997) "Social Structure and Competition in Interfirm Networks: The Paradox of Embeddedness," *Administrative Science Quarterly* 42:35–67.

White, H. (2002) "Markets and Firms," in M. Guillen, R. Collins, P. England, and M. Meyer (eds.) *The New Economic Sociology*, New York: Russell Sage Foundation.

Wu, J. L. (2003) *China's Economic Reform* (Dangdai Zhongguo Jingji Gaige), Shanghai: Shanghai Fareast Press (Shanghai Yuandong Chubanshe).

Zhou, X. G., Zhao, W., Li, Q., and Cai, H. (2003) "Embeddedness and Contractual Relationships in China's Transitional Economy," *American Sociological Review* 68: 75–102.

9 The spirit of Chinese entrepreneurship

Management practices and philosophy among business owners in Hong Kong[1]

Raymond Sin-Kwok Wong

Introduction

During the first half of 1997, the economy of Hong Kong was performing extremely well. In fact, throughout the 1990s, Hong Kong enjoyed a robust double-digit growth in its gross domestic product, though it was somewhat tamed by rampant inflation as well (Census and Statistics Department 1998). There was no immediate alarm from either government officials or the public regarding the seriousness of the impending economic crisis. The then-British colony was preoccupied in preparing for a peaceful transition to a Special Administration Region (SAR) under Chinese rule. Besides, Hong Kong has weathered several major economic crises before, including those in the late 1960s and early 1980s. If history could be its guide, there was little reason to doubt its resilience to survive and perhaps emerge even stronger after the crisis, given its huge foreign capital reserve and strong political and economic backing from the Chinese government.

Much of the robust growth in the postwar Hong Kong economy has been credited to, in both popular and academic literature, the government's positive *non-intervention* policies and, more importantly, its hard working labor force and the entrepreneurial spirit of big and small Chinese business owners. Compared to many advanced industrial societies, a relatively high proportion of the labor force is engaged in entrepreneurial activities. According to government statistics, about 10 percent of the economically active population has employment status either as employers or self-employed workers in the 1990s (Census and Statistics Department 1998). For instance, about 296,600 of the 2.75 million workers were business owners or self-employed workers in 1991. The number increased steadily to 301,100 in 1997, though its proportional share declined from 10.8 percent to 9.6 percent due to rapid expansion of the labor force. The vibrant activities of these entrepreneurs not only create jobs for themselves and others, but also provide flexibility and dynamism to the Hong Kong economy, adapting well to the ever-changing global economy.

To some, this entrepreneurial spirit (also found among the Chinese diaspora in Taiwan, Singapore, Thailand, Malaysia, and elsewhere in the world) can be partly credited to the common salutary Chinese cultural traditions, particularly (post-)Confucian ethics that stress the importance of inter-personal relatedness, harmony, obligations, and responsibility (Berger and Hsiao 1988; Bond and Hofstede 1990; Hofstede 1980; Kahn 1979; Rozman 1991; Vogel 1991). To others, drawing on the work of Fei (1992) regarding how the Chinese relational logic produces a society based largely on social networks, its economic success is due to the strong family relations in Chi-nese business organizations and the development of entrepreneurial network skills. Business ties are structured by pre-existing interpersonal ties, and these personalized networks (*quanxi*) are instrumental in facilitating and enhancing economic transactions (Chen 1986; Fukuyama 1995; Hamilton and Kao 1990; Huang 1988; Redding 1988). They further contend that since lineage (family and kinship) is important in structuring horizontal networks, Chinese businesses tend to be small family-run firms that are linked together by a complex web of personal networks (Chan 1982; Lau 1982; Omohundro 1981, Wong 1985). It is these dense and interrelated personal networks that account for the flexibility and dynamism of the economy in Hong Kong and elsewhere.

In sum, the conventional wisdom of the spirit of Chinese entrepreneur-ship is that Chinese businesses are believed to: (1) be small with relatively simple organizational structure; (2) have centralized decision making with heavy reliance on one dominant executive; (3) have a close overlap of own-ership, control, and family; (4) have a paternalistic organizational climate; and (5) be linked to the environment through networks of interpersonal obligations (Redding 1990).[2]

As the economic troubles deepened and unfolded rapidly to include many other East Asian countries including Hong Kong, Western observers were quick to blame the imploding problem to the dark side of the previous vir-tues—Chinese cultural values and personal social networks—that breed cronyism as well as an inability to embrace universalistic practices in man-agement. While it is reasonable to blame part of the problem on the irra-tional exuberance and speculative excesses in these economies in the 1990s, particularly in the stock and property markets, the association with one's roots as some kind of cultural predisposition or cultural predetermination is a completely different matter.

Previous discussion of Chinese firms and entrepreneurs in Hong Kong and elsewhere tended to be based on conjecture rather than systematic empirical inquiry. Even for those who draw their findings from empirical investigations, many suffer from the problem of nonrepresentative and/or homogeneous samples, that is, firms and/or entrepreneurs drawn from a single industry or sector rather than representations from the entire popu-lation. For instance, it is difficult to generalize findings from small manu-facturing owners who tend to be less educated and male-dominated to, say, owners in the financial, insurance, and real estate (FIRE) sector. While it might be reasonable to study industrial owners in the 1970s and early 1980s when they made significant contributions to the overall Hong Kong economy, this selective approach is becoming less and less compelling today when the importance of the industrial sector has declined precipitously, representing less than 13 percent of the labor force and only 9.1 percent of the establishments in 1997 (Census and Statistics Department 1998). Just like other advanced industrial societies, the Hong Kong economy has been rapidly transformed from a manufacturing to a service economy.

Furthermore, the changing demographic can have profound implications for business entrepreneurs and their management strategies (see Chapter 4 for details). Unlike their immigrant parents, the majority of citizens today are born, raised, and educated in Hong Kong. The continuous educational upgrading, with record numbers of eligible college-bound students, means that modern entrepreneurs are not only indigenous, but they are also better educated, more exposed to Western management practices and philosophies, and more inclined to adopt Western methods of organizing economic activities. With the rise of the nuclear family and the call for gender equality, the notion of passing on the family business to sons may become less compelling, as is the idea of relying on children for the labor pool. As a result, many old and traditional practices of the family business may no longer be functional, and conventional images of Chinese firms and entrepreneurs may no longer hold in the contemporary setting. Does it mean the changing social demography will lead to the making of a new breed of Chinese entrepreneur? How many of today's entrepreneurs exhibit such a modern outlook? Finally, if the development is indeed real, then our understanding of their social composition, motivations, and management styles are all important in shedding new light on the modern Chinese entrepreneurs.

My earlier work (Wong 2004) on similar issues has already cast some doubts on prior received wisdom. Using the citywide probability samples of organizations and business owners (*HKBOS* and *HKBES*) collected in the late 1990s, I found that the organizational structure of firms in contemporary Hong Kong no longer conforms to the conventional images as small, flat, and undifferentiated. In fact, the degree of organizational complexity of Hong Kong firms, in terms of number of vertical levels, formalization, decentralization, and departmentalization, has become remarkably similar to firms in the United States.[3] Also, contrary to the notion that the typical Chinese firms is a *family* firm, only about one third of the Hong Kong firms surveyed in both surveys actually have family members and relatives working in the company (see also King and Leung 1975); less than one third of the owners identify their businesses as family firms; and less than 40 percent of owners intend to pass their businesses to their children. Taken together, no more than two thirds of firms in the entrepreneur survey satisfy at least one of the three criteria and can therefore be broadly defined as family firms. While the number is high, it is by no means phenomenal and is indeed comparable to that in developed economies such as Canada and the

United Kingdom (Rock 1991; see also other data in this volume). Finally, while some entrepreneurs still support hiring family members and relatives, a surprisingly large proportion, particularly those born in Hong Kong, view negatively such practices and other Chinese family firm practices. Entrepreneurs who currently employ family members tend to emphasize personal/ personality traits in identifying important attributes for successful entrepreneurs, whereas those who are older and born in Hong Kong tend to emphasize managerial/network skills. In sum, if *family firms* were indeed the norm of Chinese firms in the 1970s and 1980s, the organizational environment in the 1990s is dramatically different in contemporary Hong Kong, and Chinese business entrepreneurs nowadays are more open to Western management and organizational strategies.

Building on my previous findings, this chapter seeks to further our understanding of the spirit of Chinese entrepreneurship by examining the following issues: (a) the social composition of contemporary business owners; (b) their motivations for entrepreneurship; and (c) their management style and philosophy. The major findings from the present study can be summarized as the following: (1) the motivation of contemporary entrepreneurs is dominated by the profit motive, to be one's own boss, income self-determination, need for autonomy, and need for achievement; (2) these motives are commonly shared by owners who consider their businesses as family firms, intend to pass them on to their children, and whose parents were also business owners; (3) the motivations of women entrepreneurs are substantially lower than men; (4) the management style and philosophy of business owners can be divided into two major types: managerial/administrative versus paternalistic; (5) those who had partners, born in Hong Kong, and stressed the importance of entrepreneurial skills as successful entrepreneurs are more likely to adopt managerial/administrative practices, whereas those whose parents were owners, had favorable attitudes to Chinese family firms, and considered their companies as family businesses tend to de-emphasize its importance; (6) those who considered their companies as family business intended to pass them on to their children; and (7) Cantonese, especially those who were not born in Hong Kong, and who have had a long tenure in business ownership, are more likely to practice a paternalistic style of management.

Chinese entrepreneurship in Hong Kong

With its vibrant entrepreneurial activities, Hong Kong constitutes a rich resource for studying Chinese entrepreneurship. There have been several noteworthy studies of entrepreneurship in Hong Kong; however, past analyses were mostly based on either aggregate firm level statistics or samples of specific entrepreneurs such as the Shanghainese cotton spinners, factory owners, or large business groups, rather than a spectrum of firms covering *all* sectors and sizes (Sit 1982; Sit et al. 1979; Tuan et al. 1986; S. L. Wong

1988). Like any restricted case study, such single-type organizational studies have limited utility as their results cannot be readily generalized to the entire population of firms or owners. More importantly, even if the generalizations hold true, they are derived from the experiences of a particular period of time (from the 1960s to the early 1980s) and may no longer be relevant today. Last, previous works often rely on descriptive, not multivariate, analyses and their findings may not hold when other factors are simultaneously controlled.

The following provides a brief sketch of what we know about entrepreneurship—the social composition, motivations, and management style and philosophy of owners—in both the Western literature and the Hong Kong context. In terms of social composition, entrepreneurs, particularly those in the technical fields, are likely to be drawn from the same trade before venturing into ownership. The field is predominantly dominated by men, though women's representation has increased dramatically over time. A substantial proportion of entrepreneurs is drawn from the immigrant population, as their credentials and skills are often not recognized in the new setting (Light 1972; Light and Rosenstein 1995). In particular, Sit, Wong, and their associates (Sit et al. 1979; Sit and Wong 1989) found that an overwhelming majority of Hong Kong entrepreneurs in the 1970s and 1980s were indeed immigrants from mainland China.

There is a voluminous literature on what motivates the entrepreneurs to take control of their own destiny rather than be salaried workers. Three factors have been identified that would affect an individual's decision to start a new firm: (a) the characteristics of the economic context; (b) the characteristics of the individual's life or career context; and (c) underlying individual disposition. Most studies, however, focus on the push and pull factors. Pull factors consider the psychology of the entrepreneur, which includes the desire for independence, responsibility and power, and the need for achievement (Brockhaus and Horwitz 1986; Carland et. al. 1984; Cooper 1986; McClelland 1961). On the other hand, push factors involve being fired or laid off and being frustrated or dissatisfied in the previous jobs (Brockhaus 1982; Cooper 1971; Susbauer 1972; Thorne and Ball 1981); difficulty in getting ideas advanced, lack of reward, lack of organizational fit, and lack of advancement and promotion (Casale 1986; Myers and Hobbs 1986). The importance of push factors is found to be particularly relevant among technical entrepreneurs but relatively unimportant to those not engaged in the manufacturing and high-technology sector (Cooper and Dunkelberg 1986).

Past findings found that women entrepreneurs possess very different motivations, business skills levels, and occupational background to their male counterparts (Carr 1996; Hisrich 1986; Smith et al. 1982). Men are often motivated by the drive to control their own destiny and to make things happen. This drive often stems from disagreement with their boss or a feeling that they can run things better. Women, in contrast, tend to be

motivated by the idea of independence and achievement arising from job
frustration where they have not been allowed to perform at the level they are
capable of. Among male entrepreneurs, the transition from a past occupation to the new venture is often facilitated because of an outgrowth of a
present job, sideline, or hobby. On the other hand, women often leave an
occupation with only a high level of frustration and enthusiasm for the new
venture rather than experience. The major motivations of a woman entrepreneur are more independence, achievement, job frustration, job satisfac-
tion, and self-fulfillment rather than money and power.

There is general agreement that there is no such entity as the typical
entrepreneur that fits a single, uniform profile. However, there is considerable disagreement on how many different types of entrepreneur can be
classified. Smith (1967; 1976) found are only two major types: craftspersons
versus opportunists (see also Hornaday and Bunker 1970; Smith and Miner
1984). The craftsmen-entrepreneurs (CEs) tend to have an education limited
to technical training, mostly technical job experience, little involvement in
any professional association, and poor communication skills. In dealings
with their employees, they are paternalistic, particularistic, follow relatively
rigid strategies, and reluctant to delegate authority. Their time orientation is
to the immediate and they do not plan for future growth or change. In
contrast, the opportunistic entrepreneurs (OEs) received both technical and
non-technical formal training and had a variety of work experience beyond
technical or mechanical positions. They exhibit high social awareness, evi-
denced by membership in community as well as professional associations;
are effective in communication, hiring workers on a universalistic basis; non-
paternalistic; and exhibit an awareness of and an orientation to the future.
Authority is delegated in order to allow the organization to grow. In sum,
craftsmen-entrepreneurs tended toward rigidity and opportunistic entrepreneurs tended toward adaptiveness. It has also been found that men are more
likely to belong to the former type while women entrepreneurs are more likely
to be the latter (Smith et al. 1982; see also the works cited in Chapter 6).

On the other hand, Filley and Aldag (1978) found three ideal types of
owner: craftsman, promotion, and administration types. Craftsmen were
non-adaptive, inclined to avoid risk, and concentrated on making a comfortable living. Promotion firms were small in size and organized informally
to exploit some unique competitive advantage. They tend to be centrally
controlled by the chief executive and were often short-lived and transitional
in nature. Finally, administrative firms were the most formalized and professional; they utilized planning, written policies, and budgetary controls;
and they were larger in size and less dependent on the personal leadership
of the chief executive.

Through a large-scale study of small employers, Dunkelberg and Cooper
(1982) also found three types of entrepreneur: growth-oriented owners, desire
for independence, and craftsmen orientation. Growth-oriented owners seek
substantial growth of their businesses. Desire for independence entrepreneurs

are strongly driven to avoid working for others but have no strong desire to build an organization. Last, craftsman-oriented owners are strongly oriented toward doing the work they do best, and they are most comfortable in selling or handling a technical problem rather than in working on management issues. Note that Dunkelberg and Cooper's (1982) typology did not include a group of entrepreneurs as in Filley and Aldag (1978) who might be thought of as opportunistic, managerial, or administrative entrepreneurs.

In their study of factory owners in the industrial district of Kwun Tong in Hong Kong, King and Leung (1975) found two distinct types of authority relations: economic-rational and traditional human relation. The former puts emphasis on proper performance and efficiency but not personal relationships with workers, whereas the latter stresses the importance of establishing a "humanized relationship" or *gaan ching* between owners and workers. King and Leung (1975) labeled the latter practice as "managerial indulgence," because it signifies an owner's tolerance of some workers' deeds in the workplace that lie beyond the "official" line of behavior. These behaviors include: (1) the practice of lending money to workers who are in urgent financial difficulty; (2) the provision of a relaxing and non-rigid working environment; and (3) the entrepreneurs' desire to establish *gaan ching* with their workers. Furthermore, it appears that such distinction is ethnically based; the former is commonly found among Shanghainese owners whereas the latter among Cantonese owners. With the exception of ethnic ties, the classification developed by King and Leung is largely consistent with the craftsman and opportunistic types discussed earlier.

One major problem with these different ideal types is that their identifications are rather unstable, highly dependent on the specific items included in the type construction. Often it is unclear why a particular set of characteristics should be included (such as prior job experience, background characteristics, motives and desires, and alike) in the construction. Sometimes, the same items may then be used to adjudicate differences between the types identified in the process, thereby creating a circular or tautological argument. In the analysis below, only items that are directly related to the management style and philosophy of owners are used at the identification stage. After the construction of types of entrepreneur, I then try to understand which factors contribute to the specific patterns uncovered earlier.

Data

The present study of Chinese entrepreneurs is based on the *Hong Kong Business Entrepreneurs Survey* (*HKBES*) collected by the author in 1997. It is a citywide probability sample, funded by the National Science Foundation of the United States and conducted by the Social Science Research Centre (SSRC) at the University of Hong Kong. A common problem in generating a random sample of entrepreneurs (or organizations) is the *absence* of a complete sampling frame. Most lists of organizations are incomplete or limited to one or a few types and may omit or under-represent certain organizations, especially small or new ones. Fortunately, this does not constitute a problem here because the Hong Kong Census and Statistics Department collects periodic information of *all* registered establishments in Hong Kong. The author was able to obtain a 20 percent random sample of establishments as of March 1997.[4]

The master database contained information about the name, address, industry, district code, and establishment size. After eliminating nonprofit organizations, a stratified random sample (by over-sampling medium and large establishments) was drawn.[5] Different methods were used to trace the telephone numbers that matched the address and name of the establishment. A total of 134 telephone interviews was completed. Aside from some slight under-representation of entrepreneurs with an establishment size of 1–2 and overrepresentation of establishments with a size of 10–19 from the sampling frame, there is no indication that the sample is biased in any systematic manner, even though the response rate is less than 20 percent.

The survey collects detailed socioeconomic characteristics of owners, their work histories (first and last occupation prior to operating their own businesses), nature of their businesses, management style and philosophy, motivations for entrepreneurship, attitudes to hiring family members and relatives, attitudes to Chinese family business firms, and their assessment of factors contributing to the economic success of Hong Kong under British rule. Appropriate weights are then constructed so that the distribution might represent the population of establishments in Hong Kong and thereby the population of entrepreneurs. The results below are based on weighted analyses.

Empirical findings

Despite the negative findings from my earlier study, supporters of the culturalist argument may still be reluctant to concede that the evidence contradicts their assertions. They would continue to insist that cultural effects are less powerful in shaping formal structures and overall strategy because of economic reality, but they would be critical in shaping organizational behavior and practices relating to authority, style, and attitudes in management and administration (Child 1981). Thus, our understanding of the latter here should shed more light on the ongoing debate.

Before proceeding to the analysis of business owners, we need to understand the nature of business activities at the time of the study (see Wong, Chapter 4 of this volume, for a more thorough historical discussion). Table 9.1 reports the distribution of establishment sizes by industry in 1997, tabulated from the 20 percent sample of all registered establishments. The distribution confirms that the overwhelming majority of establishments (over 87 percent) are small with less than 10 workers. This is true for all industries, with the only exception that more than 21 percent of the establishments in the transportation and storage industry have more than 10 workers.

Table 9.1 Distribution of size of establishments by industry in Hong Kong, 1997

Established size	Manu-facturing	Construc-tion	Wholesale/ retail, import/ export, restaurant/ hotel	Transport/ storage	Finance/ insurance/ real estate/ business services	Community/ social/ personal services	Total
1–2	37.50	51.59	50.96	36.30	55.61	41.30	49.42
3–4	20.10	21.18	22.55	20.35	19.15	24.28	21.79
5–9	20.23	15.99	16.33	22.02	13.18	17.70	16.43
10–19	11.28	6.19	6.32	12.00	6.67	8.72	7.13
20–49	7.10	3.63	2.73	6.12	3.52	4.31	3.51
50–99	2.18	0.84	0.74	1.73	1.00	2.83	1.09
100+	1.62	0.59	0.38	1.48	0.87	0.86	0.64
Total	100.00	100.00	100.00	100.00	100.0	100.00	100.00
N	5419	5123	38183	2025	9991	4988	65729
	8.24	7.79	58.09	3.08	15.20	7.59	100.00

The gradual opening of China's economic door to foreign investment which began in 1978 has transformed the Hong Kong economy in two significant ways. First, more and more industrial operations were relocated across the border, initiated first by medium and large factories, and then almost in wholesale fashion by small factories as well. Many of those that stayed eventually ceased operations. As a result, the importance of manufacturing declined precipitously. By 1997, only 8.2 percent of the registered establishments were in the manufacturing industry. It has been estimated that Hong Kong business owners, directly and indirectly, employ 7–10 million workers in China, far exceeding the total working population of Hong Kong (Tang 1993:45). Second, the economy is now dominated by the service sector. More than 58 percent of establishments were in the wholesale and retail, import and export, and hotel and restaurant industry and another 15 percent were in the finance, insurance, real estate, and business services industry. With more and more contemporary owners engaging in trade and services rather than industrial manufacturing, the transformation may also alter the composition of business owners and their management practice and style.

Social composition of Chinese entrepreneurs

Given the importance of manufacturing in the immediate postwar era, it is understandable why past studies of entrepreneurs in Hong Kong focused exclusively on industrial owners. To date, there has been no single study of entrepreneurs in the city that is generalizable to the entire population. To maintain comparability with past results, the first two columns of Table 9.2 report figures from the 1978 and 1987 survey of industrial owners (Sit et al.

1979; Sit and Wong 1989) whereas columns 3 and 4 are tabulated from *HKBES* for industrial owners and the entire sample, respectively.

The mean age of respondents in *HKBES* is 42.8 among industrial owners and 40.6 in the overall sample. While most of the entrepreneurs in the 1970s and 1980s were composed largely of immigrants from mainland China, more than two thirds of them today are native-born citizens, with virtually no difference between the sub-sample of industrial owners and the entire sample. According to Sit and Wong (1989), the immigrant entrepreneurs in the 1970s and 1980s echoed closely the influx of refugees resulting from waves of political events on the mainland. If we combine the estimate of 65.7 percent of industrial owners who were also immigrants from China in 1973 (King and Leung 1975) and the role played by mainland capitalists like the Shanghai cotton spinners in shaping and transforming Hong Kong into an industrial center in the 1950s and 1960s (Wong 1988), it seems safe to conclude that immigrants undoubtedly played an important role in entrepreneurship for more than four decades. But since the beginning of the 1990s, their proportionate share dropped precipitously and now only represents about 30 percent of entrepreneurs. Among those immigrant owners today, half of them came to Hong Kong before 1978 and the other half after 1978. It should be noted that the indigenous growth of entrepreneurs applies not only to industrial owners but spreads across all industries. Undoubtedly, a sizable proportion of the owners' parents are immigrants themselves, just like the majority of the parents of the adult population as well. This group of modern entrepreneurs, born and educated under colonial rule and widely exposed to Western ideas, may belong to a new type of entrepreneur who may differ from their parent's generation.

As expected, entrepreneurial activity is still very much dominated by men. Only about 15 percent of them are women. Although the proportion is small, it represents a significant improvement over time, where only 5 and 8 percent of industrial owners were women in 1978 and 1987, respectively (Sit and Wong 1989:70). Relative to their male counterparts, the size of establishment that women entrepreneurs managed is generally smaller. This difference, however, is not statistically significant, due to insufficient cases. The average number of workers per establishment is 44.0 for manufacturing and 44.4 in the entire sample, but the medians are only three workers in both cases.

The past finding that first- and second-born children have greater propensity to become entrepreneurs appears only to be true for those who engage in industrial activities. For the entire sample, less than half of them are first- or second-born children while the remaining owners are third- and lower-order children. The difference in birth order by industrial activity is statistically significant. It is not clear why the former is more susceptible to industrial entrepreneurship. Three explanations are plausible. First, the outcome may have little to do with birth order but rather be because of economic necessity. First- and second-born children are more likely to begin

Table 9.2 The social composition of Hong Kong business entrepreneurs

Variable description	Percentage distribution			
	1978	*1987*	*1997 (Manufacturing)*	*1997 (All)*
A. Place of birth	N = 413	N = 276	N = 41	N = 130
Hong Kong	20.2	31.4	72.0	66.7
Mainland China	77.3	63.9	27.4	28.9
Elsewhere	2.4	4.7	0.6	4.4
B. Birth order	N = 413	N = 264	N = 40	N = 130
First	42.1	31.4	65.1	28.1
Second	23.2	20.1	7.1	19.9
Third	16.5	18.6	18.8	34.4
Fourth and higher	18.2	29.8	9.0	17.6
C. Father's Education	N = 388	N = 219	N = 34	N = 111
No schooling	35.8	38.8	21.2	24.8
Primary	39.2	32.0	45.0	33.6
Secondary	19.1	22.9	32.9	29.1
Tertiary	5.9	6.4	0.8	12.5
D. Individual education	N = 413	N = 276	N = 41	N = 134
No schooling	5.1	4.3	0.0	0.0
Primary	36.4	27.5	12.2	7.7
Secondary	48.9	55.8	80.9	61.3
Tertiary	9.6	12.3	6.9	31.1
E. Age when starting business	N = 398	N = 275	N = 37	N = 126
29 and below	32.0	25.2	53.7	38.5
30–39	42.3	44.4	42.8	54.4
40–49	18.1	20.4	2.2	5.1
50–59	7.1	9.1	1.3	2.0
60 and above	0.5	0.7	0.0	0.0
F. Parent owner			N = 41	N = 133
Yes			52.6	55.2
No			47.4	44.8
G. Method of acquisition			N = 41	N = 129
Start from scratch			68.1	77.4
Bought			25.1	13.0
Inherited			5.6	8.5
Other			1.2	1.1

Source: Sit and Wong (1989), see text for details.

their work careers as industrial workers and to provide economic support for the family at the time when manufacturing jobs were abundant. Second, industrial ownership may require certain characteristics and personality traits that can be commonly found among first- and second-born children. Finally, while the effect of birth-order may have been important in the past, there should be no real difference between industrial and non-industrial owners today and the observed difference is due to sampling variability.

Unfortunately, we do not have additional information or enough cases to adjudicate the validity of each explanation.

As expected, the educational attainment of entrepreneurs and their fathers is significantly higher today than their counterparts in 1978 and 1987. In 1978, more than 75 percent of entrepreneurs had fathers with no more than primary education. In 1997, only 57 percent of them attained such an educational level whereas the proportion of fathers who had tertiary education actually doubled. Whereas close to 41.5 percent of industrial owners had no more than primary education in 1978, that number declined rapidly to 31.8 percent in 1987, and 12.2 percent in 1997 among industrial owners and only 7.7 percent in the full sample. On the other hand, the number of owners with tertiary education more than tripled. A detailed breakdown of individual education by place of birth (not shown) further reveals that the educational attainment of immigrant entrepreneurs tends to be polarized (the difference is statistically significant at the 0.001 level). Over 40 percent had less than junior high school education, compared to only 23 percent among native-born entrepreneurs. On the other hand, about 40 percent of immigrants had tertiary education, significantly higher than their native-born counterparts (26.6 percent).

It should be noted that although the difference in educational attainment between native and immigrant owners is significant, it is not individual education per se that accounts for whether a particular entrepreneur will disfavor the hiring of family members and relatives or be less sympathetic with the practices of Chinese family firms. According to my previous analyses, it is those Hong Kong natives, irrespective of educational attainment, who display patterns that are contrary to the received wisdom regarding Chinese entrepreneurship and therefore lend credence to the argument that Westernization, childhood socialization, and the unique social and cultural milieu of Hong Kong all contribute to the formation of a new breed of entrepreneurs (Wong 2004). There is also no difference between natives and immigrants in terms of the size of their businesses. The validity of this claim will be illustrated further when we examine the correlates of the practice and style of management.

Most entrepreneurs started their own business before age 40 (over 90 percent did so in 1997). This is considerably higher than earlier figures reported by Sit and Wong (1989) in 1978 and 1987 (74 and 70 percent, respectively). Such a difference reflects two concurrent trends. On the one hand, since immigrants constituted the majority of entrepreneurs in the early years and they came to Hong Kong as adults, they would have to work for some time before striking out on their own. This is indeed the common route to entrepreneurship among industrial workers. The role of early socialization and parental encouragement of entrepreneurship as a way of life, on the other hand, are probably more important today. In fact, a sizable proportion of entrepreneurs (over 55 percent) had at least one of their parents also engaged in entrepreneurial activities earlier (Dunn and

Holtz-Eakin 2000; Greene 2000; Hout and Rosen 2000; Laferrere 2001; Shavit and Yuchtman-Yaar 2001). In terms of the mean age of starting one's business, however, there is virtually no difference between those whose parents were owners and non-owners (31.1 versus 31.5, results not shown) and there is also no industry-specific difference. Thus, even though parental entrepreneurship contributed to individual entrepreneurship, modern Chinese entrepreneurs simply began their entrepreneurial activities at a much younger age.

The predominant method of acquisition was to start from scratch, and more than three quarters of them did so. Even for those whose parents were also business owners, only 14.5 percent actually inherited the business. Thus, the social reproduction of the entrepreneurial class is indirect, via socialization rather than direct reproduction. Close to 75 percent of the responses listed personal savings as the largest source of their required funding and almost 91 percent of it came exclusively from such source. Many of these firms started out small and continued to be small. These findings can have profound implications for class mobility and class reproduction (Aldrich et al. 1998; Wong 1992).

Motivation for entrepreneurship

What prompts individuals to choose the uncertain path of striking out of their own rather than be a salaried/waged employees? Are push factors as important as pull factors? To answer such questions, we turn to a list of items that asked respondents to rate their importance in their decision to become entrepreneurs. The items are measured in a Likert 5-point scale, ranging from very important to not important at all. They include: to make money/profit, be one's own boss, income self-determination, need for autonomy, need for achievement, a means to survive, and loss of previous job. Obviously, the profit motive is of paramount importance, with 30 percent of entrepreneurs rating it very important and another 54.2 percent as important (Table 9.3). Two other items also receiving high marks are to be one's own boss and the need for autonomy. The promises of financial gain and control of one's destiny clearly represent the underlying appeal of entrepreneurship. Surprisingly, despite entrepreneurship being an outcome of purposive action, over 80 percent still credited opportunity and chance as important factors. They simply acknowledged that they happened to be in the right place at the right time. The push factor, on the other hand, plays only minor role, with only 22 percent of respondents saying that the loss of their previous job was critical while 60 percent regarded it as completely unimportant.

Using the conventional cutoff value of one in the eigenvalue, results from principal component factor analysis indicate that only one factor is needed (see the bottom panel of Table 9.3). In particular, five items have loadings greater than 0.30; they include: to make money/profit, be one's own boss, income self-determination, need for autonomy, and need for achievement. The remaining items—chance, a means to survive, and loss of previous job—

Table 9.3 Motivation for entrepreneurship: descriptive and factor analysis

A. Descriptive outcomes

Variable description	Very important	Important	Neutral	Not important	Not important at all	N
Profit	30.0	54.2	0.0	0.8	10.3	132
To be one's own boss	17.1	53.0	0.2	1.4	28.4	132
Income self-determination	6.6	67.4	1.7	2.2	22.2	133
Need for autonomy	16.1	76.7	0.0	0.2	7.2	133
Need for achievement	10.6	69.8	1.1	2.9	15.7	132
Chance	14.8	69.3	0.4	2.3	13.2	132
A means to survive	7.2	47.9	3.8	1.6	39.5	132
Loss of previous job	1.5	20.2	17.2	0.9	60.3	127

B. Factor analysis

Variable description	Factor loading	Uniqueness
Profit	*0.497*	0.753
To be one's own boss	*0.463*	0.786
Income self-determination	*0.758*	0.426
Need for autonomy	*0.641*	0.590
Need for achievement	*0.325*	0.895
Chance	0.040	0.998
A means to survive	−0.164	0.973
Loss of previous job	−0.078	0.994

all have extremely weak loadings. Thus, the result here not only validates that entrepreneurship is a purposive action requiring a high degree of self-determination; it also suggests that pull factors are more important than push factors. Based on the loadings, factor scores are extracted and standardized to have a mean of 0 and standard deviation of 1. The newly constructed variable, MOTIVES, has the signs of the scores reversed so that a high score means high motivation and vice versa.

To understand what characteristics are affiliated with high or low values in MOTIVES, the standardized factor scores are then regressed to a list of correlated factors. They include demographic characteristics, organizational characteristics, attitudes to Chinese family firms, attitudes to the hiring of family members and relatives, attributes of successful entrepreneurs, considering the owner's business as a family business, and the intention to pass the business to one's children.[6] It should be stressed that the variables reported here are *correlates*, not causes, of what motivates individual entrepreneurship. Because of its exploratory nature and the small sample size, the decision to omit variables is based on the backward step strategy, that is, all insignificant parameters are dropped from the full model one at a time. Only parameters that are significant at the 0.05 level (2-tailed test) are retained and reported in Table 9.4.

Generally speaking, individual education, ethnicity (Cantonese versus non-Cantonese), and birthplace are not important in order to differentiate what motivates people to be entrepreneurs. On the other hand, men are more likely than women to stress the importance of profit, need for autonomy, and need for achievement in starting their own businesses. This, of course, does not mean that women entrepreneurs are not motivated by similar factors. They probably do but, consistent with the Western literature, women entrepreneurs consider self-fulfillment and other non-pecuniary factors as well (Blanchflower 2000; Hirsrich 1986; Jurik 1998; Taylor 1999). Interestingly, younger entrepreneurs are more likely than older ones to stress the importance of these factors. It is unclear whether the result signifies that older owners are less motivated by economic necessity or that it represents some kind of generational difference.

Entrepreneurs whose parents were owners are more motivated. Relative to sole proprietors, owners with partners or those engaged in incorporated businesses tend to lay less stress on such a motivation. With close to 80 percent of the incorporated businesses having two or more partners, the presence of partners significantly relieves some of the burden of entrepreneurship. Although the burden of failures and the psychological pressures on sole proprietors can still be considerable, the promises of financial return and achievement are what keeps entrepreneurship attractive.

On the other hand, owners who value the possession of entrepreneurial skills, that is, those who emphasize the importance of organization and management skills, cultivate humanized relationships (*renqingwan*), negotiating skills, adapt to changes, have goodwill (*xinyong*), and avoid nepotism, tend

Table 9.4 Correlates of motivation for entrepreneurship

Variable	Coefficient	Standard error	p-value
Intercept	−0.467	0.551	
Female	−0.810	0.327	*
Age	−0.023	0.010	*
Parent owner	0.514	0.186	**
Business type–partnership[#]	−0.464	0.194	*
Business type–incorporated[#]	−0.464	0.194	*
Entrepreneurial skill	−0.271	0.093	**
Consider organization family business	0.513	0.214	*
Pass organization to family member	0.650	0.190	***
R^2		0.283	
Adjusted R^2		0.230	
N		102	
F-statistic		5.31	
RMSE		0.899	

Notes:
*p < 0.05, **p < 0.01, ***p < 0.001.
Equality restriction applied.

to be less motivated. This probably reflects a selection process: those who are confident that they can make it would not consider these items critical in the decision process as they are already predisposed to entrepreneurship. Finally, entrepreneurs who consider their businesses as family firms or intend to pass them on to their children are particularly more motivated. For them, the success of their business ventures reflects their own success as well as their family legacy.

Management style and philosophy

What kind of management style and philosophy do most Hong Kong business owners adopt today? Are they still as authoritarian and paternalistic as is commonly assumed in the literature? The *HKBES* contains 17 items about three different aspects of the managerial style of business owners; nine items on how owners motivate workers to perform well in the workplace (encourage teamwork, be sensitive to emotional needs, offer more money/pay, provide positive feedback, offer training opportunities, create a positive climate, reward special initiatives); four items on the relationship between owners and workers (think of me as friend, boss, equal, and one big family); and four items on the management style of successful entrepreneurs (delegate power, establish mutual trust, establish clear reward and punishment, and centralize decision making). They are all rated on a Likert 5-point scale, ranging from strongly agree to strongly disagree.

Items that show the most agreement among entrepreneurs include encourage teamwork, be sensitive to emotional needs, offer more money/pay, provide positive feedback, offer training opportunities, create a positive climate, reward special initiatives, think of us as one big family, establish mutual trust, establish clear rewards and punishments, and centralize decision making. The items showing the most disagreement include think of me as boss; and items with polarized or mixed responses include offer advancement opportunity, think of me as friend, think of me as equal, and lend money.

Results from factor analysis reveal that two underlying factors are needed to account for the relationship among the items (see bottom panel of Table 9.5). The first factor has large loadings on encourage teamwork, be sensitive to emotional needs, offer more money/pay, offer advancement opportunity, offer training opportunities, create a positive climate, delegate power, establish mutual trust, and establish clear rewards and punishments. The second factor has large loadings on lend money, reward special initiatives, think of us as one big family, and create a positive climate (in opposite direction). The first factor can be interpreted to represent a Western managerial style that is instrumental but fair, and does not rely on personal relationships with one's employees (hereafter labeled MANAGERIAL). The second factor, on the other hand, represents a more humanistic, traditional, or paternalistic style of management (hereafter labeled PATERNALISTIC). This observation is strikingly consistent with the one reported by King and

Table 9.5 Management style and philosophy: descriptive and factor analysis

A. Descriptive analysis (N = 128)

Variable description	SA	A	NA/ND	D	SD
Motivate–encourage teamwork	19.30	70.72	0.64	1.10	8.24
Motivate–sensitive to emotional need	6.59	87.82	1.88	0.33	3.38
Motivate–offer more money	9.63	81.19	4.12	1.77	3.28
Motivate–offer advancement opportunity	10.30	68.28	4.77	0.47	16.19
Motivate–lend money	0.55	43.42	15.07	10.41	30.55
Motivate–provide positive feedback	15.50	75.75	0.18	1.50	7.07
Motivate–offer training opportunity	5.92	87.63	0.29	0.14	6.03
Motivate–create positive climate	15.60	82.64	0.14	0.39	1.24
Motivate–reward special initiatives	7.52	74.11	2.53	7.75	8.10
Relation–think of me as friend	9.65	65.25	0.00	2.85	22.25
Relation–think of me as boss	5.22	25.81	5.65	5.91	57.41
Relation–think of me as equal	8.66	66.39	5.82	2.30	16.83
Relation–think of us as one big family	7.71	86.17	0.39	4.12	1.61
Success–delegate power	6.06	66.66	13.21	1.84	12.24
Success–establish mutual trust	9.41	85.37	5.22	0.00	0.00
Success–clear reward/punishment	8.12	82.79	1.24	1.21	6.64
Success–centralize decision making	13.45	73.08	1.61	3.81	8.05

B. Factor analysis	*Factor loadings*		
Variable description	Managerial	Paternalistic	Uniqueness
Motivate–encourage teamwork	*0.592*	0.045	0.648
Motivate–sensitive to emotional need	*0.462*	0.208	0.743
Motivate–offer more money	*0.471*	0.050	0.776
Motivate–offer advancement opportunity	*0.555*	−0.275	0.616
Motivate–lend money	−0.029	*0.445*	0.801
Motivate–provide positive feedback	0.143	−0.280	0.901
Motivate–offer training opportunity	*0.465*	−0.093	0.775
Motivate–create positive climate	*0.411*	*−0.333*	0.720
Motivate–reward special initiatives	−0.187	*0.314*	0.866
Relation–think of me as friend	0.065	0.288	0.913
Relation–think of me as boss	0.068	−0.172	0.966
Relation–think of me as equal	0.191	0.149	0.941
Relation–think of us as one big family	0.257	*0.526*	0.657
Success–delegate power	*0.304*	−0.098	0.898
Success–establish mutual trust	*0.536*	0.060	0.709
Success–clear reward and punishment	*0.581*	0.193	0.626
Success–centralize decision making	0.270	0.048	0.925

Note:
Values may not sum to 100 due to rounding errors; factor loadings greater than 0.30 are in italics.

Leung (1975) on a small group of industrial owners in Hong Kong.[7] The standardized scores for both factors are normed such that a high score represents a high value.

Following the analytical procedure adopted earlier, multiple regression (OLS) models are applied to assess the correlates between these two different styles of management (see Table 9.6). Relative to others, middle-aged entrepreneurs (between 30 and 49 years old) are more likely to adopt a Western managerial style to create a positive climate in the workplace. Again, better educated entrepreneurs are not particularly more susceptible to Western-style management. Rather it is native-born owners who are so, irrespective of their educational attainment. This result contrasts sharply with an earlier finding by King and Leung (1975) that immigrant owners (Shanghainese to be exact) are more likely to adopt such utilitarian management style. The finding, however, is consistent with my earlier report that native-born entrepreneurs have a closer identification with managerial skills rather than personal predispositions as important attributes of successful entrepreneurship. The common exposure to Western ideas and practices has

Table 9.6 Correlates of management style and philosophy

Variable	Managerial			Paternalistic		
	coefficient	*s.e.*	*p*	*coefficient*	*s.e.*	*p*
Intercept	0.306	0.293		−1.207	0.563	*
Age (30–49)	0.336	0.155	*			
Parent owner	−0.440	0.153	**	−0.568	0.167	***
Born in Hong Kong	0.493	0.168	**	0.571	0.212	**
Cantonese not born in Hong Kong				1.041	0.283	***
Years as business owners				0.026	0.010	*
Use English in business			.	−0.249	0.095	**
Business type – partnership[#]	0.626	0.144	***			
Business type – incorporated[#]	0.626	0.144	***			
Attitudes toward family firm	−0.351	0.107	***	−0.345	0.120	**
Entrepreneurial skill	0.306	0.080	***			
Consider organization family business	−0.704	0.162	***	0.727	0.221	***
Pass organization to family member				0.476	0.167	**
R^2		0.571			0.486	
Adjusted R^2		0.540			0.443	
N		103			105	
F-statistic		18.09			11.34	
RMSE		0.699			0.783	

Note:
*$p < 0.05$, **$p < 0.01$, ***$p < 0.001$, two-tailed test.
Equality restriction applied.

certainly contributed to a change in the entrepreneurial spirit among contemporary owners, no matter how much education they received.

Relative to sole proprietors, owners who have partners and have incorporated businesses are also more likely to adopt the Western style of management. Perhaps this is the only way to minimize conflicts among partners. Similarly, it seems logical that owners who consider the importance of managerial skills as successful entrepreneurs would be more likely to adopt the same management style. Conversely, owners whose parents were entrepreneurs adopt favorable attitudes towards Chinese family firms, and consider their businesses as family firms, are all less likely to adopt such an open style of management.[8]

While it is expected that entrepreneurs whose parents were owners are less likely to adopt Western management philosophy, it is somewhat surprising to note that they are also unlikely to adopt a paternalistic management style. If we accept past findings that Chinese owners in the past indeed were prone to adopt paternalistic management, the finding here indicates that their children are clearly ambivalent toward a similar style of management in the contemporary setting. However, they are still at a crossroads as they have not yet wholeheartedly endorsed Western management style in their own business.

Relative to other ethnic entrepreneurs, Cantonese owners indeed are more likely to adopt paternalistic attitudes towards their employees, validating King and Leung's (1975) observation that they often engage in "managerial indulgence." However, it is those Cantonese immigrant owners who have the highest proclivity, followed by native-born owners, and non-Cantonese immigrant owners. Since the majority of residents of Hong Kong are Cantonese and so are most employees, it is perhaps understandable why non-Cantonese immigrant owners are least likely to be paternalistic toward their workers. The middling position of native-born owners, disregarding their ethnic background, does not necessarily contradict an earlier observation that they are also more open and susceptible to Western-style management. The unadjusted average scores for MANAGERIAL among non-Cantonese/immigrant, non-Cantonese/native-born, Cantonese/immigrant, and Cantonese/native-born owners are −0.368, 0.191, −0.552, 0.222; and for PATERNALISTIC −0.498, −0.030, 0.541, −0.026, respectively.

The longer one stays in business ownership, the more it is likely that one will adopt the paternalistic style of management. Perhaps, as entrepreneurs become more experienced, their relationship with (long-term) employees deepens and this particular type of management style would expedite day-to-day operation. This may well reflect an age effect, though its influence is not statistically significant when the age variable is included in the statistical model. Similarly, those who intend to pass on their businesses to their children and regard their businesses as family businesses are more likely to adopt the paternalistic style of management. On the other hand, the more frequent the use of English in daily business, the less likely it is for the owners to be paternalistic. This may well be indicative of the nature of the business environment and the exposure of entrepreneurs to different clienteles and management styles. Finally, entrepreneurs who do not think that Chinese family firms are more prone to traditional problems are also less likely to adopt a paternalistic style of management. This is an unexpected finding. Perhaps one plausible explanation is that it is precisely because they themselves have not adopted the same management style and therefore can escape and circumvent the peril of traditional practices altogether. It would be interesting to test whether such an effect persists under further empirical scrutiny with a different and larger sample.

Conclusion

Entrepreneurship has played and continues to play an important role in the economy of Hong Kong. Among others, one interesting question is whether contemporary entrepreneurs share common characteristics and to what extent they are similar to their counterparts of the previous generation. Unfortunately, we do not have reliable and comparable information from the past, as previous studies are often based on homogeneous samples. But if we generalize previous findings as if they represented the entire population, then the findings from the present study of Hong Kong entrepreneurs in the late 1990s seem to suggest that they indeed deviate considerably from the conventional image of Chinese entrepreneurship.

First, there is a rapid growth of indigenous entrepreneurs. This is in part due to the stabilized and subdued flow of immigrants from China since the 1980s. Perhaps, more significantly, the change social demography also signifies that the "potential" owners are all socialized and educated in a common environment that has ample exposure to Western culture and lifestyles, as well as modern management and organization principles. They regard entrepreneurship as a way of life because it provides ample opportunity for profit, income self-determination, and autonomy. An overwhelming majority began their ownership before age 40, substantially younger than their counterparts in the 1970s and 1980s. There is a high degree of class reproduction, with more than half of them coming from a family of business owners. Yet, only a few actually inherited their family business. Instead, most chose to start from scratch with their own personal savings.

Second, according to conventional wisdom, the spirit of Chinese capitalism centers on family and networks as the backbone of organizing. As a result, the management styles of Chinese owners are often paternalistic; they centralize power and decision making, are unwilling to trust and delegate non-family members, emphasize the one-big-family principle, and are less forward-looking. My findings here and elsewhere, however, reveal that this picture is quite far from the truth. While we do find the practice of paternalistic management among entrepreneurs, the predominant mode, however, is the Western management style that emphasizes rationality and efficiency. Indeed, the pattern uncovered in this study is no different from entrepreneurs in different social contexts. More importantly, native-born owners are more likely to adopt the rational management strategy, whereas those who are more familial (have favorable attitudes toward Chinese family firms and consider their own business as a family firm) are unlikely to adopt a similar strategy. On the other hand, those who are more familial (consider their own business as a family firm and intend to pass on the company to their children) are more likely to practice a paternalistic style of management.

Third, the role of ethnicity in determining the style of management has declined, especially among native-born Cantonese. Native-born owners do not simply have favorable attitudes toward Western managerial philosophy; many actually practice it in their day-to-day operation. Considering that they also have unfavorable attitudes toward the hiring of family members and relatives, the findings clearly point to a changing social and cultural environment. The type of social capital that family used to provide as an economic unit is no longer favored and entrepreneurs have increasingly adopted Western management principles. The convergence, however, is not complete and probably will never be, since the vast majority of the firms are small and their owners still maintain control of their day-to-day operations.

In sum, the findings support the assertion that entrepreneurial activities adapt accordingly to changing social and economic conditions. To paraphrase Laurent (1986), "the art of managing and organizing has no homeland." The role played by Chinese cultural traits or Confucian ethics is really minimal in the contemporary setting. This perhaps should not be surprising, as the defining characteristics of entrepreneurship are adaptation to the changing environment and the creation of a new environment to suit one's own niche.

Notes

1 An earlier version of this paper was presented at the North American Chinese Sociological Association (NACSA) annual meeting in Chicago, August 15, 2002. The project receives financial support from the National Science Foundation (SBR9515114) and the Pacific Rim Research Program at the University of California. I am also grateful to the East-West Research Centre at the Hong Kong Baptist University and the Social Science Research Centre at the University of Hong Kong for support, and Peter Chua, Janette Kawachi, and Ming-Yan Lai for assistance.

2 Other organizational characteristics of Chinese businesses noted by Redding (1990) include their tendency to: (a) focus on one product or market with growth by opportunistic diversification; (b) be very sensitive to matters of cost and financial efficiency; (c) be linked strongly, but informally, with related but legally independent organizations handling key functions such as parts supply or marketing; (d) be relatively weak in terms of creating large-scale market recognition for brands; and (e) have a high degree of strategic adaptability.

3 The data on American firms in the United States are derived from the 1991 National Organizations Survey (NOS) collected by Kalleberg et al. (1999).

4 The database contains a total of 65,735 establishments (for-profit and nonprofit establishments), and represents about 502,400 workers. According to the official report, there was a total of 305,339 establishments with a total of 2,367,688 persons

engaged in these establishments in March 1997 (Census and Statistics Department 1997). Thus, the database appears to be quite representative of the population of establishments and the number of persons engaged in such establishments.

5 Note that establishment size refers only to the particular location and does not necessarily correspond to actual firm size because the firm may have more than one site of operation.

6 Attitudes towards Chinese family firms, hiring of family members, and hiring of relatives, and attributes of successful entrepreneurs are all constructed factors scores, based on items measured in a Likert 5-point scale. With the exception of the attributes of successful entrepreneurs, they all have one factor (see Wong 2004 for details). One factor of the attributes of successful entrepreneurs emphasizes entrepreneurial skills (such as negotiating skills, organization and management skills, cultivating networks or *quanxiwan*, goodwill or *xinyong*, adapting to changes) and the other emphasizes personal attributes (open-mindedness, hard work, frugality, risk-taking, learning from mistakes, and Confucian ethics). All extracted factors are coded so that a high score means a greater propensity.

7 By construction, the two factors are uncorrelated (r = 0.002). If we use the cutoff point of 0 or below as low and above 0 as high for both factors, slightly over 56 percent of owners belong to the first factor and the remaining to the latter.

8 Attitudes toward Chinese family firms are constructed from the following items: Chinese family firms have difficulty in lasting for more than three generations, they often face succession problems, they often diversify into unrelated businesses, and they are reluctant to give outsiders control of the company. They are all measured in a Likert 5-point scale, ranging from strongly agree to strongly disagree. Only one factor score is needed and the scores are extracted such that the higher the score, the more they disagree with the statement. In other words, entrepreneurs with higher scores are those who do not hold that these are the commonly associated problems with Chinese family business firms.

References

Aldrich, H. E., Renzulli, L. A., and Langton, N. (1998) "Passing on Privilege: Resources Provided by Self-Employed Parents to Their Self-Employed Children," in K. Leicht (ed.) *Research in Social Stratification and Mobility, Vol. 17*, Greenwich, NJ: JAI Press.

Berger, P. L. and Hsiao, H. H. M. (1988) *In Search of An East Asian Development Model*, New Brunswick, NJ: Transaction Books.

Blanchflower, D. G. (2000) "Self-Employment in OECD Countries," *Labour Economics* 7:471–505.

Bond, M. H. and Hofstede, G. (1990) "The Cash Value of Confucian Values," in S. R. Clegg and S. G. Redding (eds.) *Capitalism in Contrasting Cultures*, New York: de Gruyter.

Brockhaus, R. H. (1982) "The Psychology of the Entrepreneur," in C. A. Dent, D. L. Sexton, and K. H. Vesper (eds.) *Encyclopedia of Entrepreneurship*, Englewood Cliffs, NJ: Prentice Hall.

Brockhaus, R. H. and Horwitz, P. (1986) "The Psychology of the Entrepreneur," in D. Sexton and R. Smilor (eds.) *The Art and Science of Entrepreneurship*, Cambridge, MA: Ballinger.

Carland, J. W., Hoy, F., Boulton, W. R., and Carland, J. C. (1984) "Differentiating Entrepreneurs from Small Business Owners: A Conceptualization," *Academy of Management Review* 9:354–59.

Carr, D. (1996) "Two Paths to Self-Employment? Women's and Men's Self-Employment in the United States," *Work and Occupations* 23:26–53.

Casale, A. (1986) *Tracking Tomorrow's Trends*, Kansas City, KS: Andrews, McNeel & Parker.

Census and Statistics Department (1997) *Hong Kong Monthly Digest of Statistics, August 1997*, Hong Kong: Hong Kong Government Printing Department.

——(1998) *Hong Kong Annual Digest of Statistics 1998*, Hong Kong: Census and Statistics Department.

Chan, W. K. K. (1982) "The Organizational Structure of the Traditional Chinese Firm and Its Modern Reform," *Business History Review* 56:218–35.

Chen, C. N. (1986) "Traditional Family System and Business Organization," *Marriage, Familism and Society*, Taipei: Yun-Chen Publishing Company (in Chinese).

Child, J. (1981) "Culture, Contingency and Capitalism in the Cross-National Study of Organizations," in I. L. Cummings and B. M. Staw (eds.) *Research in Organizational Behavior, Volume 3*, Greenwich, CT: JAI Press.

Clegg, S. R., Higgins, W., and Spybey, T. (1990) "'Post-Confucianism', Social Democracy, and Economic Culture," in S. R. Clegg and S. G. Redding (eds.) *Capitalism in Contrasting Cultures*, New York: de Gruyter.

Cooper, A. C. (1971) *The Founding of Technologically-Based Firms*, Milwaukee, WI: The Center for Venture Management.

——(1986) "Entrepreneurship and High Technology," in D. L. Sexton and R. W. Smilor (eds.) *The Art and Science of Entrepreneurship*, Cambridge, MA: Ballinger Publishing Company.

Cooper, A. C. and Dunkelberg, W. C. (1986) "Entrepreneurship and Paths to Business Ownership," *Strategic Management Journal* 7:53–68.

Dunkelberg, W. C. and Cooper, A. C. (1982) "Entrepreneurial Typologies: An Empirical Study," in K. H. Vesper (ed.) *Frontiers in Entrepreneurial Research*, Wellesley, MA: Babson College.

Dunn, T. and Holtz-Eakin, D. (2000) "Financial Capital, Human Capital, and the Transition to Self-Employment: Evidence from Intergenerational Links," *Journal of Labor Economics* 18:282–305.

Fei, X. T. (1992) *From the Soil: The Foundations of Chinese Society*, translated by G. G. Hamilton and W. Zheng, Berkeley, CA: University of California Press.

Filley, A. C. and Aldag, R. J. (1978) "Characteristics and Measurement of an Organizational Typology," *Academy of Management Journal* 21:578–91.

Fukuyama, F. (1995) *Trust: The Social Virtues and the Creation of Prosperity*, New York: Free Press.

Gannon, M. J. (1979) *Organizational Behavior*, Boston, MA: Little, Brown.

Greene, P. G. (2000) "Self-Employment as an Economic Behavior: An Analysis of Self-Employed Women's Human and Social Capital," *National Journal of Sociology* 12:1–55.

Hamilton, G. G. (ed.) (1991) *Business Networks and Economic Development in East and Southeast Asia*, Hong Kong: Centre of Asian Studies, University of Hong Kong.

Hamilton, G. G. and Kao, C. S. (1990) "The Institutional Foundations of Chinese Business: The Family Firm in Taiwan," *Comparative Social Research* 12:135–57.

Herzberg, F. (1968) "One More Time: How Do You Motivate Employees?" *Harvard Business Review* 46:53–62.

Hisrich, R. D. (ed.) (1986) *Entrepreneurship, Intrapreneurship, and Venture Capital*, Lexington, MA: Lexington Books.

Hofstede, G. (1980) *Culture's Consequences*, London: Sage.

Hornaday, J. A. and Bunker, C. S. (1970) "The Nature of the Entrepreneur," *Personnel Psychology* 23:47–53.

Hout, M. and Rosen, H. S. (2000) "Self-Employment, Family Background, and Race," *Journal of Human Resources* 35:671–92.

Huang, M. H. H. (1988) "An East Asian Development Model: Empirical Exploration," in P. L. Berger and M. H. H. Hsiao (eds.) *In Search of an East Asian Development Model*, New Brunswick, NJ: Transaction.

Jurik, N. C. (1998) "Getting Away and Getting By: The Experiences of Self-Employed Homemakers," *Work and Occupations* 25:7–35.

Kahn, H. (1979) *World Economic Development: 1979 and Beyond*, Boulder, CO: Westview Press.

Kalleberg, A. L., Knoke, D., Marsden, P. V., and Spaeth, J. L. (1999) *National Organizations Survey, 1991* (computer file), second release, Champaign, IL: University of Illinois, Survey Research Laboratory (producer), 1993. Ann Arbor, MI: Inter-University Consortium for the Political and Social Research (distributor), 1994.

King, A. Y. C. and Leung, D. S. K. (1975) *The Chinese Touch in Small Industrial Organizations*, Social Science Research Centre, The Chinese University of Hong Kong.

Laferrere, A. (2001) "Self-Employment and Intergenerational Transfers: Liquidity Constraints and Family Environment," *International Journal of Sociology* 31:3–27.

Lau, S. K. (1982) *Society and Politics in Hong Kong*, Hong Kong: The Chinese University Press.

Laurent, A. (1986) "The Cross-Cultural Puzzle of International Human Resource Management," *Human Resource Management* 25:91–102.

Light, I. (1972) *Ethnic Enterprise in America*, Berkeley, CA: University of California Press.

Light, I. and Rosenstein, C. (1995) *Race, Ethnicity, and Entrepreneurship in Urban America*, New York: Aldine de Gruyter.

McClelland, D. (1961) *The Achieving Society*, Princeton, NJ: Van Nostrand.

Myers, D. and Hobbs, D. J. (1986) "Technical Entrepreneurs: Are They Different?," in D. L. Sexton and R. W. Smilor (eds.) *Frontiers of Entrepreneurship Research*, Wellesley, MA: Babson Center for Entrepreneurial Studies.

Omohundro, J. T. (1981) *Chinese Merchant Families in Iloilo*, Athens, OH: Ohio University Press.

Redding, S. G. (1988) "The Role of the Entrepreneur in the New Asian Capitalism," in P. L. Berger and M. H. H. Hsiao (eds.) *In Search of An East Asian Development Model*, New Brunswick, NJ: Transaction Books.

——(1990) *The Spirit of Chinese Capitalism*, New York: de Gruyter.

Redding, S. G. and Whitley, R. D. (1990) "Beyond Bureaucracy: Towards a Comparative Analysis of Forms of Economic Resource Co-ordination and Control," in S. R. Clegg and S. G. Redding (eds.) *Capitalism in Contrasting Cultures*, New York: de Gruyter.

Rock, S. (1991) *Family Firms*, Cambridge: Director Books.

Rozman, G. (1991) *The East Asian Region: Confucian Heritage and its Modern Adaptation*, Princeton, NJ: Princeton University Press.

Shapiro, A. (1981) "The Process of Technical Company Formation in a Local Area," in A. C. Cooper and J. L. Kolmives (eds.) *Technical Entrepreneurship: A Symposium*, Milwaukee, WI: Center for Venture Management.

Shavit, Y. and Yuchtman-Yaar, E. (2001) "Ethnicity, Education, and Other Determinants of Self-Employment in Israel," *International Journal of Sociology* 31:59–91.

Sit, V. F. S. (1982) "Dynamicism in Small Industries: The Case of Hong Kong," *Asian Survey* 22:399–409.

Sit, V. S. F., Wong, S. L., and Kiang, T. S. (1979) *Small Scale Industry in a Laissez-Faire Economy: A Hong Kong Case Study*, Centre of Asian Studies Occasional Papers and Monographs, no. 30, University of Hong Kong.

Sit, V. F. S. and Wong, S. L. (1989) *Small and Medium Industries in an Export-Oriented Economy: The Case of Hong Kong*, Hong Kong: Centre of Asian Studies, University of Hong Kong.

Smith, N. R. (1967) *The Entrepreneur and His Firms: The Relationship Between Type of Man and Type of Company*, East Lansing, MI: Michigan State University Press.

Smith, N. R., McCain, G., and Warren, A. (1982) "Women Entrepreneurs Really Are Different: A Comparison of Constructed Ideal Types of Male and Female Entrepreneurs," in K. H. Vesper (ed.) *Frontiers of Entrepreneurial Research*, Wellesley, MA: Babson Center for Entrepreneurial Studies.

Smith, N. R. and Miner, J. (1984) "Types of Entrepreneur, Type of Firms, and Managerial Motivation: Implications for Organizational Life Cycle Theory," *Strategic Management Journal* 5:325–49.

Susbauer, J. C. (1972) "The Technical Entrepreneurship Process in Austin, Texas," in A. C. Cooper and J. L. Kolmives (eds.) *Technical Entrepreneurship: A Symposium*, Milwaukee, WI: Center for Venture Management.

Tang, X. L. (1993) "Waishang touzi dalu zai xian qaochao" (A New Tide of Foreign Investment in Mainland China), *China Times Weekly* 103:44–45.

Taylor, M. P. (1999) "Survival of the Fittest? An Analysis of Self-Employment Duration in Britain," *Economic Journal* 109:C140–45.

Thorne, J. R. and Ball, J. G. (1981) "Entrepreneurs and their Companies," in K. H. Vesper (ed.) *Frontiers of Entrepreneurship Research*, Wellesley, MA: Babson Center for Entrepreneurial Studies.

Tuan, C. Y., Wong, D. S. N., and Ye, C. S. (1986) *Chinese Entrepreneurship Under Capitalism and Socialism: Hong Kong and Guangzhou Cases*, Hong Kong: Centre of Asian Studies, University of Hong Kong.

Vogel, E. F. (1991) *The Four Little Dragons: The Spread of Industrialization in East Asia*, Cambridge, MA: Harvard University Press.

Wong, R. S. K. (1992) "Vertical and Non-Vertical Effects in Class Mobility: Cross-National Variations," *American Sociological Review* 57:396–410.

——(2004) "Chinese Business Firms and Business Entrepreneurs in Hong Kong," in E. T. Gomez and H. H. M. Hsiao (eds.) *De-essentializing Capitalism: Chinese Enterprise, Transnationalism, and Identity*, London: RoutledgeCurzon.

Wong, S. L. (1985) "The Chinese Family Firm: A Model," *British Journal of Sociology* 36:58–72.

——(1988) *Emigrant Entrepreneurs: Shanghai Industrialists in Hong Kong*, New York: Oxford University Press.

Index

N.B. Figures in bold type indicate a figure or table.

220   *Index*

Western observers, Chinese cultural
  values that breed cronyism 184
Western Protestant ethic, self-interest 66
Western-centric approach, Chinese
  capital in foreign investment 149
Whitley, R. 29, 33–5, 37–9, 41, 67, 96
Williamson, O.E. 32, 103–4
women, entrepreneurship and 76–**7**, 85,
  186–8, 188, 192, 197
women with upper secondary education
  (1991), penalized 80–**81**
Wong, R. S.-K. 5–7, 12–13, 45, 67, 151,
  185, 190, 194
Wong, S.L. 33, 42, 66, 138, 184, 186–7,
  192, 194
World Bank 35
world economic crisis (1973),
  transformation of Western capitalism
  21
World Trade Organization *see* WTO
written contracts, legally binding
  according to Chinese corporate law 176
WTO agreements 11, 23n3, 151
Wu, J.L. 166, 170
Wu Tsann Kuen 61–2

Xiamen municipal government,
  Xiamen Resources Group Company
  135
Xiamen University Suntar Membrane
  Scitechnology (Xiamen) Company
  Limited (1996) 135
Xiamen Wanbao 126, 134, 139
Xiamen's Torch Industrial Park, Lan's
  Sinomem 134

Yamaha 157, 159–60
Yang, M.M.H. 37, 67
Yao, S.C. 22, 52
Yazhou Zhoukan 123, 130, 134
Yeo, George, delegation to China
  (2002) 138; on links to China, India
  and Southeast Asia 136
Yeung, H. W-C. 5–6, 30, 38; Chinese
  capitalism 41–2, 45–6; Chinese
  culture and business networks 149,
  151; Chinese entrepreneurship 117;
  Chinese family firms 35; professional
  management and inter-ethnic
  business 94; transnational
  entrepreneurship 120
Yoshihara, K 60, 95
YTL Corp. Bhd and Hong Leong
  Group 94, 112n1
Yuan-Deng 155–6, 164

Zang Jiuhuan (Chinese ambassador to
  Singapore) 141
Zhang Lu 127–8
Zhang Xuezhong, overseas students
  and 134
Zhongshan, Fushan and Jiangmen for
  research 172–4; "migrant peasant
  workers" responsible for high
  turnover rates 174; mobilization of
  financial resources 175, 181n2;
  written contracts and oral contracts
  for first orders 175–6
Zhu Rongji (Chinese Prime minister)
  133
Ziben Zazhi 128

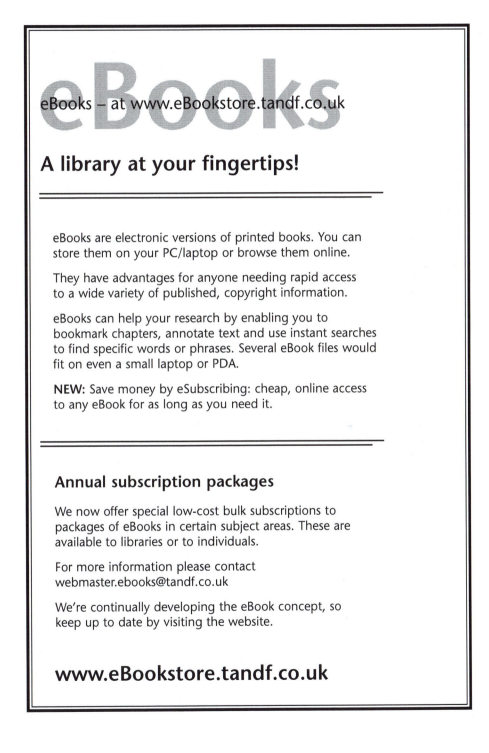